Drools Developer's Cookbook

Over 40 recipes for creating a robust business rules
implementation by using JBoss Drools rules

Lucas Amador

[PACKT] open source ✴
PUBLISHING   community experience distilled

BIRMINGHAM - MUMBAI

Drools Developer's Cookbook

First published: January 2012

Production Reference: 1201211

Published by Packt Publishing Ltd.
Livery Place
35 Livery Street
Birmingham B3 2PB, UK.

ISBN 978-1-84951-196-4

www.packtpub.com

Cover Image by Karl Swedberg (karl@englishrules.com)

Credits

Author
Lucas Amador

Reviewers
Kristy Sanders

Umamaheswaran T.G

Edson Tirelli

Acquisition Editor
Sarah Cullington

Development Editor
Hithesh Uchil

Technical Editor
Mehreen Shaikh

Copy Editor
Neha Shetty

Project Coordinator
Joel Goveya

Proofreader
Chris Smith

Indexer
Hemangini Bari

Graphics
Manu Joseph

Conidon Miranda

Production Coordinator
Arvindkumar Gupta

Cover Work
Arvindkumar Gupta

About the Author

Lucas Amador is a software developer born and raised in Buenos Aires, Argentina. His open source interest started when he was young but he finally got completely involved in it in 2008 while working with a JBoss partner giving consultancy and developing software using the JBoss middleware platform for Telco, some financial companies, and some other companies. At this time he obtained the Sun Java Developer and JBoss Advanced Developer certifications.

He got involved in the JBoss Drools community through the Google Summer of Code 2009 program, implementing a refactoring module for the Eclipse Drools Plugin, and since then he is a jBPM5/Drools committer spending his spare time implementing new features and fixing bugs. He actually works as a freelance developer and is always looking for something interesting to work on. You can check his daily works and new projects on his personal blog `lucazamador.wordpress.com` and his Github account `www.github.com/lucazamador`. He can also be contacted at `lucazamador@gmail.com`.

I would like to dedicate this book to my family who always support me in any decision taken in my life, always cheering me up in my new adventures.

About the Reviewers

Kristy Sanders has developed innovative IT solutions around the world for over 15 years. She is an expert, hands-on practitioner in Decision Management tools, approaches, practices, and technologies. Her work has helped companies increase the value of Decision Management investment and translate technological capabilities into measurable business results.

Umamaheswaran T. G is a SUN-certified Java professional with more than nine years of experience in enterprise-level implementation of the Software Development Life-Cycle (SDLC), including business analysis, functional and technical design, development, and support. He has also worked as a Consultant with industry leaders, such as Wells Fargo, USA; Citibank Japan, Bank of America, Fidelity Information Systems, and Kaiser Permanente across various business operations. He is also involved in design and development of various modules using Java, J2EE, Spring Web Services, Struts, dom4j, Drools Rule Engine, XML, XSD, Autosys, WebSphere, and Oracle.

Edson Tirelli has a Bachelor's Degree in Computer Science from the Federal University of Santa Catarina, Brazil, and has 12 years of experience in business application development, especially in the telecom industry. He is currently a senior software engineer at Red Hat where he works with AI-related research and development, and has been involved with the Drools project for the last six years. His main areas of interest are AI applied to business, middleware technologies, and compilers/language translation tools. A frequent presenter at Rules-related conferences, he is the lead designer for the Drools Fusion module for Complex Event Processing.

www.PacktPub.com

Support files, eBooks, discount offers, and more

You might want to visit www.PacktPub.com for support files and downloads related to your book.

Did you know that Packt offers eBook versions of every book published, with PDF and ePub files available? You can upgrade to the eBook version at www.PacktPub.com and as a print book customer, you are entitled to a discount on the eBook copy. Get in touch with us at service@packtpub.com for more details.

At www.PacktPub.com, you can also read a collection of free technical articles, sign up for a range of free newsletters and receive exclusive discounts and offers on Packt books and eBooks.

http://PacktLib.PacktPub.com

Do you need instant solutions to your IT questions? PacktLib is Packt's online digital book library. Here, you can access, read, and search across Packt's entire library of books.

Why Subscribe?

- ▶ Fully searchable across every book published by Packt
- ▶ Copy and paste, print, and bookmark content
- ▶ On demand and accessible via web browser

Free Access for Packt account holders

If you have an account with Packt at www.PacktPub.com, you can use this to access PacktLib today and view nine entirely free books. Simply use your login credentials for immediate access.

Table of Contents

Preface

JBoss Drools is an open source project that is always in a continuous evolution adding more modules and features to the existing ones. This evolution is possible, thanks to the vision of the core developers and the open source community that is continuously pushing it to a new level. And since version 5, Drools has been evolved to provide a unified platform for business rules, business processing, event processing, and automated planning.

With this book you will learn new features to create a robust business rules implementation, starting with tips to write business rules and ending with frameworks integration to create a full business rules solution. The recipes included in this book cover all the Drools modules and will help you to learn how your business rules can be integrated with other frameworks to create a full solution, and will also help you discover how to use complex features such as complex event processing, remote execution, declarative services, and more.

What this book covers

Chapter 1, Expert: The Rule Engine, will introduce you to new features available in the 5.2.0 release and in the previous releases to improve your expertise with the main Drools module.

Chapter 2, Expert: Behind the Rules, will cover more recipes for Drools Expert, and you will learn different ways to persist the knowledge and the use of the Drools Verifier project. You will also learn how to monitor Drools using JMX, and so on.

Chapter 3, Guvnor: Centralized Knowledge Management, contains recipes that use the Drools Guvnor as your knowledge repository using new authoring methods.

Chapter 4, Guvnor: Advanced Features and Configuration, will teach you how to back up and configure the rules repository in order to use an external database, how to interact with Guvnor using the REST API, and so on.

Chapter 5, Fusion: Processing Complex Events, will get you started with the Complex Event Processing (CEP) and Drools Fusion concepts to add event processing capabilities to your project.

Chapter 6, Executing Drools Remotely, will introduce to you all the concepts and requirements needed to use and test the Drools Server module to execute your business rules remotely using the HTTP protocol, which will enable you to interact with it using different programming languages.

Chapter 7, Integration: How to Connect Drools, covers all the possible integrations between Drools, the Spring Framework, and Apache Camel to create declarative services.

Chapter 8, Planner: Optimizing Your Automated Planning, will teach you how to optimize automated planning problems using the Drools Planner module, covering a step-by-step explanation of the configuration possibilities and how to benchmark it to improve your solution.

Chapter 9, jBPM5: Managing Business Processes, will show you how to use some features of the new jBPM5 project, such as BPMN2 process creation using the API, and testing, monitoring, and report creation.

What you need for this book

The recipes in this cookbook assume that you know the Java language pretty well and also that you have basic JBoss Drools knowledge. The latter is really important because the basic business rules authoring process and concepts aren't the main focus and we are going straight ahead into the recipes. If you do not have basic knowledge of JBoss Drools, you should consider reading Drools JBoss Rules 5.0 Developer's Guide, published by Packt, before this book. Also, you will have to know how to create Apache Maven projects to follow the recipes, and it is recommended to know about frameworks such as the Spring Framework, Apache Camel, Hibernate, and so on. However, if you don't know them don't worry because they will be minimally explained in the recipes.

- ► Java JDK 1.5 or higher (Oracle Java JDK 1.6 is recommended)
- ► Apache Maven 3.x
- ► Java IDE (Eclipse + Apache Maven plugin, Netbeans, IntelliJ IDEA or any other plugin with Apache Maven integration)

Who this book is for

This book is for experienced Java developers and architects who want to improve their current knowledge about the JBoss Drools project and also want to discover new features that can be applied in their projects.

Conventions

In this book, you will find a number of styles of text that distinguish between different kinds of information. Here are some examples of these styles, and an explanation of their meaning.

Code words in text are shown as follows: "This method returns an `org.drools.definition.type.FactType` object that is used to communicate with the `KnowledgeBase` in order to create instances of your facts."

A block of code is set as follows:

```
package drools.cookbook;

import drools.cookbook.model.FlightStatus
import drools.cookbook.model.FlightControl

global drools.cookbook.model.FlightControl control;

declare FlightStatus
    @role(event)
    @timestamp(timestamp)
end
```

When we wish to draw your attention to a particular part of a code block, the relevant lines or items are set in bold:

```
WorkingMemoryEntryPoint flightArrivalEntryPoint = ksession
    .getWorkingMemoryEntryPoint("flight-arrival");
flightArrivalEntryPoint.insert(flightStatus);
clock.advanceTime(7, TimeUnit.MINUTES);
```

Any command-line input or output is written as follows:

```
Error: Restriction LiteralRestriction from rule [rule 2] value '== 2'
and LiteralRestriction from rule [rule 2] value '!= 2'are in conflict.
Because of this, pattern that contains them can never be satisfied. type:
INCOHERENCE on: Pattern, name: Server
```

New terms and **important words** are shown in bold. Words that you see on the screen, in menus or dialog boxes for example, appear in the text like this: "clicking the **Next** button moves you to the next screen".

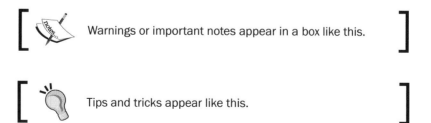

Warnings or important notes appear in a box like this.

Tips and tricks appear like this.

Reader feedback

Feedback from our readers is always welcome. Let us know what you think about this book—what you liked or may have disliked. Reader feedback is important for us to develop titles that you really get the most out of.

To send us general feedback, simply send an e-mail to `feedback@packtpub.com`, and mention the book title via the subject of your message.

If there is a book that you need and would like to see us publish, please send us a note in the **SUGGEST A TITLE** form on `www.packtpub.com` or e-mail `suggest@packtpub.com`.

If there is a topic that you have expertise in and you are interested in either writing or contributing to a book, see our author guide on `www.packtpub.com/authors`.

Customer support

Now that you are the proud owner of a Packt book, we have a number of things to help you to get the most from your purchase.

Downloading the example code

You can download the example code files for all Packt books you have purchased from your account at `http://www.PacktPub.com`. If you purchased this book elsewhere, you can visit `http://www.PacktPub.com/support` and register to have the files e-mailed directly to you.

Errata

Although we have taken every care to ensure the accuracy of our content, mistakes do happen. If you find a mistake in one of our books—maybe a mistake in the text or the code—we would be grateful if you would report this to us. By doing so, you can save other readers from frustration and help us improve subsequent versions of this book. If you find any errata, please report them by visiting `http://www.packtpub.com/support`, selecting your book, clicking on the **errata submission form** link, and entering the details of your errata. Once your errata are verified, your submission will be accepted and the errata will be uploaded on our website, or added to any list of existing errata, under the Errata section of that title. Any existing errata can be viewed by selecting your title from `http://www.packtpub.com/support`.

Piracy

Piracy of copyright material on the Internet is an ongoing problem across all media. At Packt, we take the protection of our copyright and licenses very seriously. If you come across any illegal copies of our works, in any form, on the Internet, please provide us with the location address or website name immediately so that we can pursue a remedy.

Please contact us at copyright@packtpub.com with a link to the suspected pirated material.

We appreciate your help in protecting our authors, and our ability to bring you valuable content.

Questions

You can contact us at questions@packtpub.com if you are having a problem with any aspect of the book, and we will do our best to address it.

1

Expert: The Rule Engine

In this chapter, we will cover:

- ▸ Declaring facts in the engine
- ▸ Declaring facts using XML
- ▸ Adding logging to view rules execution behavior
- ▸ Using timer-based rules
- ▸ Implementing calendar-based rules
- ▸ Monitoring query changes in real time

Introduction

Drools Expert can be considered the core of the Drools project and is used to specify, maintain, and execute your business rules. You should already know it, or at least that is expected if you are reading this cookbook. If you don't know it, then before going forward with this book I would recommend that you read **Drools JBoss Rules 5.0 Developer's Guide** written by **Michal Bali**. This book will guide you to discover the power of the main Drools modules with guided examples that will help you understand this wonderful framework.

Before going deep within the recipes, I would like to clarify that this cookbook is based on the **Drools 5.2.0.Final** release.

Back to the topic, you know that specifying rules isn't an easy task. Well, you can write rules, execute them, and see the desired results, but they may not always have the best performance. The process of writing rules has a great learning curve as well as all the knowledge you acquire, but it doesn't have to discourage you. Anyway, this chapter is not about how to create your rules and make them better. This chapter covers recipes that can help you in the process of rules writing, covering topics that begin with declarative fact creation, rules execution debugging, and creation of scheduled rules.

The idea of these recipes is not to read them through in order; you can read them in the order of your own interest. Maybe, you are an experienced Drools user and already know the concepts behind these recipes. If you are in this group, then you have the freedom of choice to refresh your memory with something that you already know or move forward to the topics that interest you the most.

Declaring facts in the engine

Instead of using regular **Plain Old Java Objects** (**POJO**s) to represent your business model, you can use another approach, such as declaring your facts directly in the engine or using the native Drools language **Drools Rule Language** (**DRL**). Also, with this alternative you can complement your existing business model by adding extra entities (such as helper classes) or adding classes that are going be used for the event processing mode.

In this recipe, we will declare two facts and show how they can be programmatically instantiated to initialize their fields with customized data. After these steps, these instantiated facts will be inserted into the working memory to generate rules activation.

How to do it...

Carry out the following steps in order to achieve this recipe:

1. Create a new DRL file and declare the facts with the following code package:

```
drools.cookbook.chapter01

import java.util.List

declare Server
    name : String
    processors : int

    memory : int // megabytes
    diskSpace : int // gigabytes
    virtualizations : List // list of Virtualization objects
    cpuUsage : int // percentage
end
```

```
declare Virtualization
    name : String
    diskSpace : int
    memory : int
end
```

Downloading the example code

You can download the example code files for all Packt books you have purchased from your account at http://www.PacktPub.com. If you purchased this book elsewhere, you can visit http://www.PacktPub.com/support and register to have the files e-mailed directly to you.

2. Add a simple rule at the end of the previously created DRL file, just to test your declared facts:

```
rule "check minimum server configuration"
dialect "mvel"
when
    $server : Server(processors < 2 ||
                    memory<=1024 ||
                diskSpace<=250)
then
    System.out.println("Server \"" + $server.name + "\" was " +
        "rejected by don't apply the minimum configuration.");
    retract($server);
end
```

3. Create a **JUnit Test Case** with the following code. This test code will create a StatefulKnowledgeSession, instantiate a rule-declared fact, and insert it into the knowledge session:

```
@Test
public void checkServerConfiguration() {

    KnowledgeBuilder kbuilder = KnowledgeBuilderFactory
        .newKnowledgeBuilder();
    kbuilder.add(new ClassPathResource("rules.drl",
        getClass()),ResourceType.DRL);

    if (kbuilder.hasErrors()) {
        if (kbuilder.getErrors().size() > 0) {
            for (KnowledgeBuilderError kerror : kbuilder.
getErrors()) {
                System.err.println(kerror);
```

```
                }
            }
        }

        KnowledgeBase kbase = kbuilder.newKnowledgeBase();
        StatefulKnowledgeSession ksession = kbase
            .newStatefulKnowledgeSession();

        FactType serverType = Kbase
            .getFactType("drools.cookbook.chapter01", "Server");

        assertNotNull(serverType);

        Object debianServer = null;
        try {
            debianServer = serverType.newInstance();
        } catch (InstantiationException e) {
            System.err.println("the class Server on drools.cookbook.
chapter01 package hasn't a constructor");
        } catch (IllegalAccessException e) {
            System.err.println("unable to access the class Server on
drools.cookbook.chapter01 package");
        }
        serverType.set(debianServer, "name", "server001");
        serverType.set(debianServer, "processors", 4);
        serverType.set(debianServer, "memory", 8192);
        serverType.set(debianServer, "diskSpace", 2048);
        serverType.set(debianServer, "cpuUsage", 3);

        ksession.insert(debianServer);

        ksession.fireAllRules();

        assertEquals(ksession.getObjects().size(), 0);

    }
```

How it works...

The engine has the ability to automatically convert these declared facts into POJO using bytecode, creating the constructors, getter and setter methods for the fields, equals and hashcode methods, and so on. However, in order to generate them we need to know how to declare them.

The first thing that you should know is that in order to declare a fact type you have to use the `declare` keyword followed by the fact name, shown as follows:

```
declare Server
```

In the next line you can declare the fact fields that the fact will contain. Each field declaration is created by the field name, followed by a colon (`:`) and finally the field type:

```
<field_name> : <field_type>
```

Remember that if you want to use a field type that is not included in the `java.lang` package, you will have to import it. Also, if you want to use a previously declared fact, it should be declared before declaring the fact that will use it:

```
name : String
processors : int
memory : int // megabytes
diskSpace : int // gigabytes
virtualizations : List // of Virtualization objects
cpuUsage : int // percentage
```

After the field declarations, you have to close the fact declaration with the `end` keyword.

Once you have the fact declared in your rules, you have to construct a `KnowledgeSession` with the rule compiled. It is assumed that you already know how to do it, but there is nothing better than being sure that we are on the same page. Anyway, the following code snippet shows how to create a knowledge session:

```
KnowledgeBuilder kbuilder = KnowledgeBuilderFactory
    .newKnowledgeBuilder();
kbuilder.add(new ClassPathResource("rules.drl", getClass()),
    ResourceType.DRL);

if (kbuilder.hasErrors()) {
    if (kbuilder.getErrors().size() > 0) {
        for (KnowledgeBuilderError kerror : kbuilder.getErrors()) {
            System.err.println(kerror);
        }
    }
```

```
}

KnowledgeBase kbase = kbuilder.newKnowledgeBase();
StatefulKnowledgeSession ksession = kbase
    .newStatefulKnowledgeSession();
```

After you have constructed a `KnowledgeBase`, you can begin to instantiate your facts in a dynamic way using the `getFactType` method of the `KnowledgeBase` object. This method needs two parameters; the first one is the package name of the rule where the fact was declared and the second one is the fact name:

```
FactType serverType = kbase.getFactType("drools.cookbook.chapter01",
"Server");
```

This method returns an `org.drools.definition.type.FactType` object that is used to communicate with the `KnowledgeBase` in order to create instances of your facts. The next step is to instantiate your fact.

```
Object debianServer = serverType.newInstance();
```

This method internally uses the Java Reflection API, so you have to be aware of the exceptions. Once you have your fact instantiated it is time to fill the fields with data. To make it possible you have to use the set method of the `FactType` object in conjunction with three parameters. The first one is the reference of your instantiated object, the second one is the name of the field, and the last one is the field value, as you can see next.

```
serverType.set(debianServer, "name", "server001");
```

After this you are ready to insert the fact (which in this example is the `debianServer` object) into the `StatefulKnowledgeSession`.

```
ksession.insert(debianServer);
```

This is all that you have to know to declare and create your facts dynamically.

 In case that you don't remember the declared fields, you can use the `getFields()` method of the `FactType` object. This method will return a list of `FactField`, which contains the field name and object type.

Declaring facts using XML

Another alternative to declare facts is using a **XSD Schema**. This simple alternative was introduced with the Drools 5.1.1 release and provides a more extensible way to model and share the business model, although it is more useful when used to create Drools commands in XML, which are going to be covered in the further chapters.

Getting ready

This feature is implemented using **JAXB** and the dependencies have to be manually added into your project if your environment doesn't provide them. If you are using Maven, the extra dependencies required are as follows:

```xml
<dependency>
  <groupId>javax.xml.bind</groupId>
  <artifactId>jaxb-api</artifactId>
  <version>2.2.1</version>
</dependency>
<dependency>
  <groupId>com.sun.xml.bind</groupId>
  <artifactId>jaxb-impl</artifactId>
  <version>2.2.1.1</version>
</dependency>
<dependency>
  <groupId>com.sun.xml.bind</groupId>
  <artifactId>jaxb-xjc</artifactId>
  <version>2.2.1.1</version>
</dependency>
```

How to do it...

Carry out the following steps to achieve this recipe:

1. The first step is to define a model using an XSD schema. In this example, three objects are configured, which can be taken as a template to create customized XSD models:

```xml
<xsd:schema xmlns:cookbook="http://cookbook.drools/chapter01"
    xmlns:xsd="http://www.w3.org/2001/XMLSchema"
targetNamespace="http://cookbook.drools/chapter01"
    elementFormDefault="qualified">

  <xsd:complexType name="server">
    <xsd:sequence>
      <xsd:element name="name" type="xsd:string" />
      <xsd:element name="processors" type="xsd:integer" />
      <xsd:element name="memory" type="xsd:integer" />
      <xsd:element name="diskSpace" type="xsd:integer" />
      <xsd:element name="cpuUsage" type="xsd:integer" />
    </xsd:sequence>
  </xsd:complexType>
```

```xml
<xsd:complexType name="serverStatus">
  <xsd:sequence>
    <xsd:element name="name" type="xsd:string" />
    <xsd:element name="freeMemory" type="xsd:integer" />
    <xsd:element name="percentageFreeMemory"
                type="xsd:integer" />
    <xsd:element name="freeDiskSpace" type="xsd:integer" />
    <xsd:element name="percentageFreeDiskSpace"
                type="xsd:integer" />
    <xsd:element name="currentCpuUsage"
                type="xsd:integer" />
  </xsd:sequence>
</xsd:complexType>

<xsd:complexType name="virtualization">
  <xsd:sequence>
    <xsd:element name="name" type="xsd:string" />
    <xsd:element name="memory" type="xsd:integer" />
    <xsd:element name="diskSpace" type="xsd:integer" />
  </xsd:sequence>
</xsd:complexType>

</xsd:schema>
```

2. Create a new DRL file with the following content, which will use the Server POJO defined in the XSD file from the previous step:

```
package drools.cookbook.chapter01

import java.util.Date
import java.util.List

rule "check minimum server configuration"
dialect "mvel"
when
        $server : Server(processors < 2 || memory<=1024 ||
                    diskSpace<=250)
then
        System.out.println("Server \"" + $server.name + "\" was " +
        "rejected by don't apply the minimum configuration.");
        retract($server);
end
```

3. Finally, the XSD model should be added into the `KnowledgeBase` as an XSD resource, together with a special JAXB configuration:

```
KnowledgeBuilder kbuilder = KnowledgeBuilderFactory
    .newKnowledgeBuilder();

Options xjcOpts = new Options();
xjcOpts.setSchemaLanguage(Language.XMLSCHEMA);

JaxbConfiguration jaxbConfiguration = KnowledgeBuilderFactory.
newJaxbConfiguration(xjcOpts, "xsd");

kbuilder.add(new ClassPathResource("model.xsd", getClass()),
    ResourceType.XSD, jaxbConfiguration);
kbuilder.add(new ClassPathResource("rules.drl", getClass()),
    ResourceType.DRL);

if (kbuilder.hasErrors()) {
  if (kbuilder.getErrors().size() > 0) {
      for (KnowledgeBuilderError kerror : kbuilder.getErrors()) {
      System.err.println(kerror);
    }
  }
}

kbase = kbuilder.newKnowledgeBase();
```

How it works...

In the process of adding XSD resources into a `KnowledgeBase` the **JAXB BindingCompiler** (**XJC**) should be notified that a XML Schema is going to be used; that is why an XJC `Options` object is created and configured:

```
com.sun.tools.xjc.Options xjcOpts = new Options();
xjcOpts.setSchemaLanguage(Language.XMLSCHEMA);
```

After this we have to create a `JaxbConfiguration` passing the previously created `Options` object and a system identifier as the parameters:

```
JaxbConfiguration jaxbConfiguration = KnowledgeBuilderFactory
    .newJaxbConfiguration(xjcOpts, "xsd");
```

Once we have the `JaxbConfiguration` object instantiated, the XSD file is ready to be added into the `KnowledgeBuilder` as a resource. As you should be aware, the XSD resource must be added before any rule that uses the model defined in the file; otherwise, you will get compilation errors for the rules:

```
kbuilder.add(new ClassPathResource("model.xsd", getClass()),
ResourceType.XSD, jaxbConfiguration);
```

Now, the tricky part is how to create instances of objects defined in the XSD file. Here, the reflection API is used to dynamically create and fill their fields with data. Internally, the `KnowledgeBuilder` compiles the `XSD` object's definition into Java objects, which reside in the Drools Classloader and can be accessed using the `KnowledgeBase` internal classloader:

```
CompositeClassLoader classLoader = ((InternalRuleBase)
((KnowledgeBaseImpl) kbase).getRuleBase()).getRootClassLoader();
```

This is an internal Drools API and could change in the future releases, which also may provide a proper public API to achieve the same results.

After following this strange way to access the Drools `CompositeClassloader`, you are ready to start using Java reflection to instantiate objects. In this example, first we have to get the Class definition, then obtain a new object instance, and finally start to fill its fields with values as is shown in the following code:

```
String className = "drools.cookbook.chapter01.Server";
Class<?> serverClass = classLoader.loadClass(className);
Object debianServer = serverClass.newInstance();
Method setName = serverClass.getMethod("setName", String.class);
setName.invoke(debianServer, "debianServer");
```

As you can see, the worst part of using XSD models is the use of the Reflection API to load the class definition and construct objects.

The idea of this recipe is to show how to use another alternative to model business objects, but if you want to know how to model objects using a XSD Schema, you should be aware that this goes beyond the recipe topic. Anyway, the Internet is a nice source to find some XSD tutorials. A particularly good and simple one can be found here: `http://www.w3schools.com/schema/default.asp`.

Adding logging to view rules execution behavior

Sometimes, you have to know what's happening inside your knowledge session to understand why your rules aren't executed as you expected. Drools gives us two possibilities to inspect their internal behavior; one is to use a `KnowledgeRuntimeLogger` and the other one is adding an `EventListener`. These loggers can be used at the same time and they should be associated to a `StatefulKnowledgeSession` to begin receiving the internal information.

These loggers have different ways to show the information. The `KnowledgeRuntimeLogger` can store all the execution logging in an XML file so it can be inspected with an external tool. On the other hand, the `EventListener` doesn't have an implementation to store the information externally, but you can implement one easily. However, as a common functionality, both loggers can show the entire internal behavior in the console.

There is nothing better than an example and a later explanation about how they work. Let's do it.

Getting ready

In this recipe, we are using `SLF4J` together with `log4j` for logging purposes. In order to use these logging frameworks, you need to add the following dependencies into your Apache Maven project:

```
<dependency>
  <groupId>org.slf4j</groupId>
  <artifactId>slf4j-api</artifactId>
  <version>1.6.1</version>
</dependency>
<dependency>
  <groupId>org.slf4j</groupId>
  <artifactId>slf4j-log4j12</artifactId>
  <version>1.6.1</version>
</dependency>
```

How to do it...

Carry out the following steps in order to complete the recipe:

1. Firstly, a custom `AgendaEventListener` implementation is needed. This is done by creating a new Java class, which implements the `org.drools.event.rule.AgendaEventListener` interface. This listener implementation will log only the events related to Activations created by facts (for further information regarding Activations you can read the *There's more...* section in this recipe). In the next listener implementation, we have to add the **SLF4J Framework** to log all the agenda behavior, but you can also store this information in a database, send it to a remote server, and so on:

```java
public class CustomAgendaEventListener
    implements AgendaEventListener {

    private static final Logger logger =
LoggerFactory.getLogger(CustomAgendaEventListener.class);

    public void activationCancelled(ActivationCancelledEvent
                                event) {
        logger.info("Activation Cancelled: " +
                        event.getActivation());
    }

    public void activationCreated(ActivationCreatedEvent
                                event) {
        logger.info("Activation Created: " +
                        event.getActivation());
    }

    public void beforeActivationFired(
        BeforeActivationFiredEvent event) {
        logger.info("Before Activation Fired: " +
                        event.getActivation());
    }

    public void afterActivationFired(AfterActivationFiredEvent
            event) {
        logger.info("After Activation Fired: " +
                        event.getActivation());
    }

    public void agendaGroupPopped(AgendaGroupPoppedEvent
                                event) {
```

```
        logger.info("Agenda Group Popped: " +
                event.getAgendaGroup());
    }


    public void agendaGroupPushed(AgendaGroupPushedEvent
                                event) {
        logger.info("Agenda Group Pushed: " +
                event.getAgendaGroup());
    }
}
```

2. Now, you can add a customized WorkingMemoryEventListener. The WorkingMemoryEventListener only knows about all the information of fact insertion/update/retraction events. In order to implement this listener, you only have to implement the org.drools.event.rule. WorkingMemoryEventListener interface:

```
public class CustomWorkingMemoryEventListener
    implements WorkingMemoryEventListener {

    private static final Logger logger = LoggerFactory
        .getLogger(CustomWorkingMemoryEventListener.class);

    public void objectInserted(ObjectInsertedEvent event) {
        logger.info("Object Inserted: " +
                event.getFactHandle() +
                " Knowledge Runtime: " +
                event.getKnowledgeRuntime());
    }

    public void objectRetracted(ObjectRetractedEvent event) {
        logger.info("Object Retracted: " +
                event.getFactHandle() +
                " Knowledge Runtime: " +
                event.getKnowledgeRuntime());
    }


    public void objectUpdated(ObjectUpdatedEvent event) {
        logger.info("Object Updated: " +
                event.getFactHandle() +
                " Knowledge Runtime: " +
                event.getKnowledgeRuntime());
    }

}
```

3. Once both the event listeners are created, they have to be registered in the StatefulKnowledgeSession:

```
ksession.addEventListener(new CustomAgendaEventListener());
ksession.addEventListener(new
                        CustomWorkingMemoryEventListener());
```

4. Optionally, you can also register a console KnowledgeRuntimeLogger, but the logging output will be similar to that generated by the registered WorkingMemoryEventListener. This KnowledgeRuntimeLogger has other output logging options that you can check in the *There's more...* section of this recipe:

```
KnowledgeRuntimeLoggerFactory.newConsoleLoggger(ksession);
```

How it works...

Internally, the Drools Framework uses an event system to expose its internal state, and that is the reason why we created and registered these event listeners. Obviously, it is not always necessary to register both listeners because this depends on the information that you want to be aware of.

As you already saw, the methods to be implemented are pretty descriptive. For example, in the activationCreated method you have access to the event created when the Activation was created. These events are ActivationEvent objects and they expose a lot of useful information; for example, you can access the KnowledgeRuntime (StatefulKnowledgeSession), and get the facts that matched the rule and caused the activation or get the name of the rule that was activated, and so on.

Once the example is executed, the event listeners will start to log every event created. Next, you will see an excerpt of a logging output with comments and information about the event:

▶ CustomAgendaEventListener: The activation of the check minimum server configuration rule was created after the fact insertion:

```
2011-09-26 18:30:32,472 INFO - Activation Created: [Activation
rule=check minimum server configuration, tuple=[fact
0:1:13813952:1:1:DEFAULT:Server( memory=2048, diskSpace=2048,
processors=1, virtualizations=null, name=server001, cpuUsage=3 )]
```

▶ CustomWorkingMemoryEventListener: The object server with name server001 was inserted into the WorkingMemory:

```
2011-09-26 18:30:32,475 INFO - Object Inserted: [fact
0:1:13813952:1:1:DEFAULT:Server( memory=2048, diskSpace=2048,
processors=1, virtualizations=null, name=server001, cpuUsage=3 )]
Knowledge Runtime: org.drools.impl.StatefulKnowledgeSessionImpl@9f
8ac1
```

- The `CustomAgendaEventListener`: `ksession.fireAllRules()` method was executed and the listener showed the information before the `fireAllRules()` method invocation:

```
2011-09-26 18:30:32,476 INFO - Before Activation Fired:
[Activation rule=check minimum server configuration, tuple=[fact
0:1:13813952:1:1:DEFAULT:Server( memory=2048, diskSpace=2048,
processors=1, virtualizations=null, name=server001, cpuUsage=3 )]
```

- The `fireAllRules()` method was invoked and the rule consequence was executed:

```
Server "server001" was rejected by don't apply the minimum
configuration.
```

- `CustomWorkingMemoryEventListener`: The rule RHS retracted the fact:

```
2011-09-26 18:30:32,494 INFO - Object Retracted: [fact
0:1:13813952:1:1:DEFAULT:Server( memory=2048, diskSpace=2048,
processors=1, virtualizations=null, name=server001, cpuUsage=3 )]
Knowledge Runtime: org.drools.impl.StatefulKnowledgeSessionImpl@9f
8ac1
```

- `CustomWorkingMemoryEventListener`: As a consequence of the fact retraction, the current activation was updated with a null object:

```
2011-09-26 18:30:32,495 INFO - After Activation Fired:
[Activation rule=check minimum server configuration, tuple=[fact
0:-1:13813952:1:1:null:null]
```

With this information about the events, you will be able to identify what is happening inside your working memory and any possible issues. There are more events related to the engine, especially the `AgendaGroup` events and the `ProcessEventListeners`. But as a sample, these ones are enough to demonstrate how you can use them to detect the internal behavior of your rules.

There's more...

KnowledgeRuntimeLogger options

Besides the console output, you can store the logging information in an external file. This logging storage can be done in two different ways, with a similar XML output but different storage behavior. After the information is captured, you would like to read what was stored; the best way to interpret this XML format is using the Audit Log View of the **Drools Eclipse Plugin**, but you also can interpret it with another XML reader tool.

The first option to store the logging is using the `newFileLogger()` method. This method has two parameters; the first one is the `StatefulKnowledgeSession` instance to be logged and the other one is the output filename:

```
KnowledgeRuntimeLoggerFactory.newFileLogger(ksession, fileName)
```

This option is not able to store the information in real time; it only does it when the logger is closed or the internal buffer is flushed. In order to store the information with a more real-time behavior, you can use the `newThreadedFileLogger()` method, which has an extra parameter to indicate the time interval (milliseconds) at which to flush the information to the file:

```
KnowledgeRuntimeLoggerFactory.newThreadedFileLogger(session, fileName,
interval)
```

Both methods return a `KnowledgeRuntimeLogger` instance that exposes a `close()` method, which should be invoked when you don't want to use the loggers anymore. Just as a caveat, don't forget to invoke this method or you could lose all the information gathered when using the non-threaded file logger.

Activations

People quite often misunderstand how Drools works internally. So, let's try to clarify how rules are "executed" really. Each time an object is inserted/updated/retracted in the working memory, or the facts are update/retracted within the rules, the rules are re-evaluated with the new working memory state. If a rule matches, it generates an `Activation` object, which contains the following information:

- The rule name
- The objects that made this rules match
- The action that generated this new Activation
- The associated object `FactHandles`
- The declaration identifiers

This `Activation` object is stored inside the Agenda until the `fireAllRules()` method is invoked. These objects are also evaluated when the `WorkingMemory` state changes to be possibly cancelled. Finally, when the `fireAllRules()` method is invoked the Agenda is cleared, executing the associated rule consequence of each Activation object. The following figure shows this:

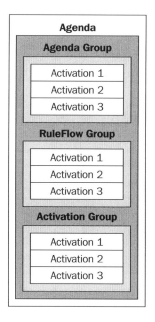

Using timer-based rules

In the latest Drools release, you will find a new powerful timer to schedule rules. With this new implementation, you can create more personalized scheduled rules, thanks to the support of **cron timers**. Remember that the previous implementation that only supports a single value is still available for backward compatibility. These timers are useful when you want to create rules to be executed during certain periods of time, for example, if you need to keep checking the reliability of an external service, and take actions if it doesn't return the expected values.

How to do it...

Carry out the following steps to use a timer inside your rules:

1. Create a rule with a timer configured, using a `cron` expression. The new timer attribute will use a `cron` expression that is going to re-evaluate this rule every five seconds. As you can see, this simple rule is going to check the availability of the server asserted into the working memory every five seconds:

```
package drools.cookbook.chapter01

import java.util.Date
import java.util.List
```

```
global drools.cookbook.chapter01.ServerAlert alerts

rule "Server status"
dialect "mvel"
timer (cron:0/5 * * * ?)
when
    $server : Server(online==false)
then
    System.out.println("WARNING: Server \"" + $server.name + "\" is
offline at " + $server.lastTimeOnline);
    alerts.addEvent(new ServerEvent($server, $server.
lastTimeOnline, ServerStatus.OFFLINE));
end
```

2. After you have created your rule, you have to create a unit test in which you have to invoke the `fireUntilHalt()` method of the `StatefulKnowledgeSession` instance to autofire the activations as they are created, instead of invoking the `fireAllRules()` method.

3. Put this method invocation inside a new thread because it will block the current thread. In this example, we are simulating the availability of a server, for a period of 30 seconds, where the server starts with an online status and after 7 seconds it goes offline for a period of 16 seconds. The next unit test code simulates this behavior in a non-deterministic way:

```
@Test
public void historicalCpuUsageTest() throws InterruptedException {

    KnowledgeBuilder kbuilder = KnowledgeBuilderFactory
        .newKnowledgeBuilder();
    kbuilder.add(new ClassPathResource("rules.drl",
                getClass()), ResourceType.DRL);

    if (kbuilder.hasErrors()) {
        if (kbuilder.getErrors().size() > 0) {
            for (KnowledgeBuilderError kerror : kbuilder.
getErrors()) {
                System.err.println(kerror);
            }
        }
    }

    KnowledgeBase kbase = kbuilder.newKnowledgeBase();
    final StatefulKnowledgeSession ksession = kbase
        .newStatefulKnowledgeSession();
```

```
        final Server debianServer = new Server("debianServer",
            new Date(), 4, 2048, 2048, 4);
        debianServer.setOnline(true);

        new Thread(new Runnable() {
            public void run() {
                ksession.fireUntilHalt();
            }
        }).start();

        debianServerFactHandle = ksession.insert(debianServer);

        Thread simulationThread = new Thread(new Runnable() {
            public void run() {
                try {
                    Thread.sleep(7000);
                    debianServer.setOnline(false);
                    ksession.update(debianServerFactHandle,
                                    debianServer);
                    Thread.sleep(16000);
                    debianServer.setOnline(true);
 debianServer.setLastTimeOnline(new Date());
                    ksession.update(debianServerFactHandle,
                                    debianServer);
                } catch (InterruptedException e) {
                    System.err.println("An error ocurrs in the " +
                                        "simulation thread");
                }
            }
        });

        simulationThread.start();

        // sleep the main thread 30 seconds
        Thread.sleep(30000);
        simulationThread.interrupt();
        ksession.halt();
}
```

How it works...

When you set a `cron`-based timer in a rule, you are actually scheduling a sort of job that will recheck the rule patterns during a certain period of time, based on the `cron` date pattern.

In order to complete the `cron` timer's functionality, it is necessary to maintain the working memory continually checking if there are activations created to automatically fire them. To implement it you can to use the `fireUntilHalt()` method.

The `fireUntilHalt()` method will keep firing the activations created until none remains in the agenda. When no more activations are found in the agenda, it will wait until more activations appear in the active agenda group or `ruleflow` group.

If you have executed the previous test, maybe you expected only three alerts to be raised. However, sometimes you will see three or four alerts, because the `cron` job execution depends on the computer clock. This pattern specifies that the rule is going to be executed every five seconds, but not every five seconds counting from when the knowledge session is instantiated, because it takes the computer time as reference.

There's more

The `cron` pattern uses the standard `cron` syntax, which is used in UNIX-like systems to schedule jobs, and is implemented using the **Quartz Framework**. However, in this customized implementation seconds support was added. As a brief introduction, the `cron` scheduler has the following syntax where you can declare a point in time, or time intervals:

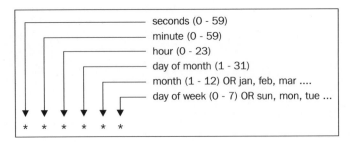

An example of a point in time is the pattern: `0 0 17 * * fri`, which executes exactly at 18:00:00 every Friday. And, if you change the last field to `mon-fri` we are specifying a time interval, when the job is going to be executed from Monday to Friday at 18:00:00.

See also

In order to understand more about the `cron` syntax, you can use the Wikipedia page `http://en.wikipedia.org/wiki/Cron` as a starting point and then read the tutorials linked in its *Reference* section.

Implementing calendar-based rules

Along with the implementation of timers explained in the previous recipe, another way to schedule rules is using the calendar support. This functionality is also implemented using the Quartz Framework and is very useful to define blocks of time in which rules cannot be executed. For example, with this feature a set of rules can be defined to be executed only on the weekdays, all the non-holidays, or not on specific dates when you need to avoid the rules' execution.

Getting ready

If you want to use this feature, you need to add another dependency in your project. Along with the minimal and required Drools dependencies (`knowledge-api`, `drools-core`, and `drools-compiler`), the quartz library is needed to create the calendars.

In a project managed using Apache Maven, you have to add the following XML with the dependency declaration into the POM file. Keep in mind than the minimum required quartz version is 1.6.1:

```xml
<dependency>
    <groupId>org.opensymphony.quartz</groupId>
    <artifactId>quartz</artifactId>
    <version>1.6.1</version>
</dependency>
```

How to do it...

Carry out the following steps in order to complete the recipe:

1. Create a new DRL file and add the following rule, which is configured with a calendar using the `calendar` keyword followed by a calendar identifier that will be registered in the next step:

```
rule "New virtualization request"
calendars "only-weekdays"
when
    $request : VirtualizationRequest($serverName : serverName)
    $server : Server(name==$serverName)
then
    System.out.println("New virtualization added on server " +
$serverName);
    $server.getVirtualizations().add(
        $request.getVirtualization());
    $request.setSuccessful(true);
    retract($request);
end
```

2. Create a new unit test in this example using JUnit, where a Quartz Calendar object is registered with the same identifier. It is used in the rule that was previously created into the knowledge session before beginning to insert facts into it:

```
@Test
public void virtualizationRequestTest() throws
InterruptedException {

    StatefulKnowledgeSession ksession =
        createKnowledgeSession();

    WeeklyCalendar calendar = new WeeklyCalendar();
    org.drools.time.Calendar onlyWeekDays = QuartzHelper
        .quartzCalendarAdapter(calendar);

    ksession.getCalendars().set("only-weekdays",
                                onlyWeekDays);

    Server debianServer = new Server("debianServer", 4,
                                4096, 1024, 0);
    ksession.insert(debianServer);

    Virtualization rhel = new Virtualization("rhel",
        "debianServer", 2048, 160);
    VirtualizationRequest virtualizationRequest =
        new VirtualizationRequest(rhel);

    ksession.insert(virtualizationRequest);

    ksession.fireAllRules();

    if (isWeekday()) {
        Assert.assertEquals(true,
            virtualizationRequest.isSuccessful());
        System.out.println("The virtualization request was " +
            "accepted on server: " + rhel.getServerName());
    }
    else {
        Assert.assertEquals(false,
            virtualizationRequest.isSuccessful());
        System.out.println("The virtualization request was " +
            "rejected because is weekend.");
    }

}
```

How it works...

As was said in the recipe introduction, the calendar feature allows you to specify a block of time in which the rule cannot be executed. When an object is inserted into the working memory, or the working memory internal state changes because other rules are being fired, such as updating/deleting/retracting facts, it generates a new full pattern matching of the rules and the inserted facts. Once this process happens, the rules that have a calendar declaration with a `false` value cannot be matched, and by consequence they cannot generate new activations.

 The rule's calendar assignment doesn't make the rule false, it just prevents the generation of rule activations.

In order to configure a Drools Calendar, an `org.quartz.Calendar` implementation is needed. Quartz has several implementations that are ready to be used, such as a `WeeklyCalendar`, a `HolidayCalendar`, a `MonthlyCalendar`, and so on. It also has a customizable calendar that can be created so as to implement the `org.quartz.Calendar` interface.

For example, the `WeeklyCalendar` returns `true` by default when it is a weekday, but it can be personalized to exclude/include another day:

```
WeeklyCalendar calendar = new WeeklyCalendar();
```

Then the Drools `QuartzHelper` is used to create an `org.drools.time.Calendar` object, passed as a first parameter to the previously instantiated Quartz Calendar:

```
org.drools.time.Calendar onlyWeekDays = QuartzHelper.quartzCalendarAda
pter(calendar);
```

After these steps, the calendar is ready to be registered into the `StatefulKnowledgeSession` object, which should be done before any object insertion. In order to register the calendar, we have to use the `set(String calendarIdentifier, Calendar calendar)` method of the `getCalendars()` KnowledgeSession method, passing the rule calendar identifier as the first parameter and the previously created `org.drools.timer.Calendar` as the second one.

```
ksession.getCalendars().set("only-weekdays", onlyWeekDays);
```

These are all the steps needed to register and configure the calendar. After this the `StatefulKnowledgeSession` is ready to be used as you normally do.

Monitoring query changes in real time

In the previous Drools release it was not possible to follow how a query changes when the working memory is updated; however, now with the implementation of **Live Queries** it is possible to monitor how a query changes over time. This feature is useful for monitoring purposes, because it allows following the evolution of the facts' fields in real time.

How to do it...

Carry out the following steps in order to achieve this recipe:

1. Create a DRL file and add the following rule definition to it. As you can see, the rule query syntax is still the same as for the previous Drools release and has not changed to implement this feature:

```
package drools.cookbook.chapter01

query serverCpuUsage(int maxValue)
    $server : Server(cpuUsage <= maxValue)
end


rule "Check the minimum server configuration"
dialect "mvel"
when
    $server : Server(processors < 2 || memory<=1024 ||
diskSpace<=250)
then
    System.out.println("Server \"" + $server.name + "\" was
rejected by don't apply the minimum configuration.");
    retract($server);
end
```

2. Now you have to create a custom `ViewChangedEventListener` implementation to store the query's Change events:

```
import org.drools.runtime.rule.Row;
import org.drools.runtime.rule.ViewChangedEventListener;

public class CustomViewChangedEventListener implements
ViewChangedEventListener {

    private List<Server> updatedServers;
    private List<Server> removedServers;
    private List<Server> currentServers;

    public CustomViewChangedEventListener() {
```

```
        updatedServers = new ArrayList<Server>();
        removedServers = new ArrayList<Server>();
        currentServers = new ArrayList<Server>();
    }

    public void rowUpdated(Row row) {
        updatedServers.add((Server)row.get("$server"));
    }

    public void rowRemoved(Row row) {
        removedServers.add((Server)row.get("$server"));
    }

    public void rowAdded(Row row) {
        currentServers.add((Server)row.get("$server"));
    }

    public List<Server> getUpdatedServers() {
        return updatedServers;
    }

    public List<Server> getRemovedServers() {
        return removedServers;
    }

    public List<Server> getCurrentServers() {
        return currentServers;
    }

}
```

3. In the last step, you have to register the listener created in the previous step in the query that needs to be monitored. In order to register a listener, you have to open a LiveQuery using the openLiveQuery(queryName, params, listener) method of the StatefulKnowledgeSession:

```
StatefulKnowledgeSession ksession = createKnowledgeSession();

Server winServer = new Server("winServer", 4, 4096, 2048, 25);
ksession.insert(winServer);

Server ubuntuServer = new Server("ubuntuServer", 4, 2048, 1024,
70);
FactHandle ubuntuServerFactHandle = ksession.insert(ubuntuServer);
```

```
Server debianServer = new Server("debianServer", 4, 2048, 1024,
10);
ksession.insert(debianServer);

CustomViewChangedEventListener listener = new
CustomViewChangedEventListener();
LiveQuery query = ksession.openLiveQuery("serverCpuUsage", new
Object[]{20}, listener);

// only 1 server object in the query results
System.out.println(listener.getCurrentServers().size());

ubuntuServer.setCpuUsage(10);
ksession.update(ubuntuServerFactHandle, ubuntuServer);

// now there are 2 server objects in the query results
System.out.println(listener.getCurrentServers().size());

ubuntuServer.setCpuUsage(5);
ksession.update(ubuntuServerFactHandle, ubuntuServer);

// 2 server objects still in the query results
System.out.println(listener.getCurrentServers().size());
// but one of them was updated
System.out.println(listener.getUpdatedServers().size());

query.close();
ksession.dispose();
```

How it works...

Live Queries work by opening a view and publishing events, which are pushed into the registered custom `ViewChangedEventListener` implementation every time the working memory's internal status changes.

In order to use the Live Queries feature it is necessary to implement a custom listener, which should implement the `org.drools.runtime.rule.ViewChangedEventListener` interface. This interface has three methods that should be implemented to store and update the query events. As a simple approach, a listener implementation could store the information internally in a Java Collection.

Once the `ViewChangedEventListener` implementation is done, it should be registered with the associated query using the `openLiveQuery(String query, Object[] params, ViewChangedEventListener listener)` method of the `StatefulKnowledgeSession` where it will be registered:

```
LiveQuery query = ksession.openLiveQuery("serverCpuUsage", new
Object[]{20}, listener);
```

Here the parameters of the method are as follows:

- ▶ `query`: The name of the query to be monitored
- ▶ `parameters`: The parameters required by the query
- ▶ `listener`: The listener used to monitor the query

Once the query is "opened", every time the working memory's internal state changes, the opened query results can be potentially refreshed. When the query results change, the listener is pushed with the associated information, which invokes one of the three methods implemented.

And finally, the query results are ready to be consumed based in the listener storage implementation. In this example, the server objects from the query results are stored in three different collections to know which are the current, updated, and removed servers.

There's more...

Another useful feature is integration with `GlazedList` libraries to process the `LiveQuery` results. The goal of `GlazedList` is to let us apply transformations on List objects, such as sorting, filtering, and multiple transformations.

As a simple use in the current example, we are going to sort the output of the `serverCpuUsage` query based on the CPU usage.

In order to start using `GlazedList`, it is necessary to import the required library; it can be done using the following Apache Maven XML code snippet.

```xml
<dependency>
  <groupId>net.java.dev.glazedlists</groupId>
  <artifactId>glazedlists_java15</artifactId>
  <version>1.8.0</version>
</dependency>
```

Now, we have to create another custom `ViewChangedEventListener` implementation, but this time it also should extend the `AbstractEventList` class. Next, you will see an example of a listener implementation:

```java
public class GlazedListViewChangedEventListener
                        extends AbstractEventList<Row>
                        implements ViewChangedEventListener {

    private List<Row> data = new ArrayList<Row>();

    public void rowUpdated(Row row) {
        int index = this.data.indexOf( row );
        updates.beginEvent();
```

```java
        updates.elementUpdated(index, row, row);
        updates.commitEvent();
    }

    public void rowRemoved(Row row) {
        int index = this.data.indexOf(row);
        updates.beginEvent();
        data.remove(row);
        updates.elementDeleted(index, row);
        updates.commitEvent();
    }

    public void rowAdded(Row row) {
        int index = size();
        updates.beginEvent();
        updates.elementInserted(index, row);
        data.add(row);
        updates.commitEvent();
    }

    public void dispose() {
        data.clear();
    }

    @Override
    public Row get(int index) {
        return data.get(index);
    }

    @Override
    public int size() {
        return data.size();
    }

}
```

The difference with the previous listener implemented is that using `GlazedList` now you have to store, update, and delete the elements into the `updates` field provided by the `AbstractEventList` class.

Now, after opening the `LiveQuery` as we saw previously in this recipe, it is time to create the customized `GlazedList` object. In this example, a `GlazedList` `SortedList` object was used to order the list using the `cpuUsage` field as reference, as you can see in the following code snippet:

```
SortedList<Row> serverSortedList = new
SortedList<Row>(listener, new Comparator<Row>() {
    public int compare(Row r1, Row r2) {
    Server server1 = (Server) r1.get("$server");
        Server server2 = (Server) r2.get("$server");
        return (server1.getCpuUsage() - server2.getCpuUsage());
}
});
```

In this `SortedList` instance, a custom `Comparator` was implemented to override the default behavior, in which the objects to be compared must implement the `Comparator` interface. In the `compare(Row r1, Row r2)` method the row object is used to obtain the variable bounded in the query, in this case the `$server` variable name.

Once the customized `GlazedList` is implemented it's ready to be used to query the results, as you can see in the following code snippet:

```
for (Row row : serverSortedList) {
    System.out.println(row.get("$server"));
}
```

And lastly, don't forget to check out the examples provided with the book to complement the recipes.

2
Expert: Behind the Rules

In this chapter, we will cover:

- ▶ Marshalling knowledge sessions
- ▶ Using persistence to store knowledge
- ▶ How to discard duplicated facts on insertion
- ▶ Using a custom classloader in knowledge agent
- ▶ Verifying the quality of rules with the Drools Verifier
- ▶ Monitoring knowledge with JMX

Introduction

Beyond knowing and using rules, it is necessary to know what other tasks can be performed with the knowledge of using the Drools API. These tasks begin with two possible ways to store knowledge, to how monitor the knowledge sessions to know their internal state and its behavior. This chapter will be focused on recipes that are not completely related to rules authoring, but will help in the integration process.

Marshalling knowledge sessions

Knowledge storage can be an important feature of your application if you want to resume the execution with the previous working memory state. This recipe will cover a simple approach to how you can store your knowledge sessions using the Drools API and how to recover them so that they can used immediately.

How to do it...

Follow the steps given here in order to complete this recipe:

1. Create your business rules, knowledge base, and knowledge session as you normally do.

2. Implement the `java.io.Serializable` interface in all your business objects, so that they can be marshalled.

3. Obtain a `Marshaller` instance using the Drools `MarshallerFactory` object, create a `java.io.File` object, and save the working memory data in a `ksession.info` file. Don't forget to close the file stream. The following code shows this:

```
ByteArrayOutputStream baos = new ByteArrayOutputStream();
Marshaller marshaller = MarshallerFactory
    .newMarshaller(kbase);
File file = new File("ksession.info");
FileOutputStream foStream;
foStream = new FileOutputStream(file);
marshaller.marshall(baos, ksession);
baos.writeTo(foStream);
baos.close();
```

4. At this point of the recipe the working memory data was stored in the `ksession.info` file. Now, to unmarshall the stored knowledge session it is necessary to use a `Marshaller` object that is created with the same knowledge base used to create the knowledge session, which is now going to be unmarshalled. It can be the same one used to store the knowledge session or a new instance:

```
Marshaller marshaller = MarshallerFactory
    .newMarshaller(kbase);
```

5. The last step is to invoke the `unmarshall(InputStream is)` method of the `Marshaller` object, which will return the restored `StatefulKnowledgeSession`:

```
FileInputStream fileInputStream =
    new FileInputStream("ksession.info");
StatefulKnowledgeSession ksession = marshaller
    .unmarshall(fileInputStream);
```

How it works...

The process of marshalling/unmarshalling a working memory is relatively easy because Drools provides the entire API to do it. In order to do this, it is necessary to use a `MarshallerFactory` together with the `KnowledgeBase` and the `StatefulKnowledgeSession` that is going to be stored:

Obtain an `org.drools.marshalling.Marshaller` object instance through the `newMarshaller(KnowledgeBase kbase)` static method of the `org.drools.marshalling.MarshallerFactory` class.

```
Marshaller marshaller = MarshallerFactory
    .newMarshaller(kbase);
```

The marshaller can use different strategies to know how to marshall your business objects and these strategies can be specified using the `newMarshaller(KnowledgeBase kbase, ObjectMarshallingStrategy[] strategies)` method, but the usage of strategies will be covered later in the *There's more* section of this recipe. The only thing that you should know at this moment is that the default strategy is the **SerializeMarshallingStrategy** and works using the `writeObject()` method of your business classes that implement the `Serializable` interface.

The next step is the creation of a `java.io.File` and a `FileOutputStream` object to store the `StatefulKnowledgeSession`:

```
File file = new File("ksession.info");
FileOutputStream foStream = new FileOutputStream(file);
```

Once it's done, the `StatefulKnowledgeSession` is ready to be marshalled. In this step a `ByteArrayOutputStream` is necessary to convert the `KnowledgeSession` into `bytes[]` objects and then write it into the `FileOutputStream`.

```
ByteArrayOutputStream baos = new ByteArrayOutputStream();
marshaller.marshall(baos, ksession);
baos.writeTo(foStream)
baos.close();
```

After these lines of code, the current state of the `StatefulKnowledgeSession` is stored into the `ksession.info` file. Keep in mind that any working memory modifications that happen after the marshalling process aren't going to be stored in the file unless the marshalling process is executed again.

There's more...

Unmarshalling is the inverse process that will allow us to restore our knowledge session from the disk and it's important to understand how to do it to be able to save and restore our working memory data. The following sections explain how to achieve this.

Unmarshalling the knowledge session

Now, it is time to unmarshall the stored `StatefulKnowledgeSession`. As said before, it's necessary to have a `Marshaller` created with the same `KnowledgeBase` with which the `StatefulKnowledgeSession` was marshalled (for example, the `KnowledgeBase` needs to have the same rules):

```
Marshaller marshaller = MarshallerFactory
    .newMarshaller(kbase);
```

Once the marshaller is created, the `unmarshall(InputStream is)` method is used to obtain the `StatefulKnowledgeSession`. This code snippet shows how this method receives an `InputStream` object, and how the knowledge was stored into a file. We are now going to use a `FileInputStream` created with the name of the file in which the `StatefulKnowledgeSession` was stored:

```
FileInputStream fis = new FileInputStream("ksession.info");
StatefulKnowledgeSession ksession = marshaller
    .unmarshall(fis);
```

Once this method is invoked, it returns a `StatefulKnowledgeSession` that is ready to be used as you usually use it.

If you take a look into the `Marshaller` methods, you will find that there are other umarshaller methods with different parameters, for example, the `unmarshall(InputStream is, StatefulKnowledgeSession ksession)` method. This will unmarshall the `InputStream` into the `StatefulKnowledgeSession` that is passed as the second parameter, losing the current session state.

Session can be marshalled using different strategies to serialize the data in different ways. Next, you will see how to use another type of marshalling without implementing the `Serializable` interface in your domain objects.

Using marshalling strategies

Marshalling strategies allow you to specify how the session is marshalled. By default there are two implementations, `IdentityMarshallingStrategy` and `SerializeMarshallingStrategy`, but the users can implement their own strategy implementing the `ObjectMarshallingStrategy` interface (for example, one possible implementation is the creation of a `XMLMarshallingStrategy` that uses XStream to marshall/unmarshall your Plain Old Java Objects, that is, POJOs).

In the previous example, only the `SerializeMarshallingStrategy` was used, which needs the user POJOs to implement the `Serializable` interface. However, if you don't want to implement this interface, then the `IdentityMarshallingStrategy` can be your choice. In this case, you must keep in mind that you have to use the same `Marshaller` to unmarshall the knowledge session, because this strategy works by marshalling/unmarshalling a `Map` object in which only the object's ID is stored. However, it keeps the object references in another object, which isn't marshalled.

In order to use an `IdentityMarshallingStrategy`, follow the steps given below:

1. Create a `ClassFilterAcceptor` to specify the packages in which the strategy is going to be applied. Otherwise the default `*.*` pattern is going to be used and all the files will use the strategy. In this example, the classes inside the `drools.cookbook.chapter02.virtualization` do not implement `Serializable` because these classes are going to be marshalled using an `IdentityMarshallingStrategy`.

    ```
    String[] patters = new String[]
        {"drools.cookbook.chapter02.virtualization.*" }
    ObjectMarshallingStrategyAcceptor identityAcceptor =
    MarshallerFactory.newClassFilterAcceptor(patterns);
    ```

2. After the `ClassFilterAcceptor` creation, obtain the `ObjectMarshallingStrategy` objects. Here two strategies are obtained, one using the *identity* approach together with the `ClassFileAcceptor` and the other one using the *serialize* strategy to serialize all the others packages.

    ```
    ObjectMarshallingStrategy identityStrategy = MarshallerFactory
        .newIdentityMarshallingStrategy(identityAcceptor);
    ObjectMarshallingStrategy serializeStrategy = MarshallerFactory.
    newSerializeMarshallingStrategy();
    ```

3. The final step consists of obtaining a `Marshaller` instance, and letting the `MarshallerFactory` know that these two strategies are going to be used.

    ```
    Marshaller = MarshallerFactory.newMarshaller(kbase,
        new ObjectmarshallingStrategy[]{identityStrategy,
    serializeStrategy});
    ```

And that is all that needs to be done to use marshalling strategies. Now you can start using the marshaller as was seen in this recipe.

Using persistence to store knowledge

Another option to store the working memory state is using the JPA persistence provided by the **drools-persistence-jpa module**, which will basically store all the inserted facts in a relational database. This recipe will cover the configuration that can only be used with business rules. However, in the next chapter, it will be explained how to configure it to be used together with business processes.

Getting ready

The only preliminary step is to add the extra dependencies needed by the project and that is going to be described in the following Apache Maven dependencies code snippet. In addition to the **drools-persistence-jpa**, which is the module that provides the JPA feature, the two more dependencies that are required are: the **Bitronix Transaction Manager**, a simple and embeddable JTA Transaction Manager, and a **JDBC** Driver, in this case, the embedded and in-memory **H2** database engine driver.

```
<dependencies>
  <dependency>
    <groupId>org.drools</groupId>
    <artifactId>drools-persistence-jpa</artifactId>
    <version>5.2.0.Final</version>
  </dependency>
  <dependency>
    <groupId>org.codehaus.btm</groupId>
    <artifactId>btm</artifactId>
    <version>1.3.3</version>
  </dependency>
  <dependency>
    <groupId>com.h2database</groupId>
    <artifactId>h2</artifactId>
    <version>1.2.128</version>
  </dependency>
</dependencies>
```

How to do it...

Follow the steps given here in order to complete this recipe:

1. After adding the required dependencies in the Apache Maven project, implement the `java.io.Serializable` interface in all the classes that are going to be inserted into the working memory.

2. Create a `persistence.xml` file into the `META-INF` directory of the project with the following code:

```xml
<?xml version="1.0" encoding="UTF-8"?>
<persistence version="1.0"
    xmlns="http://java.sun.com/xml/ns/persistence"
    xmlns:orm="http://java.sun.com/xml/ns/persistence/orm"
    xmlns:xsi="http://www.w3.org/2001/XMLSchema-instance"
    xsi:schemaLocation="http://java.sun.com/xml/ns/persistence
    http://java.sun.com/xml/ns/persistence/persistence_1_0.xsd
                    http://java.sun.com/xml/ns/persistence/orm
http://java.sun.com/xml/ns/persistence/orm_1_0.xsd">
  <persistence-unit name="drools.cookbook.persistence.jpa"
      transaction-type="JTA">
   <provider>org.hibernate.ejb.HibernatePersistence</provider>
   <jta-data-source>jdbc/testDatasource</jta-data-source>
   <class>org.drools.persistence.info.SessionInfo</class>
   <properties>
     <property name="hibernate.dialect"
               value="org.hibernate.dialect.H2Dialect" />
     <property name="hibernate.max_fetch_depth" value="3" />
     <property name="hibernate.hbm2ddl.auto"
               value="create" />
     <property name="hibernate.show_sql" value="true" />
     <property name="hibernate.connection.autocommit"
               value="true" />
     <property
       name="hibernate.transaction.manager_lookup_class"
value= "org.hibernate.transaction.BTMTransactionManagerLookup"
     />
   </properties>
  </persistence-unit>
</persistence>
```

3. Create a `jndi.properties` file inside the `resources` folder with the following content:

```
java.naming.factory.initial=bitronix.tm.jndi.
BitronixInitialContextFactory
```

4. Now is the time to configure and initialize the data source. Configure the environment, and create a `StatefulKnowledgeSession` through the `JPAKnowledgeService`. Create a new Java class and add the following code inside the `main` method:

```java
PoolingDataSource dataSource = new PoolingDataSource();
dataSource.setUniqueName("jdbc/testDatasource");
dataSource.setMaxPoolSize(5);
dataSource.setAllowLocalTransactions(true);

dataSource.setClassName("org.h2.jdbcx.JdbcDataSource");
dataSource.setMaxPoolSize(3);
dataSource.getDriverProperties().put("user", "sa");
dataSource.getDriverProperties().put("password", "sa");
dataSource.getDriverProperties().put("URL","jdbc:h2:mem:");

dataSource.init();

Environment env = KnowledgeBaseFactory.newEnvironment();
EntityManagerFactory emf = Persistence
.createEntityManagerFactory("drools.cookbook.persistence.jpa");

env.set(EnvironmentName.ENTITY_MANAGER_FACTORY, emf);
env.set(EnvironmentName.TRANSACTION_MANAGER,
    TransactionManagerServices.getTransactionManager());
env.set(EnvironmentName.GLOBALS, new MapGlobalResolver());

KnowledgeBuilder kbuilder = KnowledgeBuilderFactory
    .newKnowledgeBuilder();
kbuilder.add(new ClassPathResource("rules.drl", getClass()),
    ResourceType.DRL);

if (kbuilder.hasErrors()) {
    if (kbuilder.getErrors().size() > 0) {
        for (KnowledgeBuilderError kerror : kbuilder.getErrors())
{
            System.err.println(kerror);
        }
    }
}

kbase = kbuilder.newKnowledgeBase();
ksession = JPAKnowledgeService
    .newStatefulKnowledgeSession(kbase, null, env);
```

5. Once the `StatefulKnowledgeSession` is created, you can start to insert/modify/ retract facts into the working memory. But in order to use the JPA persistence, a `UserTransaction` should be started before inserting a fact into the working memory and should be committed after it:

```
UserTransaction ut = (UserTransaction) new InitialContext()
    .lookup("java:comp/UserTransaction");

ut.begin();
Server debianServer = new Server("debianServer", 4, 4096, 1024, 0);
ksession.insert(debianServer);
ksession.fireAllRules();
ut.commit();
```

How it works...

Once you have implemented the `java.io.Serializable` interface in your domain model, we have to configure the JPA persistence. In the second step, we created a `persistence.xml` file, which creates a persistence unit and configures the JPA `EntityManager` provider, and this file will be explained next in order to detail the most important parameters of this configuration file.

One of most important parameters is the `provider`, where you can specify which JPA implementation you would like to use. The recommended implementation is the one provided by Hibernate, which is currently used in the Drools JPA Persistence internal tests:

```
<provider>org.hibernate.ejb.HibernatePersistence</provider>
```

Another parameter is the configuration of the JNDI name of the database. Choose a name that is easy to remember to later programmatically configure the datasource.

```
<jta-data-source>jdbc/testDatasource</jta-data-source>
```

Then a class XML tag will be added to make a reference to the Drools object that will store all the information about the working memory state. The jBPM5 business processes are not going to be used in this recipe and hence, we only need to add the `SessionInfo` object, which will contain the working memory state serialized in one of its fields:

```
<class>org.drools.persistence.info.SessionInfo</class>
```

Now, it is time to configure the Hibernate properties, where the most important configurations are: the Hibernate Dialect and the Transaction Manager configuration, which will depend on your database engine (for example, H2), and the JTA Transaction Manager (for example, Bitronix).

Follow the steps given here to configure the Hibernate properties:

1. The following code snippet shows a complete Hibernate configuration using an H2 database and a Bitronix Transaction Manager:

```
<properties>
  <property name="hibernate.dialect"
            value="org.hibernate.dialect.H2Dialect" />
  <property name="hibernate.max_fetch_depth" value="3" />
  <property name="hibernate.hbm2ddl.auto" value="create" />
  <property name="hibernate.show_sql" value="true" />
  <property name="hibernate.connection.autocommit"
            value="true" />
  <property name="hibernate.transaction.manager_lookup_class"
 value="org.hibernate.transaction.BTMTransactionManagerLookup" />
</properties>
```

At this point the `persistence.xml` file is already configured and now you can move to the next step.

The `jndi.properties` file created in the `resources` folder will register the Bitronix Transaction Manager inside the JNDI directory, which is mostly used in plain J2SE applications running outside an application server. In this step you only have to add the following code in the `jndi.properties` file:

```
java.naming.factory.initial=bitronix.tm.jndi.
BitronixInitialContextFactory
```

2. Once all the configuration files are created, you are ready to create a `StatefulKnowledgeSession` to start interacting with. This process involves the creation of various resources such as the `PoolingDataSource`, an `Environment`, and the `StatefulKnowledgeSession` itself.

3. Create a new Java class file and add the following code inside a Java `main` method. In this example, we are using Bitronix as the transaction manager, and hence it is necessary to create the datasource using a `bitronix.tm.resource.jdbc.PoolingDataSource` object. To configure this datasource properly, it is necessary to at least configure the following properties:

   - **Unique name**: This will be the same value as the `<jta-data-source/>` `persistence.xml` property.
   - **Class name**: This is the canonical name of the database engine JDBC datasource class.
   - **Driver properties**: These are the user, password, and URL of the JDBC engine, which depend of the database engine driver.

```
PoolingDataSource dataSource = new PoolingDataSource();
dataSource.setUniqueName("jdbc/testDatasource");
```

```
dataSource.setMaxPoolSize(5);
dataSource.setAllowLocalTransactions(true);

dataSource.setClassName("org.h2.jdbcx.JdbcDataSource");
dataSource.setMaxPoolSize(3);
dataSource.getDriverProperties().put("user", "sa");
dataSource.getDriverProperties().put("password", "sa");
dataSource.getDriverProperties().put("URL", "jdbc:h2:mem:");
```

4. After this configuration, the datasource must be started and stopped once the application execution is finished:

```
datasource.init();
```

5. Once the datasource is started, it is time to create an `EntityManagerFactory` using the JPA API that will load the `persistence.xml` file with the definitions of the persistent units, and create the `EntityManagerFactory` if the `drools.cookbook.persistence.jpa` persistence unit definition is found.

```
EntiManagerFactory emf = Persistence
    .createEntityManagerFactory(
        "drools.cookbook.persistence.jpa");
```

6. After the `EntityManagerFactory` creation, it is time to configure the Drools Environment using the `newEnvironment()` static method of `KnowledgeBaseFactory` to obtain a new instance, shown in the following code snippet. The `Environment` object needs at least these two properties configured:

   □ **EnvironmentName.ENTITY_MANAGER_FACTORY**: The `EntityManagerFactory` object that was created in the previous step

   □ **EnvironmentName.TRANSACTION_MANAGER**: The property that holds the `TransactionManager` object created with the selected implementation

```
Environment env = KnowledgeBaseFactory.newEnvironment();
env.set(EnvironmentName.ENTITY_MANAGER_FACTORY, emf);
env.set(EnvironmentName.TRANSACTION_MANAGER,
        TransactionManagerServices.getTransactionManager());
```

7. Once the `Environment` object is configured, it is time to create the `StatefulKnowledgeSession` using a different API; but the `KnowledgeBase` must be created using the common API. To create a JPA-enabled `StatefulKnowledgeSession`, you need to invoke the `newStatefulKnowledgeSession(args..)` static method of the `JPAKnowledgeService` class, and pass the `KnowledgeBase`, the `KnowledgeSessionConfiguration` (if required), and the `Environment` objects as the method arguments:

```
StatefulKnowledgeSession ksession = JPAKnowledgeService
    .newStatefulKnowledgeSession(kbase, null, env);
```

After these steps, the `StatefulKnowledgeSession` is ready to save the working memory state using JPA, but to do this, it is necessary to use JTA `UserTransactions` when objects are inserted/modified/retracted into the `KnowledgeSession`. If no `UserTransaction` is started or committed, then the working memory state is not going to be stored, losing all the information:

```
UserTransaction ut = (UserTransaction) new InitialContext()
    .lookup("java:comp/UserTransaction");

ut.begin();
Server debianServer = new Server("debianServer", 4, 4096, 1024, 0);
Ksession.insert(debianServer);

Ut.commit();
```

There's more...

In a production environment, it is recommended to use another database engine rather than the in-memory and embeddable H2 due to obvious reasons. In this section, we are going to see the configuration changes needed to use **MySQL** as the database engine:

1. The initial step is to add the MySQL driver dependency into the project. If you are using Apache Maven, you can add the following XML code in your Project Object Model (POM), which is also referred to as `pom.xml` file:

```
<dependency>
  <groupId>mysql</groupId>
  <artifactId>mysql-connector-java</artifactId>
  <version>5.0.8</version>
</dependency>
```

2. Next, you will see all the necessary modifications in the previously-created files. The `hibernate.dialect` property in the `persistence.xml` file needs to be modified with the `MySQLDialect` class canonical name:

```
<property name="hibernate.dialect"
    value="org.hibernate.dialect.MySQLDialect" />;
```

3. The last step is to change the datasource driver properties, in this case, modifying the classname property value, removing the URL property, and adding the database and `serverName` properties.

```
dataSource.setClassName("com.mysql.jdbc.jdbc2.optional.
MysqlXADataSource");

dataSource.setMaxPoolSize(3);
dataSource.getDriverProperties().put("user", "user");
```

```
dataSource.getDriverProperties().put("password", "password");
dataSource.getDriverProperties().put("databaseName",
                                    "databaseName");
dataSource.getDriverProperties().put("serverName ", "localhost");
```

After these modifications you are ready to start using MySQL as your JPA database engine.

How to discard duplicated facts on insertion

In some scenarios, you will have to discard equal objects (objects of the same type and values) when they are inserted into the working memory, to avoid data inconsistency and unnecessary activations. In this recipe, we will see how to change the insert behavior just by changing one configuration property.

How to do it...

Follow the steps given here in order to complete this recipe:

1. Override the `hashcode()` and `equals(Object obj)` methods in your business classes, as shown in the following code:

```
public class Server {

    private String name;
    private int processors;
    private int memory;
    private int diskSpace;
    private int cpuUsage;


    @Override
    public boolean equals(Object obj) {
        if (obj == null) {
            return false;
        }
        if (!(obj instanceof Server)) {
            return false;
        }
        Server server = (Server) obj;
        return server.name.equals(name)
                && server.processors == processors
                && server.memory == memory
                && server.diskSpace == diskSpace
```

```
                          && server.virtualizations.size() ==
                              virtualizations.size();
        }


        @Override
        public int hashCode() {
            int result = 17;
            result = 31 * result + name.hashCode();
            result = 31 * result + processors;
            result = 31 * result + memory;
            result = 31 * result + diskSpace;
            return result;
        }


    }
```

2. In order to configure the default assert behavior property to equality, you have to configure it using a `KnowledgeBaseConfiguration` object, which will be also used to create `KnowledgeBase`. Create a new Java class and add the following code inside the `main` method:

```
KnowledgeBaseConfiguration kbaseConfig = KnowledgeBaseFactory
    .newKnowledgeBaseConfiguration();
kbaseConfig.setOption(AssertBehaviorOption.EQUALITY);
KnowledgeBase kbase = KnowledgeBaseFactory
    .newKnowledgeBase(kbaseConfig);
StatefulKnowledgeSession ksession = kbase
    .newStatefulKnowledgeSession();
```

3. Now that the `StatefulKnowledgeSession` is created, you can start to instantiate facts with the same data and insert them into the knowledge session.

```
Server debianServer = new Server("debianServer", 8, 8192, 2048, 0);
ksession.insert(debianServer);

Server anotherDebianServer = new Server("debianServer", 8,
                                        8192, 2048, 0);
ksession.insert(anotherDebianServer);

System.out.println(ksession.getObjects().size());
```

4. Once you execute the `main` method, you will see how the `StatefulKnowledgeSession` discards the facts with the same data using the overridden `equals()` and `hashCode(object)` methods.

How it works...

As discussed earlier, it is possible to modify the default insert behavior to discard duplicated facts. To do so, follow the steps given here:

The first step involves the overrides of the hashcode() and equals(object) methods of the objects of which you want to discard the duplications.

Once your domain objects override the hashCode() and equals(object) methods, it is time to configure the assertion behavior using a KnowledgeBaseConfiguration object, and this is done by setting the AssertBehaviorOption.EQUALITY option:

```
KnowledgeBaseConfiguration kbaseConfig = KnowledgeBaseFactory
    .newKnowledgeBaseConfiguration();
kbaseConfig.setOption(AssertBehaviorOption.EQUALITY);
KnowledgeBase kbase = KnowledgeBaseFactory.
newKnowledgeBase(kbaseConfig);
kbase.addKnowledgePackages(kbuilder.getKnowledgePackages());
```

Once the KnowledgeBase is configured to use the equality assert behavior, the KnowledgeSession is ready to discard duplicated inserted objects. Internally, the working memory uses a HashMap to store all the inserted facts and every new inserted object will return a new FactHandle object, the one that was inserted into the working memory, if it isn't already present in the HashMap.

By default the working memory works using the EQUALITY assertion mode. This means that the working memory uses an IdentityHashMap to store the inserted facts, which uses the equality operator (==) to compare the keys and doesn't use the hashCode() method. Using this assertion mode, new fact insertions will always return a new FactHandle object, but when a fact is inserted again, the original FactHandle object will be returned.

Using a custom classloader in a knowledge agent

Knowledge agents were created to monitor resources and dynamically rebuild the KnowledgeBase when these resources are modified, removed, and even new resources are added. Now, it is possible to add or modify rules with new fact types that the KnowledgeAgent classloader cannot recognize without ending in compilation errors when the resources are compiled. This can be done using the custom classloaders feature that will be explained in the next recipe.

How to do it...

Follow the steps given here in order to complete this recipe:

1. Create a new Change Set resource file named `change-set.xml` and add your business rules resources files. In this example, only one DRL file is declared:

```xml
<?xml version="1.0" encoding="UTF-8"?>
<change-set xmlns='http://drools.org/drools-5.0/change-set'
  xmlns:xs='http://www.w3.org/2001/XMLSchema-instance'
  xs:schemaLocation='http://drools.org/drools-5.0/change-set.xsd'>

  <add>
    <resource source =
      'classpath:drools/cookbook/chapter02/rules.drl'
      type='DRL' />
  </add>

</change-set>
```

2. Once you have configured the Change Set resource, create a new Java class file and inside the `main` method add the following code snippet. This code is used to create a custom `URLClassLoader` object using a JAR file named `model.jar`, which will contain your business model:

```java
URL modelJarURL = getClass().getResource("model.jar");
URLClassLoader customURLClassloader =
  new URLClassLoader(new URL[] { modelJarURL });
```

3. Create a knowledge base using the previously created `URLClassLoader` object as shown in the following code. All this code must be included in the previously created `URLClassLoader` object:

```java
KnowledgeBuilderConfiguration kbuilderConfig =
KnowledgeBuilderFactory.newKnowledgeBuilderConfiguration(null,
    customURLClassloader);
KnowledgeBaseConfiguration kbaseConfig = KnowledgeBaseFactory
    .newKnowledgeBaseConfiguration(null,
    customURLClassloader);
KnowledgeBase kbase = KnowledgeBaseFactory
    .newKnowledgeBase(kbaseConfig);
```

4. Next, you have to create a `KnowledgeAgent` object using the previously created `KnowledgeBase` and `KnowledgeBuilderConfiguration` objects:

```
KnowledgeAgentConfiguration aconf =
    KnowledgeAgentFactory.newKnowledgeAgentConfiguration();
KnowledgeAgent kagent =
    KnowledgeAgentFactory.newKnowledgeAgent("test", kbase,
                                            aconf,
                                            kbuilderConfig);
```

5. Finally, it is time to add the knowledge resources and obtain the `KnowledgeBase` updated by the knowledge agent:

```
kagent.applyChangeSet(
    new ClassPathResource("change-set.xml", getClass()));
kbase = kagent.getKnowledgeBase();
```

How it works...

In order to use a custom classloader, it is necessary to have a business model packaged in a JAR file, which can be located in the project structure or in an external directory.

In this case, a `java.net.URLClassLoader` object is used to point to resources loaded by a `java.net.URL` object, which will point to the JAR file:

```
URL modelJarURL = getClass().getResource("model.jar");
URLClassLoader customURLClassloader = new URLClassLoader(new URL[] {
modelJarURL });
```

Once the custom classloader is created, you have to configure a `KnowledgeBuilder` object using a `KnowledgeBuilderConfiguration` object, which will be instantiated with the custom classloader, which was created previously. If you are wondering why it is necessary to configure the `KnowledgeBuilder`, remember that all the resources are compiled using it and the `KnowledgeAgent` doesn't make an exception. The first parameter of the `new KnowledgeBuilderConfiguration(Properties properties, ClassLoader... classLoaders)` static method is used to configure settings as your own accumulate functions, disable MVEL strict mode, change the Java dialect compiler, and so on. The second parameter, which is the one that we are interested in, is used to pass the classloader being used to compile the rules, which can be more than one if required:

```
KnowledgeBuilderConfiguration kbuilderConfig = KnowledgeBuilderFactory
    .newKnowledgeBuilderConfiguration(null, customURLClassloader);
```

Once it is done, the next step is to create an initial and empty `KnowledgeBase` using the `KnowledgeBaseConfiguration` object that was created with the custom classloader:

```
KnowledgeBaseConfiguration kbaseConfig = KnowledgeBaseFactory
    .newKnowledgeBaseConfiguration(null, customURLClassloader);
KnowledgeBase kbase = KnowledgeBaseFactory
    .newKnowledgeBase(kbaseConfig);
```

The last step on the knowledge agent creation process is to create a `KnowledgeAgentConfiguration` object, which in this case doesn't have to be configured, and obtain a `KnowledgeAgent` instance using the `newKnowledgeAgent(String name, KnowledgeBase kbase, KnowledgeAgentConfiguration configuration, KnowledgeBuilderConfiguration builderConfiguration)` static method of the `KnowledgeAgentFactory` together with all the previously created objects:

```
KnowledgeAgentConfiguration aconf = KnowledgeAgentFactory
    .newKnowledgeAgentConfiguration();
KnowledgeAgent kagent = KnowledgeAgentFactory
    .newKnowledgeAgent("test", kbase, aconf, kbuilderConfig);
```

Once the knowledge agent is created, it is time to apply the change set and obtain the generated knowledge base:

```
kagent.applyChangeSet(new ClassPathResource("change-set.xml",
                                            getClass()));
kbase = kagent.getKnowledgeBase();
```

Finally, the knowledge agent is ready to compile the knowledge resources files using the custom classloader generated in the first step. As you may have figured out, the only restriction in this approach is that the configuration could only be passed on the creation instance, without a way to add your classloader in runtime.

Verifying the quality of rules with the Drools Verifier

This recipe will cover how to verify the quality of knowledge packages using the **Drools Verifier** project, which is also built using rules (to verify the quality of rules). Drools Verifier already comes with a full set of verification rules that can be used to test incoherence, equivalence, incompatibility patterns, and so on. It also allows you to create and add your own verification rules.

How to do it...

Follow the steps given here in order to understand how to verify the quality of your business rules:

1. Add the Drools Verifier dependency into the `pom.xml` file of your Apache Maven project:

```
<dependency>
  <groupId>org.drools</groupId>
  <artifactId>drools-verifier</artifactId>
  <version>5.2.0.Final</version>
</dependency>
```

2. Create your business rules and be ready to verify them. In this example, we are going to use really simple rules with visible problems, only for the purpose of showing which information can be collected:

```
package drools.cookbook.chapter02

import drools.cookbook.chapter02.Server
import java.util.Date
import java.util.List

rule "rule 1"
when
    $server : Server(processors==2, memory==1024)
then
    retract($server);
end

rule "rule 2"
when
    $server : Server(processors==2, processors!=2)
then
    retract($server);
end

rule "rule 3"
when
    $server : Server(processors==2, memory==1024)
then
    retract($server);
end
```

3. Create a new Java class named `RulesVerification` and add the following code. Here, we are going to configure Drools Verifier to analyze the quality of the rules:

```java
package drools.cookbook.chapter02;

public class RulesVerification {

    public static void main(String[] args) {

        VerifierBuilder vbuilder = VerifierBuilderFactory
            .newVerifierBuilder();

        Verifier verifier = vbuilder.newVerifier();

        verifier.addResourcesToVerify(new
            ClassPathResource("rules.drl",
                              RulesVerification.class),
                              ResourceType.DRL);

        if (verifier.hasErrors()) {
            List<VerifierError> errors = verifier.getErrors();
            for (VerifierError ve : errors) {
                System.err.println(ve.getMessage());
            }
            throw new RuntimeException("rules with errors");
        }

        verifier.fireAnalysis();

        VerifierReport result = verifier.getResult();

        Collection<VerifierMessageBase> noteMessages = result
                .getBySeverity(Severity.NOTE);
        for (VerifierMessageBase msg : noteMessages) {
            System.out.println("Note: " + msg.getMessage() +
                " type: " + msg.getMessageType() +
                " on: " + msg.getFaulty());
        }

        Collection<VerifierMessageBase> errorMessages = result
                .getBySeverity(Severity.ERROR);
        for (VerifierMessageBase msg : errorMessages) {
            System.out.println("Note: " + msg.getMessage() +
                " type: " + msg.getMessageType() +
                " on: " + msg.getFaulty());
```

```
        }

        Collection<VerifierMessageBase> warningMessages =
            result.getBySeverity(Severity.WARNING);
        for (VerifierMessageBase msg : warningMessages) {
            System.out.println("Note: " + msg.getMessage() +
                " type: " + msg.getMessageType() +
                " on: " + msg.getFaulty());
        }

        Collection<MissingRange> rangeCheckCauses = result
            .getRangeCheckCauses();
        for (MissingRange missingRange : rangeCheckCauses) {
            System.out.println(missingRange);
        }

        verifier.dispose();

    }

}
```

4. Execute the Java `main` method to visualize the analysis output.

How it works...

As we discussed in the introduction of this recipe, the Drools Verifier module works using a specific set of rules that analyzes the rules added using their API. These rules are added by default when the `Verifier` module is initialized into its internal `StatefulKnowledgeSession` (remember that Verifier is built by rules and it is wrapping a knowledge session and its knowledge base) and also the API gives us the possibility to create more verification rules using the Fact Types provided by Drools Verifier.

In the second step, after declaring some rules to use as example, we created a new Java class with the necessary code to analyze the rules.

Next, you will see an explanation about how it was configured and how Verifier works:

1. The first step is to start analyzing rules using the Verifier API to obtain an `org.drools.verifier.Verifier` object instance using the `VerifierBuilder` obtained through the `VerifierBuilderFactory` object factory.

```
VerifierBuilder vbuilder = VerifierBuilderFactory
    .newVerifierBuilder();
Verifier verifier = vbuilder.newVerifier();
```

2. Once it is done, you can start adding the knowledge resources as DRL and Change Set using the `addResourcesToVerify(Resource resource, ResourceType type)` method in the same way as you add resources to a `KnowledgeBuilder`. When you use a `KnowledgeBuilder` to compile the rules, you can know when there are compilation errors, and it also can be done using `Verifier`:

```
verifier.addResourcesToVerify(new
    ClassPathResource("rules.drl", getClass()),
                    ResourceType.DRL);


if (verifier.hasErrors()) {
    List<VerifierError> errors = verifier.getErrors();
    for (VerifierError verifierError : errors) {
        System.err.println(verifierError.getMessage());
    }
    throw new RuntimeException("rules with errors");
}
```

3. After all the rules that needed to be analyzed are added, it is time to initiate the analysis process using the `fireAnalysis()` method, which will return true if no analysis errors occur:

```
boolean works = verifier.fireAnalysis();
```

4. Once the analysis is completed, the next step is to obtain the rules analysis information output:

```
VerifierReport result = verifier.getResult();
```

Using this `VerifierReport` object, you can obtain the information about the analysis invoking its `getBySeverity(Severity serverity)` method, where `Severity` is one of the next three predefined Verification Severity types:

- **NOTE**: Messages that can be ignored (for example, a repeated constraint in a rule pattern)
- **WARNING**: A possible problem, (for example, an inexistent restriction or a missing complement pattern)
- **ERROR**: Something that needs correction (for example, a pattern that could never be satisfied)

For example, the following code is used to obtain and display the ERROR severity types:

```
Collection<VerifierMessageBase> errorMessages = result
    .getBySeverity(Severity.ERROR);
for (VerifierMessageBase msg : errorMessages) {
    System.out.println("Error: " + msg.getMessage() +
                    " type: " + msg.getMessageType() +
                    " on: " + msg.getFaulty());
}
```

Using this code with the rules added in the example, the following output is obtained:

```
Error: Restriction LiteralRestriction from rule [rule 2] value '== 2'
and LiteralRestriction from rule [rule 2] value '!= 2'are in conflict.
Because of this, pattern that contains them can never be satisfied. type:
INCOHERENCE on: Pattern, name: Server


Error: Restriction LiteralRestriction from rule [rule 2] value '!= 2'
and LiteralRestriction from rule [rule 2] value '== 2'are in conflict.
Because of this, pattern that contains them can never be satisfied. type:
INCOHERENCE on: Pattern, name: Server


Error: Pattern, name: Server in Rule 'rule 2' can never be satisfied.
type: ALWAYS_FALSE on: Pattern, name: Server
```

As we can see in the preceding output, the first two error message outputs are pretty similar because the rules are analyzed in all the pattern constraints, and one constraint is in conflict with another one, due to which, the second one will be also in conflict with the first one. Also, this execution output shows that these errors are an *incoherence* and can be found on the `name: Server` pattern of the rule named `rule 2`. As a consequence of this pattern analysis, the last error message confirms that it is an `ALWAYS_FALSE` type and will never be satisfied.

```
Warning: Rule base covers == 1024, but it is missing != 1024 type:
MISSING_EQUALITY on: LiteralRestriction from rule [rule 3] value '==
1024'


Warning: Rule base covers == 1024, but it is missing != 1024 type:
MISSING_EQUALITY on: LiteralRestriction from rule [rule 1] value '==
1024'


Warning: Rules rule 3 and rule 1 are redundant. type: REDUNDANCY on: null
```

As we can see in the preceding output, by obtaining the WARNING type analysis messages, we can discover that the first two messages are again similar. But it is only because the rules `rule 1` and `rule 3` are equals, and this message says that the pattern is only being applied to the 1024 memory value and all the other values aren't going to be analyzed by other rules. This shows a possible point where the knowledge processing is not going to be applied. Earlier, I said that there are two equals rules, and I also told you about how Drools Verifier has the knowledge to detect *redundancy*. This *redundancy* was detected and it gave us a warning.

In this example, we didn't get any **NOTE** analysis message; however, we are going to obtain the field gaps to know which field restrictions are missing. Think about this as more detailed information than the generic WARNING message obtained earlier, which can be obtained using the `getRangeCheckCauses()` method, shown as follows:

```
Collection<MissingRange> rangeCheckCauses = result
    .getRangeCheckCauses();
for (MissingRange missingRange : rangeCheckCauses) {
    System.out.println(missingRange);
}
```

The output will be as follows:

```
Gap: (Field 'memory' from object type 'Server') Operator = '<' 1024 from
rule: [rule 3]

Gap: (Field 'memory' from object type 'Server') Operator = '>' 1024 from
rule: [rule 3]

Gap: (Field 'processors' from object type 'Server') Operator = '<' 2 from
rule: [rule 3]

Gap: (Field 'processors' from object type 'Server') Operator = '>' 2 from
rule: [rule 3]

Gap: (Field 'processors' from object type 'Server') Operator = '>' 2 from
rule: [rule 2]

Gap: (Field 'memory' from object type 'Server') Operator = '<' 1024 from
rule: [rule 1]

Gap: (Field 'memory' from object type 'Server') Operator = '>' 1024 from
rule: [rule 1]

Gap: (Field 'processors' from object type 'Server') Operator = '<' 2 from
rule: [rule 1]

Gap: (Field 'processors' from object type 'Server') Operator = '>' 2 from
rule: [rule 1]

Gap: (Field 'processors' from object type 'Server') Operator = '<' 2 from
rule: [rule 2]
```

All the fields gap message outputs are pretty similar. For example, from the first two messages, we can discern that the memory field of the `Server` object is not being compared in rules with values less than 1024 and greater than 1024, leaving a nonexistent pattern where `Server` objects aren't going to be evaluated by the inference engine.

As you have seen in this recipe, Drools Verifier is a powerful module to analyze the quality of your knowledge, detecting possible points of failure, and also is integrated in Guvnor to build a complete set of rules authoring.

There's more...

Drools Verifier also has the feature to create HTML/TXT reports of the analysis results and, as you can imagine, the reports can only be created once the analysis execution is done. To create these reports, the `VerifierReportWriterFactory` is used to obtain a `VerifierReportWriter` instance, which depends on the report style needed. In the following steps, you will learn quickly how to create your Verifier reports:

1. In this case, an HTML report is going to be generated, so the `newHTMLReportWriter()` static method is invoked to obtain a `VerifierReportWriter`:

   ```
   VerifierReportWriter htmlWriter = VerifierReportWriterFactory
       .newHTMLReportWriter();
   ```

2. The next step is to specify the output file creating a `FileOutputStream` object with the filename as the constructor parameter. In this case, the file extension is ZIP because the `HTMLReportWriter` generates a ZIP file with all the HTML files compressed.

   ```
   FileOutputStream htmlOut = new
       FileOutputStream("htmlReport.zip");
   ```

3. The last step of the report generation is to use the `VerifierReportWriter` instance to write the report, using the previously created `FileOutputStream` object as the first parameter and the verifier execution result as the second one.

   ```
   htmlWriter.writeReport(htmlOut, verifier.getResult());
   ```

   Once this method is invoked, the report should appear in the specified directory path, ready to be unzipped and read with any HTML browser/editor.

Monitoring knowledge with JMX

In this recipe, we will see how to enable the Drools monitoring features and how knowledge bases and knowledge sessions can be monitored. This feature is useful to obtain internal state information about the number of inserted facts in the working memory, fired/created/cancelled activations, rules state information, and so on that was implemented using the JMX technology, which is an industry standard, used to manage and monitor applications/resources.

Getting ready

Before you start enabling the monitoring features, we need to download a **JMX** monitoring tool. In this case, we are going to use **VisualVM**, which actually is more than a JMX monitoring tool as it is primarily used as a profiling application. Download VisualVM 1.3.1 or higher version (if available) from `https://visualvm.dev.java.net/download.html`. It is possible that VisualVM is already installed in your environment because it is bundled in Sun JDK 6 since update 7 and Apple's Java for Mac OS X 10.5 Update 4.

The minimal requisite to execute VisualVM is to have
Oracle/Sun JDK 6+ installed.

Once the application has been downloaded, decompress the ZIP file and execute the
`visualvm` binary file located in the bin directory. After the License Agreement has been
accepted, it's time to install the MBean Plugin (for more information about MBeans refer to
the *There's more...* section of this recipe) to access to the Drools metrics information. The
plugins installation options can be accessed through the **Tools | Plugins** menu, in which the
Available Plugins tab is the one of most interest to us. Check the install column's checkbox
of the **VisualVM-Mbeans** plugin in the list. Click the **Install** button and proceed with the
installation, as shown in the following screenshot:

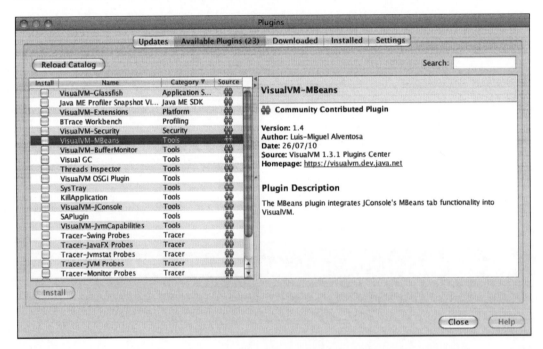

Once the installation is done, we are ready to enable the monitoring feature in our
Drools-enabled application.

How to do it...

Follow the steps given here, in order to monitor your knowledge session using JMX.

1. First, you have to enable the Drools MBean management. This is done configuring the knowledge base using the `MBeansOption.ENABLED` option.

```
KnowledgeBaseConfiguration config = KnowledgeBaseFactory
    .newKnowledgeBaseConfiguration();
config.setOption(MBeansOption.ENABLED);

KnowledgeBase kbase = KnowledgeBaseFactory
    .newKnowledgeBase("kbase", config);
        kbase.addKnowledgePackages(kbuilder.
getKnowledgePackages());
```

2. After the knowledge base is configured, and before executing the application, the JVM must be configured with the following arguments to enable the JMX remote management:

```
-Dcom.sun.management.jmxremote
-Dcom.sun.management.jmxremote.port=3000
-Dcom.sun.management.jmxremote.ssl=false
-Dcom.sun.management.jmxremote.authenticate=false
```

3. Once the application is executed, VisualVM is ready to be started. In the left panel, there is a list of the applications ready to be monitored. Select your application and the **MBeans** tab to see the drools-related information, as shown in the following screenshot:

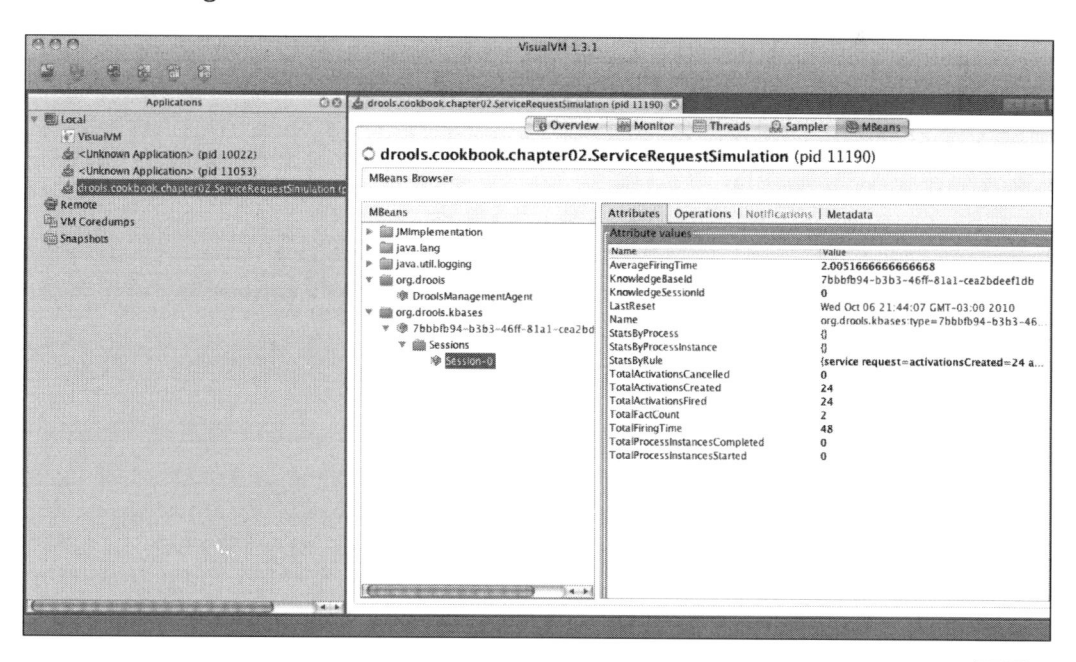

How it works...

Configuring a knowledge base with the `MBeansOption.ENABLED` option enables the Drools JMX feature and it will start an internal `MBeanServer` that will register all the knowledge sessions created from this knowledge base. In this implementation, the resources can be knowledge bases and stateful knowledge sessions. Stateless knowledge sessions can't be monitored because of their nature. It is a wrapped stateful knowledge session that is regenerated each time the rules are fired, and as a consequence the working memory state is lost.

There's more...

There is a lot of information exposed and this will be explained in detail in the following sections:

KnowledgeBase information

This information can be accessed in the `org.drools.kbases` tree node, where each knowledge base is identified by a unique UID.

The following information is displayed in the **Attributes** tab:

- ▶ `Globals`: Globals defined into the knowledge rules
- ▶ `Id`: Auto-generated or specified knowledge base UID
- ▶ `Packages`: Rules packages names that are part of the knowledge rules
- ▶ `SessionCount`: Count of knowledge sessions created from this knowledge base

Also, you will notice that there are three more tabs available. In this case, the **Operations** tab has two methods that can be used to initialize internal MBeans to gather extra configuration regarding the knowledge base (these MBeans methods are commonly used to configure the MBeans). The **Metadata** tab displays information about operations and attributes, and the **Notifications** tab is used to subscribe to MBeans notifications and this functionality is not implemented in Drools MBeans.

The knowledge base MBean available methods are as follows:

- ▶ `startInternalMBeans()`: Starts the internal MBeans that display the knowledge base configuration and entry points related information
- ▶ `stopInternalMBeans()`: Used to stop the previously started internal MBeans

KnowledgeSession information

In each knowledge base tree node and inside the `Sessions` folder, you will discover all the knowledge sessions that were created from it.

The following information is displayed in the **attributes** tab:

- ▶ `TotalProcessInstancesStarted`: Total number of process instances started

- ▶ `TotalProcessInstancesCompleted`: Total number of process instances completed
- ▶ `TotalFiringTime`: Total activations firing time
- ▶ `TotalFactCount`: Total working memory fact count
- ▶ `TotalActivationsFired`: Total number of activations fired in the knowledge session
- ▶ `TotalActivationsCreated`: Total number of activations created in the knowledge session
- ▶ `TotalActivationsCancelled`: Total number of activations cancelled in the knowledge session
- ▶ `StatsByRule`: Description of total number of fired/created/cancelled activations generated by each rule
- ▶ `StatsByProcessInstance`: Description of total number of fired/created/cancelled activations generated by each process instance
- ▶ `StatsByProcess`: Description of total number of fired/created/cancelled activations generated by each process
- ▶ `Name`: Knowledge session name
- ▶ `LastReset`: Last time that the information was reset
- ▶ `KnowledgeSessionId`: Autogenerated knowledge session UID
- ▶ `KnowledgeBaseId`: Autogenerated or specified UID of the knowledge base from which the knowledge session was created
- ▶ `AverageFiringTime`: Average activation firing time

Also, in the **Operations** tab there are four methods that can be used to retrieve specific information about rule/process/process instance statistics and one to reset the metrics statistics.

With this information, you are able to monitor the framework's internal state, visualizing the data, creating simple graphics, and also monitoring the JVM performance.

Another option to consume the Drools MBeans information is using the JMX API. To achieve this, you have to create the connection URL that will contain the IP address and port of the JMX-enabled application, which was previously configured through the JVM arguments.

```
String url = "service:jmx:rmi:///jndi/rmi://ip_address:port/jmxrmi"
```

Once the connection URL is defined, it is time to create the connection to be able to consume the knowledge information.

```
JMXConnector jmxConnector = JMXConnectorFactory.connect(
    new JMXServiceURL(url));
MbeanServerConnection connection = jmxConnector.
getMBeanServerConnection();
```

If the connection was successful, it is time to begin retrieving the MBean information. This is the most complicated step because you have to discover which MBeans were registered (each knowledge base and knowledge session has its associated MBean) and how to consume the attributes.

The registered knowledge base MBeans can be discovered using the following namespace: `org.drools.kbases:type=*` , where the * is the wildcard to discover all of them, using the following code snippet:

```
String resourceFilter = "org.drools.kbases:types=*";
Set<ObjectName> names = connection.queryNames(new
ObjectName(resourceFilter), null);
```

Once we have the `ObjectNames` objects, they can be used to consume the MBean attributes of their associated `KnowledgeBase` using their `getAttribute()` method (where the `attributeName` is the attribute's name that can be viewed using VisualVM, for example, Packages attribute):

```
Object value = connection.getAttribute(objectName, attributeName);
```

Finally, to discover the knowledge session MBeans the following namespace can be used, in the same way as the knowledge base MBeans were discovered: `org.drools.kbases:type =*,group=Sessions,sessionId=Session-*`

3
Guvnor: Centralized Knowledge Management

In this chapter, we will cover:

- ▶ Creating our model definition with the Model Editor
- ▶ Importing our model definition
- ▶ Creating data enumerations
- ▶ Using From Collect patterns in the Guided BRL Editor
- ▶ Organizing knowledge with Working Sets
- ▶ Creating rules templates
- ▶ Creating knowledge snapshots

Introduction

Guvnor is the business rules manager included with Drools to manage knowledge and to be a centralized repository for Drools knowledge bases. However, it is not just used to manage rules, because it has extra features that make it a robust business rules manager ready to be used in any production environment.

This chapter will cover recipes more oriented to rules authoring and knowledge management, showing the latest features included in the 5.2.0 release, and the next chapter will cover tasks related to administration and configuration of this BRMS.

Creating our model definition with the Model Editor

One of the first tasks before starting to write rules inside Guvnor is to define our domain model. This model can be defined by uploading a JAR file containing the model or by modeling using the **Model Editor** included in Guvnor. In this recipe, you will see how to use the Model Editor to define your fact definition.

Getting ready

Before starting to use Guvnor, you should install it inside a Servlet container or Application Server. In this book, we are going to use the JBoss Application Server 5.1 to deploy this web application. The Guvnor 5.2.0 distribution file, available at `http://www.jboss.org/drools/downloads` already comes with a version ready to be deployed in a JBoss AS 5.1, and it also comes with WAR files compatible with JBoss AS 6.0 and Apache Tomcat 6.0.

How to do it...

Carry out the following steps in order to create a model definition using the Model Editor:

1. Open Guvnor in your favorite web browser and create a new package. Once the application is loaded, you need to create a **New Declarative Model** using this option from the **Create New** contextual menu. This is shown in the following screenshot:

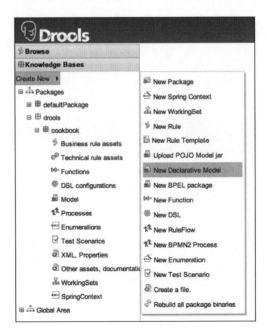

2. The next step is to create a new declarative model that will be used to group your declared facts. A pop-up will be displayed to choose the name and the package where the facts are going to belong, as shown in the following screenshot:

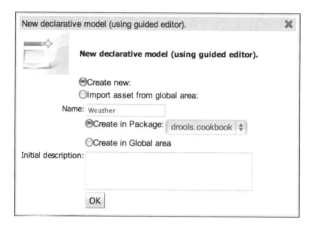

3. Click on **Add a new fact type** to create a new fact. After you insert the fact name, in this example we will define a **Temperature** fact, and press **OK**. Then you will be able to define the **Temperature** fact field's name and types, as shown in the following screenshot:

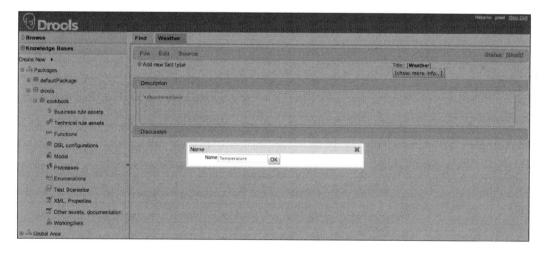

4. Once you have declared the fact, you can start adding fields by clicking on the **Add new fact type** link. This link will show a pop-up where you have to choose the field name and field type. The **Type** combobox comes with a few predefined types, but you can write your own custom type if none of them fits your needs, as shown in the following screenshot:

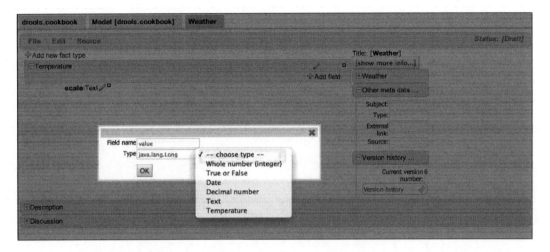

5. Once you are finished with the modeling of the fact, save the changes with the **Save changes** option from the **File** menu to make it available in your package.

How it works...

The declaration of facts using the Guvnor Model Editor is an alternative that we can use in different situations. For example, when we don't have access to the Java model to create facts in order to hold internal states that don't need to be declared in your real domain model, or for testing purposes, and so on. This Model Editor is a graphical interface, so you don't have to manually write the declaration of facts using metadata, as this feature internally defines the facts using metadata.

The only thing to keep in mind is that after adding a field, the field type is not going to be shown correctly in the fact field list. However, the type value is still correctly assigned to the field name, and you can check it by pressing the pencil button to modify the values.

Importing our model definition

The basic way to be able to write rules using our domain model is by uploading our Java model into Guvnor. In the examples files, you will find a JAR file with the domain model, which is used in this recipe. Let's take a look at how to do it.

How to do it...

Carry out the following steps in order to import your Java model definition into Guvnor:

1. In your package definition, create a new model archive (JAR) choosing the **Upload POJO Model jar** option, as shown in the following screenshot:

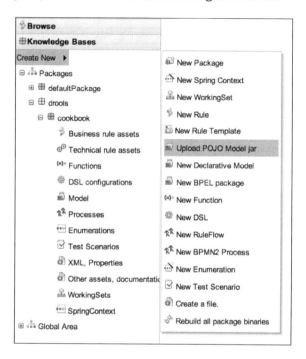

2. Once you have selected this menu option, one pop-up, **New model archive (jar)**, will be displayed on the screen. In this pop-up, you can choose a name for the model archive that is going to be created. This can also be used to import a previous JAR model created in the global area, as shown in the following screenshot:

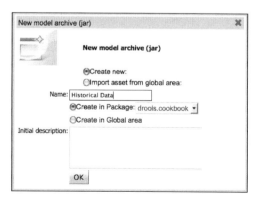

3. A new tab, **Historical Data**, will appear to upload your JAR model. In this tab, you will see a standard file upload component to choose your file name and one **Upload** button to start the uploading process, as shown in the following screenshot:

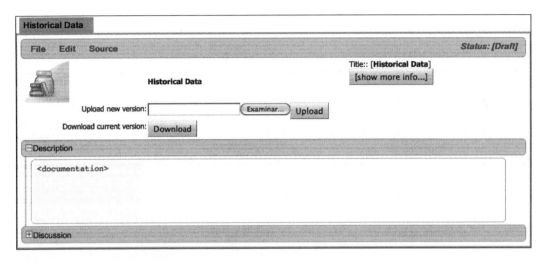

How it works...

This feature simply works as a file uploader that should be used to upload a JAR model that contains the domain to be used in writing rules. There is also an extra button to download the uploaded model. The declaration of the domain model is a preliminary and non-exclusive step that should be executed before starting the rules authoring.

See also

▶ Refer to the *Creating our model definition with the Model Editor* recipe.

Creating data enumerations

Enumerations are useful to map fact fields to a list of predefined values. The Guvnor integration will make the rule authoring process a friendly task for non-technical people, using common values that will restrict the possible fact values instead of using internal fact values that can be confusing for business analysts. This recipe will show you how to take advantage of this.

How to do it...

Carry out the following steps in order to create a new data enumeration in your knowledge declaration:

1. In your package definition, choose the **New Enumeration** option to create a new declarative enumeration, as shown in the following screenshot:

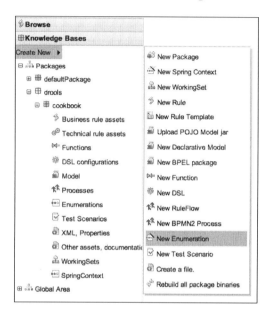

2. Once you have selected this menu option, one pop-up, **Create a new enumeration (drop down mapping)**, will be displayed on the screen. Then, choose the name and package destination for this new asset. As you can see in the following screenshot, there is also an option to import previously defined enumerations into the selected package:

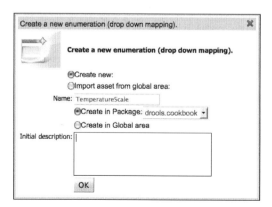

3. Next, start writing the enumeration mappings inside a simple textbox, as shown in the following screenshot. In this example, you can see the possible values of the scale field from the Temperature fact. Once the enumeration is saved, these values are going to be displayed when you start to write rules using the BRL editor:

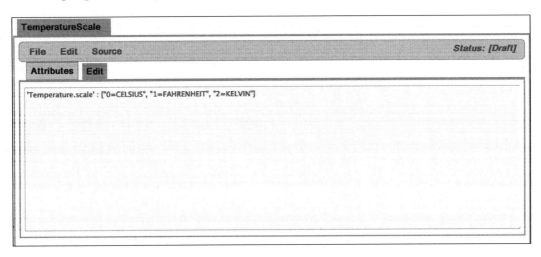

4. Once you have finished writing the enumerations, save your changes using the **Save** option from the **File** menu.

How it works...

Data enumerations are useful to use in guided editor drop-down lists. These enumerations are nothing more than a set of values to be displayed in the guided rules editor, where these values can be statically or dynamically defined in the text field from the enumeration editor.

In order to define the values, you can use two different approaches, which are as follows:

▶ The first one is to declare the string values directly on the editor.

▶ The other approach is to obtain the string values from an external datasource. Using the datasource approach will consist of a Java helper class with a method that should return a `java.util.List` of String types. This helper class will have to reside in Guvnor's classpath.

The simple approach to define the data enumeration values is to write them directly in the editor:

```
'Temperature.scale' : ["0-CELSIUS", "1-FAHRENHEIT", "2-KELVIN"]
```

Each of these enumeration components is defined using a key-value tuple using a minus character as the separator. With this declaration, the scale field of the previously defined Temperature fact can be assigned with the values 0, 1, or 2 in the guided editor. As you can see in the following screenshot, the **CELSIUS**, **FAHRENHEIT**, and **KELVIN** values are mapped inside the editor in a combo list selection:

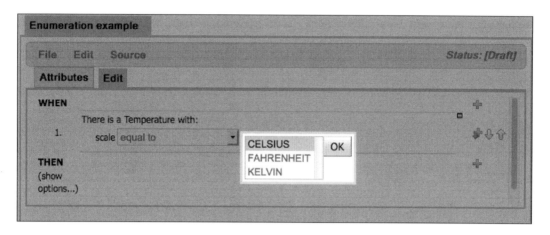

The enumeration values mapping can be more complex. One example of this is using the previously defined enumeration values to restrict another enumeration mapping:

```
'Temperature.scale' : ["0-CELSIUS", "1-FAHRENHEIT", "2-KELVIN"]
'Temperature.humidity[scale==0]' : ['NORMAL']
'Temperature.humidity[scale==1]' : ['HIGH']
'Temperature.humidity[scale==2]' : ['NORMAL', 'HIGH']
```

In this case, the humidity field will have different values that are going to depend on the scale field value, and the guided editor will be affected, only displaying the humidity field values according to the selected scale value.

The datasource option relies on an extra helper class that will provide the enumeration string values that could implement the values extraction in different ways. For example, statically written inside the helper class or reading them from an external source such as a database, an XML file, and so on:

```
'Temperature.scale' : (new drools.cookbook.TemperatureScaleHelper()).
getActiveScales()
```

In the previous snippet of code, the helper class should be instantiated in the enumeration declaration to invoke the method that will return the string values list.

Keep in mind that the data enumerations are loaded the first time you open a rule with the guided editor, and if you already had a guided editor open before the data enumeration declaration it should be reopened to display these changes in the field editors.

Using From Collect patterns in the Guided BRL Editor

From Collect patterns are useful to gather a set of facts from the working memory, bringing a reduced set of your working memory facts to the engine. These patterns were not supported in the previous Guvnor releases; however, thanks to the community effort, it is now possible to use them in the **Guided BRL Editor**.

How to do it...

Carry out the following steps in order to use a From Collect pattern in the Guided BRL Editor:

1. As always, first you have to create a new asset. In this case, you will have to create a new rule by selecting the **New Rule** option, as shown in the following screenshot:

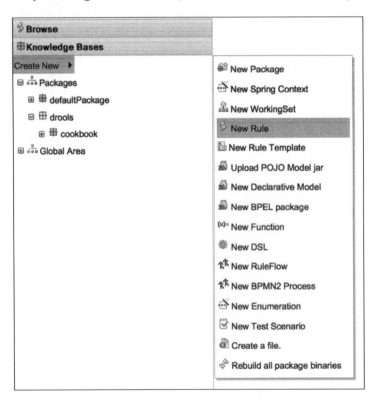

2. After this step, a new pop-up, **New Rule**, will show up to configure the rule properties, such as category, package, description, rule format, and so on. However, the only requirement to write the rules is the Business Rule (Guided Editor) format selection, as shown in the following screenshot:

3. Now it is time to add patterns to our guided rule editor by clicking on the green cross, as shown in the following screenshot:

4. Once you have clicked, a new pop-up will show up with all the possible conditions that you can use in your LHS. In this case, we are going to select **Temperature** and confirm the selection by clicking on the **OK** button:

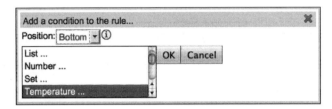

5. Once the Temperature fact is selected, a new LHS pattern will be added into the **TemperatureWatcher** rule editor. Clicking on the **There is a Temperature WHEN** rule pattern link will show up another pop-up, **Modify constraints for Temperature**, in which you can start adding constraints to the pattern.

For this rule example, we are going to add a constraint to know if this was the last Temperature fact inserted into the working memory and another one to match the Temperature scale. As shown in the following screenshot, the only options that are going to be used are the **Add a restriction on a field** to add the constraints to the Temperature fact, and the **Variable name** to set a name to the matched pattern (in this case, **$last_record** will be the variable name for the matched patterns):

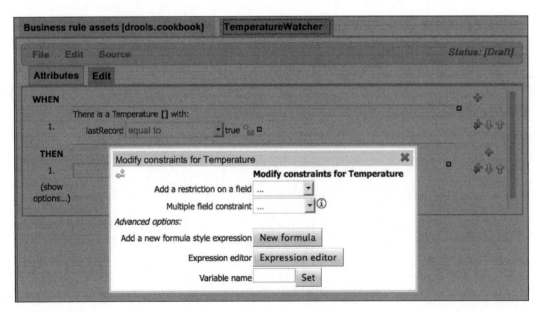

6. Once we have the first pattern done, we can start writing the second and more interesting pattern, which will be the pattern using a From Collect constraint. To do this, you have to click on the green cross and select the **From Collect** condition from the conditions list. Click on the **OK** button to confirm it, as shown in the following screenshot:

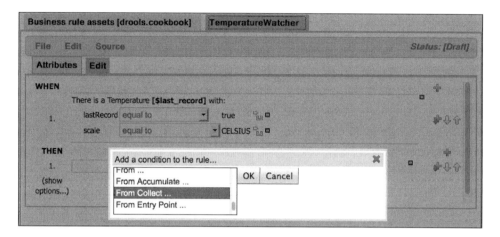

At this point you will see another pattern in the Guided Editor with two sections to be completed with patterns. The first section is to bind the output of the pattern to a `java.util.Collection`, a `java.util.Set`, or a `java.util.List` fact type, as shown in the following screenshot:

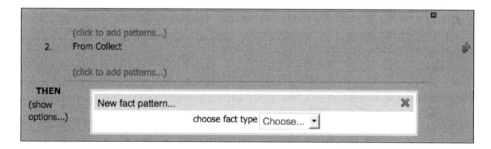

After the pattern creation, this is going to be assigned to a `java.util.List` fact type and also its size field will be restricted, as shown in the following screenshot:

7. The next step is to complete the second part of the pattern, where a new pop-up, **New fact pattern**, will be shown displaying all the possibilities to complete it, as shown in the following screenshot:

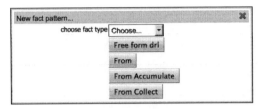

In this example, we are going to do a simple pattern to match with the Temperature facts inside the working memory, by selecting **Temprature** from the **choose fact type** drop-down, as shown in the following screenshot:

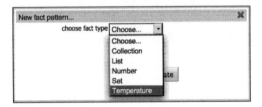

8. Now it is time to add constraints to the From Collect Temperature fact, and add a pattern to match all the previously inserted Temperature facts (`lastRecord==false` constraint) with the same temperature measurement scale (`scale==$last_record.scale` constraint), within the last hour ((`$last_record.timestamp - timestamp) <= 3600` constraint), as shown in the following screenshot:

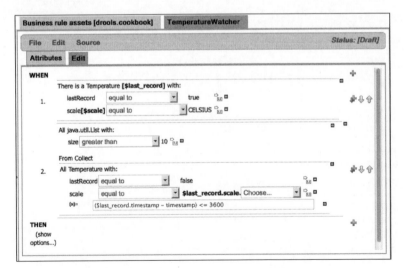

9. Don't forget to complete the RHS pattern and save the changes.

How it works...

As we discussed in the recipe introduction, these From Collect pattern constraints allow us to define a subset of working memory facts to act as a pattern data source. In this recipe, we are using the new From Collect Guvnor constraint support to create more powerful LHS patterns instead of the common pattern constraints.

As a last tip, you can see in the following screenshot that the second part of the pattern can be completed with a lot of options, that is, it will allow us to concatenate **From**, **From Accumulate**, and **From Collect** constraints, to create a data source of really complex facts:

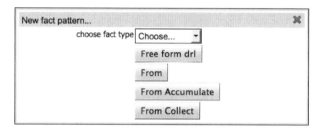

Remember that you can preview the rule being generated using the **View source** option from the **Source** menu. The following screenshot shows the TemperatureWatcher rule:

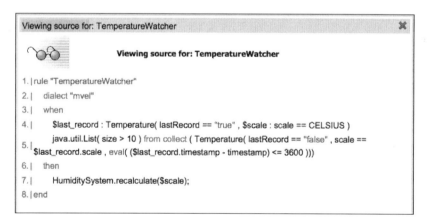

Organizing knowledge with Working Sets

Another feature of the new Guvnor is **Working Sets**. Suppose that you have a really big domain model, and all these fact definitions belong to the same domain but they could be grouped into fine grained subdomains. You would like to explicitly define these subdomains to create rules with a more specific fact model group in order to improve the design efficiency, adding restrictions in rule authoring.

However, there is nothing better than an example to show how it can be used. So, let's look at it.

How to do it...

Carry out the following steps in order to create a Working Set for your domain model:

1. First, you will have to create a new asset. In this case, we need to choose the **Working Set** option.

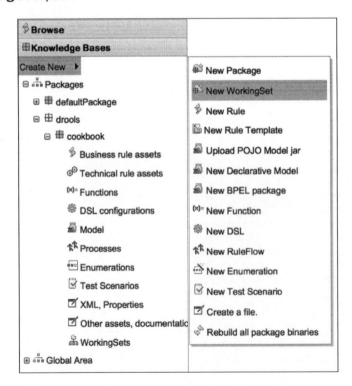

2. A new pop-up, **New WorkingSet** will appear on the screen. Choose a name for the Working Set and select the package destination. In this recipe, we are going to use **WeatherWS** as our Working Set name, as shown in the following screenshot:

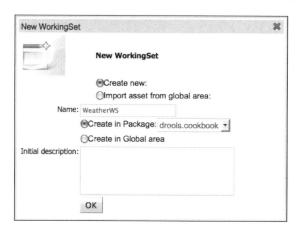

Once the created working set tab is opened, you have to add the fact types that are going to belong to your subdomain/package of types. In this case, we created a Working Set to group all the facts relative to Weather, where **Temperature**, **Humidity**, and **Wind** fact types were added, as shown in the following screenshot. This domain model is pretty simple, with only six fact types, but it will be enough to show the Working Sets' capabilities on rules authoring:

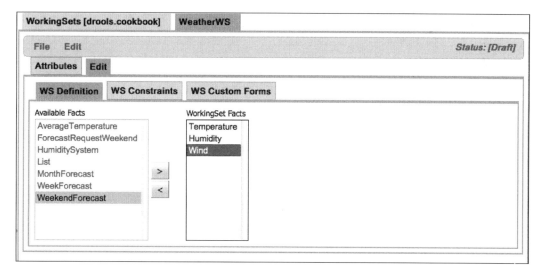

3. Then we have to create another working set named **ForecastWS** to group the **Weekend**, **Week**, and **Monthly** weather forecast, as shown in the following screenshot:

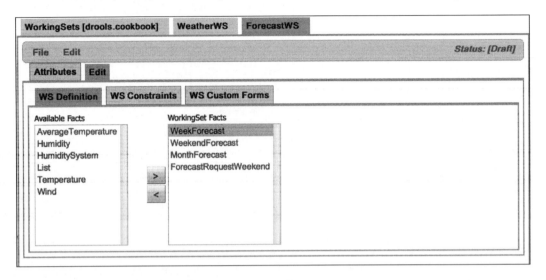

4. Once they are created, we can start to write rules using Working Sets to restrict the rules domain. Once you have created a rule using the Guided Editor, you will see a new option to **Select Working Sets** in the **Edit** menu, where the Working Sets can be assigned to the rule, as shown in the following screenshot:

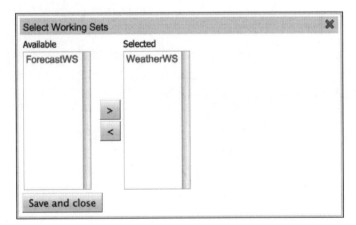

5. Once you have selected which working sets are going to be available for the current rule, you will see how this impacts the rule authoring. When you add a new condition (LHS) or action (RHS) to the rule, you will see how the available facts are restricted to the selected working sets. In this case, only **Humidity**, **Temperature**, and **Wind** facts are available to be used, as shown in the following screenshot:

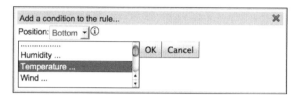

How it works...

When you define a Working Set and assign it to a rule, you will see how the available facts reduce further, impacting in the conditions and consequences that can be written.

Also, this will impact in another way when a Working Set is assigned to a rule that currently had conditions or consequences with no available facts. These conditions/consequences are not going to disappear or be removed; they will only turn into read-only mode, as you can see in the following screenshots:

Before Working Sets selection:

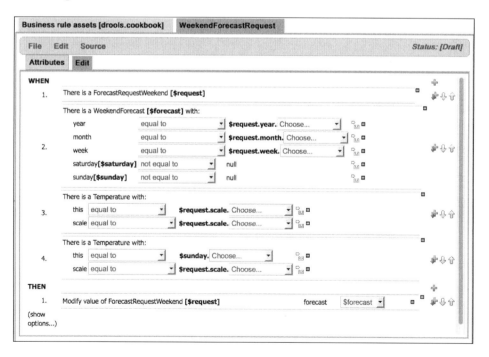

After Working Sets selection:

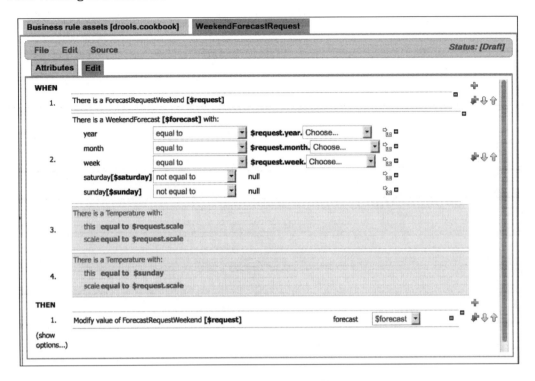

As you can see the preceding screenshot, patterns **3** and **4** were converted to read-only mode, disabling all possibilities to edit, move, or remove the patterns.

Working Sets currently can only be assigned to rules and not to packages or users. However, these improvements are supposed to be supported in the coming releases.

Another thing to keep in mind is about the nature of Working Sets and how they are strictly related to the packages assignment, instead of the rules assignment. Technically, it is not possible to assign different Working Sets to different rules in the same package, because they are internally related to packages and the assignment will affect all the rules in them.

Creating rules templates

This is also one of latest features included in Guvnor, which allows you to write rule templates in a graphical way using a combination of a Guided Editor together with a custom spreadsheet editor to complete the template data. As you may know, rules templates can be used when in your knowledge, you have a group of rules following the same patterns, constraints, and consequences in the RHS, only with differences in the constants, names for objects, or fields. In this recipe, you will see how to create the rules, how to assign the values to the template keys, and how to preview the rules that are being generated.

How to do it...

1. Create a new Rule Template asset with a name, initial category, and package.

2. Once the created rule template is loaded, you will see an editor that is almost identical to the Rule Guided Editor, as shown in the following screenshot. However, it also has a button that will open a pop-up to add the template data, which will be covered in the following steps:

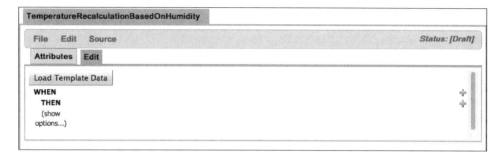

3. At this point you can start adding patterns in the conditional section as is usually done in the Guided Editor. However, in the process to assign a value to a field constraint, you will see the option to assign a **Template key** to the field value, as shown in the following screenshot:

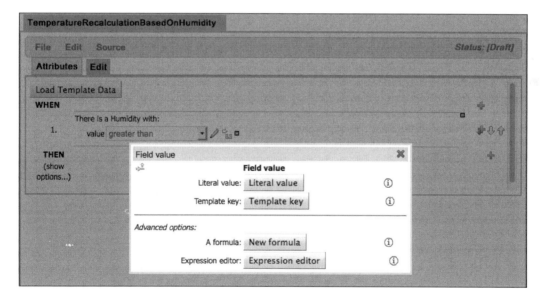

4. After assigning a template key, the **Field value** pop-up will be displayed on the screen. It will display a label **value** with a value text. Once you click on this label, it will be transformed into a text box, where a template key identifier can be assigned, as shown in the following screenshot:

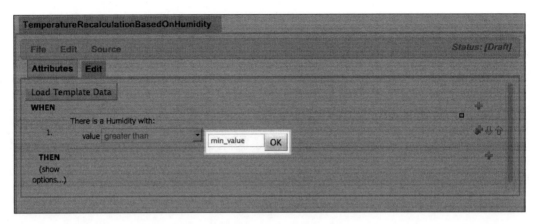

5. These template keys also can also assigned in the consequence patterns, in the same way as they are assigned in the conditional section:

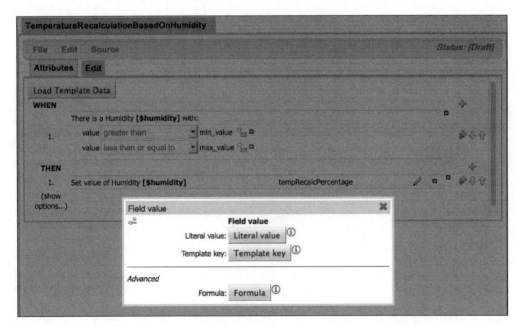

6. Once the rule authoring is done and the template keys are assigned, you can start to add the template data using the custom spreadsheet editor, which will be displayed in a pop-up when you click on the **Load Template Data** button, as shown in the following screenshot:

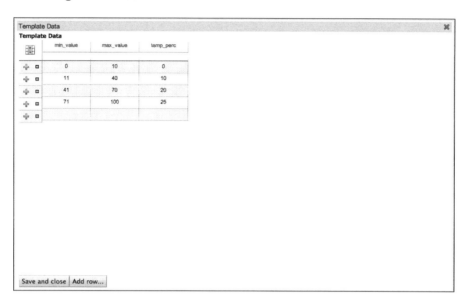

7. In this template data editor, you can start assigning all the possible values that the template keys can have. To assign the values, you have to add a row, by clicking on the **Add row...** button, and then you only have to assign the values to each of the template key fields, as shown in the following screenshot:

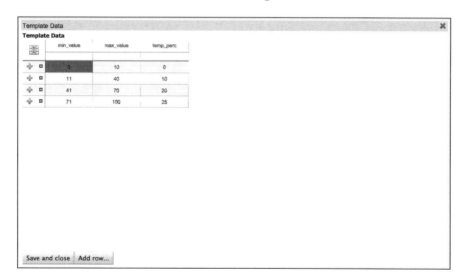

> Don't forget that each of these template data rows represents a rule that will be generated when the package is compiled.

8. Once you have added all your rows, close and save the rows data by clicking on the **Save** and **Close** button. Also remember to save the rule template changes.

9. Finally, after saving all the changes, you can get a preview of the rules to be generated using the **View source** option that can be found in the **Source** menu of the Rule Template editor, as shown in the following screenshot:

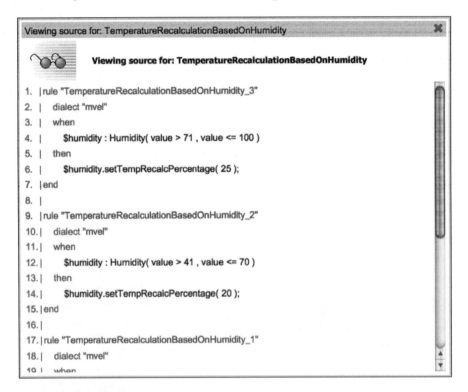

How it works...

Rules templates can be created with regular DRL files, creating the rule file, adding tags, and then expanding the rule file before adding it to the `KnowledgeBuilder` to compile the rules. However, the integration with Guvnor simplifies this process by automatically generating the rules without the need to manually expand them. It also adds a nice graphical editor that converts the rule authoring process.

As we discussed in this recipe, the pattern constraint values can be assigned to a static identifier, known as the **template key**. These template keys are later used to replace the constraint values with the values assigned in the template data editor.

 Template keys can be mixed with regular constraint values when you are adding patterns in a rule template.

After all the template keys and patterns are defined, the process continues filling the template data using the graphical editor. This editor simplifies the expansion of the rules, hiding the process to manually create the object and assigns them to expand the rules, as this has to be done when using regular DRL files. Each row that is added in the template data editor will generate a new rule when the package is compiled, but the rule will be only generated correctly if all the row fields have values. Otherwise, the rule can be expanded incorrectly, with only the consequences, conditions, or neither, as shown in the following screenshot:

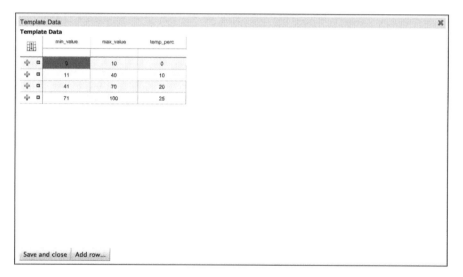

 Custom enumerations are also supported in the template data editor giving more flexibility to the rules authoring process.

Once all the necessary rows are added and the template data and rule template are saved, the rules are ready to be consumed for an external application.

This is the most important piece of knowledge needed to start using rule templates inside Guvnor, which really simplifies the process to author rules, thanks to all these graphical editors.

Creating knowledge snapshots

In the process of adding, modifying, and deleting your rules, you would like to create snapshots to store the evolution of your stored knowledge and to have incremental deployments. Guvnor allows you to accomplish this in an easy way giving us a tool to create deployment snapshots, freezing the knowledge in that point of time and also giving us the possibility to compare the differences between previously created snapshots.

How to do it...

Follow the steps given here, in order to create snapshots of your knowledge:

1. The **Package Snapshots** section is accessed in the main menu. It displays all the existing packages and all the created deployment snapshots. Select **New Deployment snapshot** from the list. It also allows us to create a new snapshot and rebuild all the existing ones, as shown in the following screenshot:

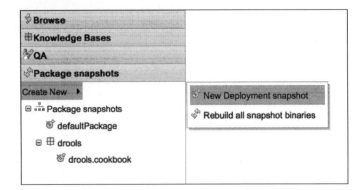

2. Once the selection is done, a pop-up, **New snapshot**, will appear on the screen. Select a package to generate a snapshot. You can use any package created in the previous recipes or the **defaultPackage** provided by Guvnor to follow the further steps:

3. Once the package is selected, you have to assign a name for the snapshot, as shown in the following screenshot:

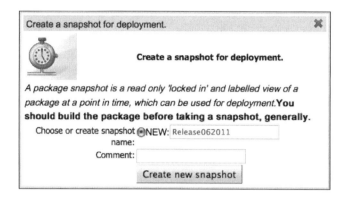

4. After pressing the **Create new snapshot** button, a pop-up will be displayed informing us that the snapshot was successfully created and the package snapshot will be displayed in the Package Snapshots tree view under the generated package name snapshot, as shown in the following screenshot:

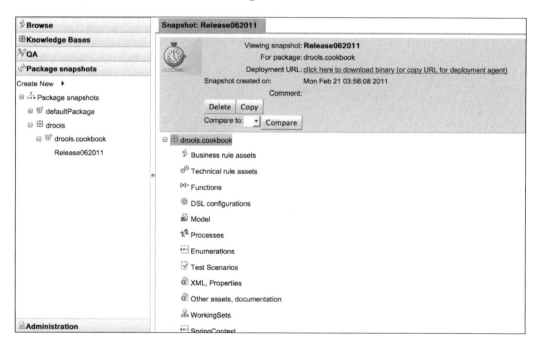

5. Once the package snapshot is created, it is ready to be used. As you can see in the previous screenshot, it provides a custom deployment URL to be used by your application.

How it works...

The deployment snapshots simply freeze the knowledge for when you need it, saving a state of the knowledge that cannot be modified. Of course, you can still modify the knowledge through the **Knowledge Bases**, but any change will not be reflected in the snapshots.

These package snapshots can also be explored to visualize their content, but all the knowledge will be displayed in the read-only mode. For example, the **Business Rules assets** section of the **Snapshot items** tab can be explored to see the rules that were included in it:

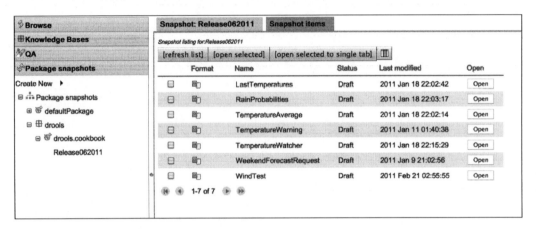

Now, all the assets included in the snapshot can be opened to visualize their content, but they cannot be modified or deleted. As you can see in the following screenshot, all the options to edit the rules are disabled making it impossible to make any modification:

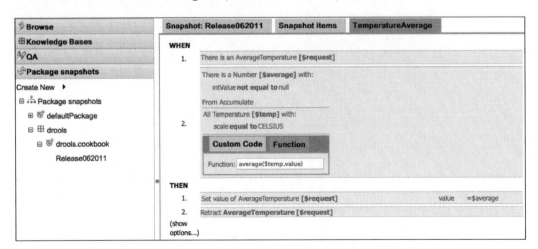

After this recipe, hopefully you understand how useful the creation of deployment snapshots is and you now understand how to create them. They are a critical feature to improve the quality of rules development giving us the possibility to create incremental knowledge without interfering in the rules authoring process.

There's more...

Each time you create a new snapshot, you may like to know the evolution of the knowledge, which rules were added, modified, or removed from the package. This comparison is only possible when you have more than one snapshot in the package, for obvious reasons.

When you open a package snapshot, you will see an option to create a comparison between snapshots. This comparison can be made by selecting the package snapshot that is going to be compared with the current one selected in the **Compare to** combobox and then clicking on the **Compare** button. After the Package snapshots module compares the snapshots, it will display a table view with the differences between them, as shown in the following screenshot:

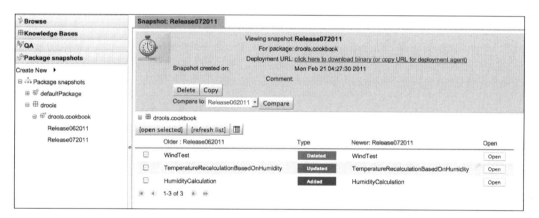

In this case, it displays that some rules were deleted, updated, and also that a new rule was added in the snapshot, showing the knowledge evolution between the deployment snapshots.

4

Guvnor: Advanced Features and Configuration

In this chapter, we will cover:

- ▶ Setting and creating a GUI language
- ▶ Backing up your knowledge
- ▶ Configuring MySQL as default rules repository
- ▶ Configuring the repository files location
- ▶ Obtaining resources using the REST API

Introduction

Beyond rules authoring and knowledge centralization, which are the main purposes of **Guvnor**, there are some extra features that can help you in the rules management process. This chapter is focused on these non-authoring features, such as repository files storage configuration, external interaction with the repository using the REST API, and so on.

Setting and creating a GUI language

Guvnor allows us to change the default GUI language thanks to it being developed using internationalization support. In this recipe, we will see how to change the default language and how to create our own translation.

How to do it...

Carry out the following steps in order to change the default language:

1. Download Drools Guvnor 5.2.0.Final from `http://www.jboss.org/drools/downloads/`. Copy the `guvnor-5.2.0.Final-jboss-as-5.1.war` file in a JBoss Application Server 5.1 and start it.

2. Open your web browser and type `http://127.0.0.1:8080/guvnor-5.2.0.Final-jboss-as-5.1/` in the URL address bar, which will redirect you to the full URL address `http://127.0.0.1:8080/guvnor-5.2.0.Final-jboss-as-5.1/org.drools.guvnor.Guvnor/Guvnor.html`. The following screenshot shows this.

> If your JBoss Application Server or servlet container port is bound to another IP address and/or port, you will have to modify the URL in order to access it.

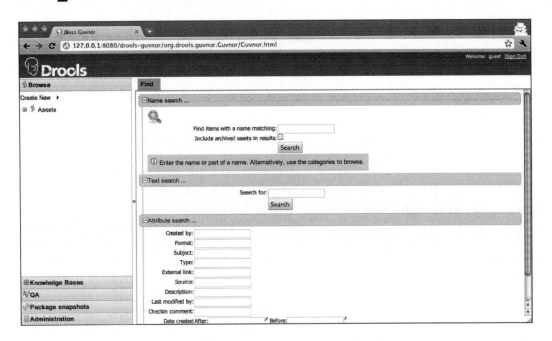

3. Add the `locale=pt_BR` parameter at the end of the URL to change the language to, for example, Brazilian Portuguese. In this case, the full URL will be `http://127.0.0.1:8080/guvnor-5.2.0.Final-jboss-as-5.1/org.drools.guvnor.Guvnor/Guvnor.html?locale=pt_BR`. This is shown in the following screenshot:

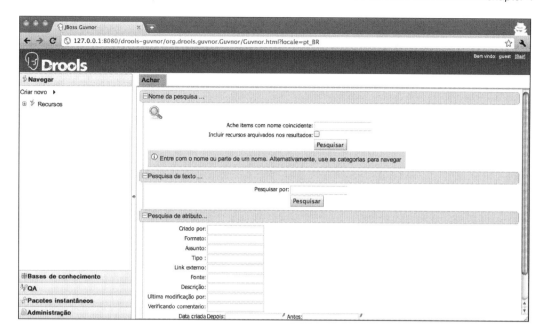

 English is the language that is used in the Guvnor interface by default.

4. Now, you are ready to use **Drools Guvnor** in another language. But if your language isn't available, you may like to take a look at the following sections in order to create your own customized GUI language resource.

How it works...

Drools Guvnor was designed to support internationalization and localization to adapt the user interface to different languages. As you saw in the *How to do it...* section of this recipe, to use this feature you have to add the `locale=$language` parameter at the end of the URL, where `$language` can be one of the following supported languages:

▸ `es_ES`: Spanish

▸ `fr_FR`: French

▸ `ja_JP`: Japanese

▸ `pt_BR`: Brazilian Portuguese

▸ `zh_CN`: Chinese

There's more...

What if Guvnor doesn't currently support your language? Well, you can always translate and create your custom bundle, and of course show your appreciation to the community by donating your translation.

In order to create your Guvnor translation, first you will have to obtain the source code following the latest available instructions at `http://www.jboss.org/drools/`. Once you obtain the source code, you will find the `I8N` resource files inside the `drools-webapp/src/main/java/org/drools/guvnor/client/messages/folder`, as shown in the following screenshot:

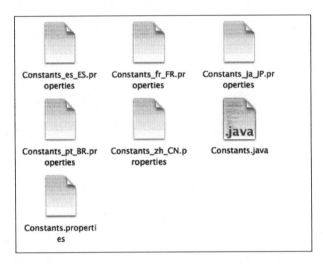

Each of these properties files represents one translation bundle and the language can be discovered by taking a look at the filename (as you already figured out), where the `Constants.properties` file is the default English translation.

The easiest step to start the translation is by creating a copy of the `Constants.properties` file and changing the name by adding the localization ID at the end (for example, `Constants_de_DE.properties` for a German translation). With this new file you can start to translate the values by opening it with a text editor or your favorite IDE resource bundles editor.

It has a simple format, as you can see in the following code snippet, where each line represents one of the strings to be replaced in the Guvnor UI and the right side is the current translation. If your language has non-standard characters they have to be replaced using Unicode characters, as you can see in the following Spanish translation excerpt:

```
Pattern=Patr\u00f3n\:
Assets=Recurso
CreateNew=Crear Nuevo
Category=Categor\u00eda
```

Once you have finished all the translation, which will take some time because at this moment there are more than 1000 lines, you will have to compile the Guvnor source code to make the language available. To compile the source code, you need some knowledge about Apache Maven, but as a quick hint you can use the following command line to do a full build:

```
mvn clean package -Dfull
```

However, if you would like to skip the testing phase you can add the -DskipTests parameter, shown as follows:

```
mvn clean package -Dfull -DskipTests
```

Once the compilation is successful, the generated war file can be deployed into a JBoss Application Server or a servlet container, and the translation can be accessed by adding the locale parameter into the URL address.

Lastly, don't forget to donate your translation to the community!

Backing up your knowledge

One of the most important tasks when you store data is backup, and this recipe will show how it can be done in Guvnor when you are using the default Jackrabbit file-based repository. This feature allows you to manually export all your data to back up your knowledge in case of information loss.

How to do it...

Carry out the following steps in order to create a backup of your knowledge stored in Drools Guvnor:

1. It's a simple task; open your favorite web browser. Type `http://localhost:8080/drools-guvnor/` and once the application is loaded, select the **Import Export** option in the **Administration** section, as shown in the following screenshot:

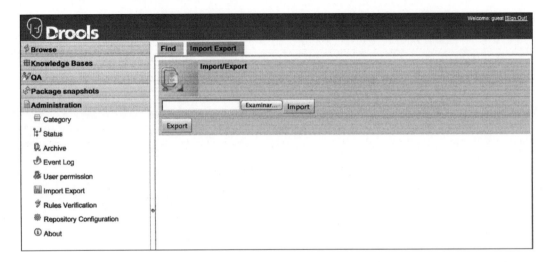

2. In this new tab, you will see the options to import and export backups. Click on the **Export** button and a pop-up will appear on the screen, which will ask you for a confirmation. Once you agree, a database backup will be generated in a zipped file. Finally, the web browser will ask you to save the backup with a common save dialog.

How it works...

The Guvnor data storage API is based on the **Java Content Repository** (**JCR**) standard, using the **Apache Jackrabbit** (`http://jackrabbit.apache.org/`) as the default implementation. Using a standard implementation, it's possible to interchange the JCR implementation without any issue.

Getting back on track, the backup option in Guvnor exports all the assets created with the UI in a ZIP file that contains a single XML file. In order to import this data, you will only have to use the **Import** option from the backup module.

Configuring MySQL as the default rules repository

Another optimization that can be added to Guvnor storage configuration is to use an RDBMS instead of storing the assets in a file directory. With this configuration, Guvnor will have a more solid storage engine and also will obtain more advanced storage features such as clustering, advanced backup system, and so on. This recipe will cover the configuration needed to change the JCR repository storage to use a MySQL database, but as you will see at the end of the recipe it's also possible to use another RDBMS.

Getting ready

The only requirement is to install a MySQL database on your computer. The latest Community Server can be downloaded from `http://dev.mysql.com/downloads/mysql/`. The installation and configuration procedure is far from the scope of this recipe, but instead you can follow the official documentation `http://dev.mysql.com/doc/refman/5.5/en/` to achieve it.

Once the MySQL database is up and running, it is time to create the database and user permissions. Open a terminal or command-line console and carry out the following steps:

1. Log in as the root user using the MySQL command-line client:

   ```
   shell>mysql -u root -p
   Enter password:
   ```

2. Once you are logged in, create a `guvnordb` database/schema with the following SQL query:

   ```
   mysql> CREATE DATABASE guvnordb;
   ```

3. If you want to verify the schema creation, the available schemas can be displayed by executing the following query:

   ```
   mysql>SHOW DATABASES;
   ```

4. After the schema creation you have to create the `guvnor user`, which in this example only can connect to the database server from the `localhost` host, and also assign an access password to the user:

   ```
   mysql> CREATE USER 'guvnor'@'localhost' IDENTIFIED BY 'guvnor';
   ```

5. Once the user is created, the only remaining step is assigning it the full access permissions to the `guvnordb` schema:

   ```
   mysql>GRANT ALL PRIVILEGES ON guvnordb.* TO 'guvnor'@'localhost'
   WITH GRANT OPTION;
   ```

After the configuration of the MySQL database, you can start the migration of the current Guvnor storage configuration.

How to do it...

Carry out the following steps in order to configure a MySQL database to store your knowledge instead of using the default Apache Jackrabbit file-based storage:

1. In order to migrate to an existing repository, you will have to generate an information export, as was seen in the previous recipe, which will be used later to restore the information previously stored using the Apache Jackrabbit file-based storage. If you didn't start Drools Guvnor earlier, you will need to execute it once to create the default `repository.xml` file that will be later modified.

2. Shut down the JBoss Application Server or the Servlet container where Guvnor is deployed if it's currently running.

3. Open the `repository.xml` file with your favorite text editor, generated by default in the `bin/` folder of the JBoss Application Server or the Servlet container directory, and be ready to search and replace XML tags.

 Remember to always create a backup of the `repository.xml` file and the `repository` folder in order to prevent information loss.

4. Replace all the `<FileSystem />` tags with the following configuration:

```
<FileSystem class="org.apache.jackrabbit.core.fs.db.DbFileSystem">
    <param name="driver" value="com.mysql.jdbc.Driver"/>
    <param name="url" value="jdbc:mysql://localhost/guvnodb"/>
    <param name="user" value="guvnor"/>
    <param name="password" value="guvnor"/>
    <param name="schema" value="mysql"/>
    <param name="schemaObjectPrefix" value="FS_"/>
</FileSystem>
```

5. Replace all the `<PersistenceManager />` tags with the following configuration:

```
<PersistenceManager class="org.apache.jackrabbit.core.persistence.
bundle.MySqlPersistenceManager">
    <param name="driver" value="com.mysql.jdbc.Driver"/>
    <param name="url"
    value="jdbc:mysql://localhost/guvnordb"/>
    <param name="user" value="guvnor"/>
    <param name="password" value="guvnor"/>
    <param name="schema" value="mysql"/>
    <param name="schemaObjectPrefix"
    value="PM_WS_${wsp.name}_" />
</PersistenceManager>
```

6. Save the `repository.xml` file and remove the `repository` folder, which is going to be replaced with new data.

7. Download the latest MySQL Java Connector from `http://dev.mysql.com/downloads/connector/j/5.1.html` and copy the JAR file into the `lib` directory of the JBoss Application Server or the Servlet container common libraries folder.

8. Start the JBoss Application or Servlet Container, and if applicable, import the backup generated in the first step as we saw in the previous recipe.

How it works...

The default Guvnor storage implementation, Apache Jackrabbit, makes it possible to interchange the backend engine storage. By default, it uses an embeddable Java open source relational database, **Apache Derby**, as its Persistence Manager to store the Guvnor's assets into the file system. This Persistence Manager lets us configure it in an easy way to be used with one of the following RDBMS:

- Apache Derby
- H2 Database Engine
- MySQL
- PostgreSQL
- Oracle 10g or newer
- Oracle 9

 If your database engine isn't listed it is also possible to configure it using a generic Jackrabbit Persistence Manager.

In order to configure Apache Jackrabbit to use a different database, in this case MySQL, you have to configure the virtual file system, workspace, and versioning features configuration. Carry out the following steps in order to configure all the requirements:

1. The Virtual File System configuration is one level below the initial `<Repository/>` XML tag under the `<FileSystem/>` XML tag, and you can deduce how it simply stores the assets into the file system:

```
<Repository>
  <FileSystem   class="org.apache.jackrabbit.core.fs.local.
LocalFileSystem">
    <param name="path" value="${rep.home}/repository"/>
  </FileSystem>
    <!-- more configurations -->
<Repository/>
```

2. Then, the first step to start the configuration is to change the `FileSystem` class value to `org.apache.jackrabbit.core.fs.db.DbFileSystem` and add the connection parameters, which are pretty similar to any JDBC configuration:

```
<Repository>
  <FileSystem class="org.apache.jackrabbit.core.fs.db.
DbFileSystem">
     <param name="driver" value="com.mysql.jdbc.Driver"/>
     <param name="url" value="jdbc:mysql://localhost/guvnordb"/>
     <param name="user" value="guvnor"/>
     <param name="password" value="guvnor"/>
     <param name="schema" value="mysql"/>
     <param name="schemaObjectPrefix" value="FS_"/>
  </FileSystem>
  <!-- more configurations -->
<Repository />
```

3. There are three places where the `FileSystem` configuration must be modified and all of them must have the same configuration. The other two are used to configure the workspace and versioning, and can be founded under the `<Workspace />` and `<Versioning />` tags respectively.

4. Once all the `<FileSystem/>` tags are modified, it's time to configure the Persistence Manager. In this case, the `<PersistenceManager/>` tag can only be modified in the workspace and versioning sections, which with the default file storage have the following configuration:

```
<PersistenceManager class="org.apache.jackrabbit.core.persistence.
pool.DerbyPersistenceManager">
  <param name="url" value="jdbc:derby:${wsp.home}/
db;create=true"/>
  <param name="schemaObjectPrefix" value="${wsp.name}_"/>
</PersistenceManager>
```

5. As you can see, the Persistence Manager relies on an Apache Derby Persistence Manager to store the assets, so we are going to change this to use a `MySQLPersistenceManager` object and also configure the parameters' connections:

```
<PersistenceManager class="org.apache.jackrabbit.core.persistence.
bundle.MySqlPersistenceManager">
  <param name="driver" value="com.mysql.jdbc.Driver"/>
  <param name="url" value="jdbc:mysql://localhost/guvnordb"/>
  <param name="user" value="guvnor"/>
  <param name="password" value="guvnor"/>
  <param name="schema" value="mysql"/>
  <param name="schemaObjectPrefix" value="PM_WS_${wsp.name}_" />
</PersistenceManager>
```

6. Once the Persistence Manager is configured in the workspace and versioning sections, you have finished the repository XML configuration. Now, you will only have to download and copy the Java JDBC connector library of MySQL into the `lib` directory of the JBoss Application Server or your Servlet container.

7. Finally, you can see an almost complete `repository.xml` file with the relevant persistence modifications, shown as follows:

```xml
<?xml version="1.0"?>
<Repository>
  <FileSystem class="org.apache.jackrabbit.core.fs.db.
    DbFileSystem">
     <param name="driver" value="com.mysql.jdbc.Driver"/>
    <param name="url" value="jdbc:mysql://localhost/guvnordb"/>
    <param name="user" value="guvnor"/>
    <param name="password" value="guvnor"/>
    <param name="schema" value="mysql"/>
    <param name="schemaObjectPrefix" value="FS_"/>
  </FileSystem>

  <!-- securityconfiguration -->
  <Security appName="Jackrabbit">
    <SecurityManager class=
"org.apache.jackrabbit.core.security.simple.SimpleSecurityManager"
workspaceName="security">
    </SecurityManager>
    <AccessManager class=
"org.apache.jackrabbit.core.security.simple.SimpleAccessManager">
    </AccessManager>
    <LoginModule class=
"org.apache.jackrabbit.core.security.simple.SimpleLoginModule">
      <param name="anonymousId" value="anonymous"/>
      <param name="adminId" value="admin"/>
    </LoginModule>
  </Security>

<Workspaces rootPath="${rep.home}/workspaces"
defaultWorkspace="default"/>

<!--workspace configuration -->
<Workspace name="${wsp.name}">
<FileSystem class="org.apache.jackrabbit.core.fs.db.DbFileSystem">
  <param name="driver" value="com.mysql.jdbc.Driver"/>
  <param name="url" value="jdbc:mysql://localhost/guvnordb"/>
  <param name="user" value="guvnor"/>
  <param name="password" value="guvnor"/>
```

```xml
        <param name="schema" value="mysql"/>
        <param name="schemaObjectPrefix" value="FS_WS_${wsp.
name}_"/>
</FileSystem>
<PersistenceManager class="org.apache.jackrabbit.core.persistence.
bundle.MySqlPersistenceManager">
   <param name="driver" value="com.mysql.jdbc.Driver"/>
   <param name="url" value="jdbc:mysql://localhost/guvnordb"/>
   <param name="user" value="guvnor"/>
   <param name="password" value="guvnor"/>
   <param name="schema" value="mysql"/>
   <param name="schemaObjectPrefix" value="PM_WS_${wsp.name}_" />
</PersistenceManager>
<SearchIndex class="org.apache.jackrabbit.core.query.lucene.
SearchIndex">
   <param name="path" value="${wsp.home}/index"/>
   <param name="supportHighlighting" value="true"/>
</SearchIndex>
<!-- more configurations -->
</Workspace>
<Versioning rootPath="${rep.home}/version">
<FileSystem class="org.apache.jackrabbit.core.fs.db.DbFileSystem">
   <param name="driver" value="com.mysql.jdbc.Driver"/>
   <param name="url" value="jdbc:mysql://localhost/guvnordb"/>
   <param name="user" value="guvnor"/>
   <param name="password" value="guvnor"/>
   <param name="schema" value="mysql"/>
<param name="schemaObjectPrefix" value="Versioning_FS_"/>
</FileSystem>
<PersistenceManager class="org.apache.jackrabbit.core.persistence.
bundle.MySqlPersistenceManager">
   <param name="driver" value="com.mysql.jdbc.Driver"/>
   <param name="url" value="jdbc:mysql://localhost/guvnordb"/>
   <param name="user" value="guvnor"/>
   <param name="password" value="guvnor"/>
   <param name="schema" value="mysql"/>
   <param name="schemaObjectPrefix" value="Versioning_PM_" />
</PersistenceManager>
   </Versioning>
     <SearchIndex class=
"org.apache.jackrabbit.core.query.lucene.SearchIndex">
     <param name="path" value="${rep.home}/repository/index"/>
     <param name="supportHighlighting" value="true"/>
   </SearchIndex>

</Repository>
```

For further information about the `PersistenceManager` configuration you can take a look at `http://wiki.apache.org/jackrabbit/PersistenceManagerFAQ`.

There's more...

Another option to create JCR database persistence configurations is using the **Repository Configuration** option that can be found in the **Administration** section, as shown in the following screenshot:

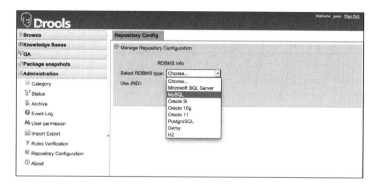

It comes with several predefined configurations that can be used to migrate the repository storage, and also allows you to create JNDI configurations to use together with data sources. Once you have selected the RDBMS, and clicked on the **Continue** button, four text boxes will be displayed to complete with the same information that was configured in the *How to do it...* section of this recipe, which is as follows and is also shown in the following screenshot:

- ▶ **Driver**: `com.mysql.jdbc.Driver`
- ▶ **URL**: `jdbc:mysql://localhost/guvnordb`
- ▶ **User**: `guvnor`
- ▶ **Password**: `guvnor`

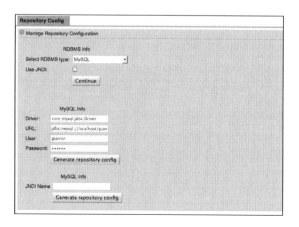

When the **Generate repository config** is clicked, a ready-to-use `repository.xml` file configuration will be displayed on the right side of the screen, as shown in the following screenshot, which can be saved by clicking on the **Save Configuration** button:

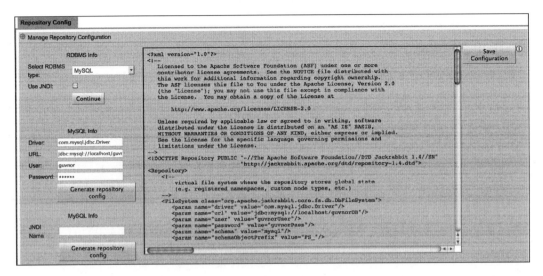

Once the file is saved into your hard drive, it is ready to replace the default Guvnor repository configuration file. Don't forget to add the appropriate JDBC library into the `servlet container library` folder.

See also

▶ Refer to the *Configuring the repository files location* recipe.

Configuring the repository files location

When you start the JBoss Application Server or servlet container where Guvnor was deployed, you will see how the repository configurations files are created in the directory where the servlet container was started. Instead of this, the best approach is to store the configuration in a secure and easy-to-identify directory. Let's see how this can be done.

How to do it...

The following steps will explain how to modify the default directory where the repository files are going to be stored:

1. First, you have to unzip the `guvnor-5.2.0.Final-jboss-as-5.1.war` file and then delete or move this file to another directory.

2. Open the `components.xml` file, located in the `WEB-INF` folder, with your favorite text editor and identify the section where the repository component is configured, as you can see in the following XML code snippet:

```
<component name="repositoryConfiguration">
<!-- JackRabbit  -->
<property name="properties">
<key>org.drools.repository.configurator</key>
<value>org.drools.repository.jackrabbit.
JackrabbitRepositoryConfigurator</value>
<!--<key>repository.root.directory</key><value>/opt/yourpath</
value>  -->
</property>
</component>
```

3. Uncomment the `repository.root.directory` property key and assign the directory where you want to store the repository configuration files as the property value:

```
<key>repository.root.directory</key><value>/opt/configurations/</
value>
```

4. Once the file is modified, zip the `guvnor-5.2.0.Final-jboss-as-5.1` folder and rename the generated ZIP file with a `.war` extension.

5. If you have data that was previously stored, you should move the files generated in the `bin/` folder to the new storage folder. After this you are ready to start the JBoss Application Server or the Servlet Container where it was deployed.

How it works...

Guvnor depends on **JBoss Seam** to configure features, such as the security management and the repository component. All these components are installed when the deployment scanner discovers a Java Bean annotated with an `@Name` Seam annotation, and these components use the `components.xml` configuration file to override or add the default properties.

Inside the `components.xml` file you will find a section where the `repositoryConfiguration` component is configured:

```
<component name="repositoryConfiguration">
<!-- JackRabbit  -->
<property name="properties">
<key>org.drools.repository.configurator</key>
<value>org.drools.repository.jackrabbit.
JackrabbitRepositoryConfigurator</value>
<!--  <key>repository.root.directory</key><value>/opt/yourpath</value>
-->
</property>
</component>
```

The important property here is `repository.root.directory`, which is disabled by default, and is the one in which we are interested. By enabling this property key, you can specify the directory where the JCR repository files are going to be stored. Actually, it is really useful to know the location where these files are located instead of having them inside the `bin` directory of the servlet container, where they can be accidently removed or can get lost in a migration.

Unzip the `guvnor-5.2.0.Final-jboss-as-5.1.war` file and modify the files. Alternatively, you can use the GNU Midnight Commander to edit the `components.xml` file (no need to unzip). Once you are done with modifying the files, you are ready to move your `repository.xml` file and the `repository` folder to the new location.

Obtaining resources using the REST API

The Drools Guvnor 5.2.0.Final release includes a new **REST API** created to remotely interact with the repository to obtain resources such as packages, assets, and categories, update assets, invoke package compilation, and so on, without the need to use the GUI. In this recipe, you will learn how to interact with the repository using the API and the different format responses available.

How to do it...

Carry out the following steps in order to obtain the generated rule package using the REST API:

1. Create a new Maven project and add the following dependencies in the `pom.xml` file:

```
<dependencies>
  <dependency>
    <groupId>org.drools</groupId>
    <artifactId>knowledge-api</artifactId>
    <version>5.2.0.Final</version>
  </dependency>
  <dependency>
    <groupId>org.drools</groupId>
    <artifactId>drools-core</artifactId>
    <version>5.2.0.Final</version>
  </dependency>
</dependencies>
```

2. Create a `GuvnorRestApi` Java class file in your project with the following code:

```
package.drools.cookbook;

public class GuvnorRestApi {
```

```
private String guvnorURI;

public GuvnorRestApi(String guvnorURI) {
This.guvnorURI = guvnorURI;
    }


}
```

3. Add the following method in the same class file. This method will be used to create the connection with Drools Guvnor to obtain a compiled binary package:

```
publicInputStreamgetBinaryPackage(String packageName) throws
Exception {
    URL url = new URL(guvnorURI + "/rest/packages/" + packageName
+ "/binary");
    HttpURLConnection connection = (HttpURLConnection)
url.openConnection();
    connection.setRequestMethod("GET");
    connection.setRequestProperty("Accept",
MediaType.APPLICATION_OCTET_STREAM);
    connection.connect();
    if (connection.getResponseCode() != 200) {
        throw new Exception("Bad response code: " +
connection.getResponseCode());
    }
    if (!connection.getContentType().equalsIgnoreCase(
MediaType.APPLICATION_OCTET_STREAM)) {
        throw new Exception("Bad response content type: " +
connection.getContentType());
    }
    returnconnection.getInputStream();
}
```

4. Use the following code in a Java `main` method to instantiate a `GuvnorRestApi` object and interact with the repository using the REST API:

```
String guvnorURI = "http://localhost:8080/guvnor-5.2.0.Final-
jboss-as-5.1";
GuvnorRestApi guvnorRestApi = new GuvnorRestApi(guvnorURI);
InputStream binaryPackage = guvnorRestApi
.getBinaryPackage("drools.cookbook");

KnowledgeBuilderkbuilder = KnowledgeBuilderFactory.
  newKnowledgeBuilder();
kbuilder.add(new InputStreamResource(binaryPackage),
  ResourceType.PKG);
KnowledgeBase kbase = kbuilder.newKnowledgeBase();
StatefulKnowledgeSessionksession =
  kbase.newStatefulKnowledgeSession();
```

How it works...

The Guvnor REST API is implemented using the JAX-RS standard that allows you to communicate using the HTTP protocol, using the common PUT, GET, POST, and DELETE methods.

At this moment there are two exposed resources to interact with the repository:

- ▶ Packages and Assets
- ▶ Categories

The Packages and Assets resource is used to obtain the available packages and assets by sending a GET method to the Guvnor REST URI. There are many available possibilities to obtain different information, for example, you can:

- ▶ Obtain all the available packages and their assets using the following URI:

  ```
  http://address:port/guvnor-5.2.0.Final-jboss-as-5.1/rest/
  packages
  ```

- ▶ Obtain specific information about a package with all its assets:

  ```
  http://address:port/guvnor-5.2.0.Final-jboss-as-5.1/rest/
  packages/drools.cookbook
  ```

- ▶ Obtain the generated rules of a package:

  ```
  http://address:port/guvnor-5.2.0.Final-jboss-as-5.1/rest/
  packages/drools.cookbook/source
  ```

- ▶ Obtain a package compilation:

  ```
  http://address:port/guvnor-5.2.0.Final-jboss-as-5.1/rest/
  packages/drools.cookbook/binary
  ```

- ▶ Obtain all the assets from a specific package:

  ```
  http://address:port/guvnor-5.2.0.Final-jboss-as-5.1/rest/
  packages/drools.cookbook/assets
  ```

Using this URI, you can obtain specific information from an asset adding its name after it, and also you can add the /source and /binary parameters, as seen earlier, to obtain the source code or the binary compilation.

 These URIs can be used in a web browser to display the output in XML format.

This API also can be used to create new assets or packages by sending a POST message to the following URI:

```
http://address:port/guvnor-webapp/rest/packages
```

The assets and packages are also updateable by sending a `PUT` message to the correct one of the following URIs:

```
http://address:port/guvnor-webapp/rest/packages/name/
```

```
http://address:port/guvnor-webapp/rest/packages/name/assets/name
```

Also, these resources can also be deleted with a `DELETE` message to the previous URIs.

Those are almost all the available interfaces to interact with Guvnor using an HTTP communication. The last thing you should know is that these exposed resources expect information in one of the following formats:

- Application/ATOM+XML
- Application/XML
- Application/JSON

Getting back on the recipe content, carry out the followings steps:

The first thing that you have to do is the configuration of the project dependencies. In this case, you have to add the minimum Drools dependencies, because in this recipe we are going to create a `StatefulKnowledgeSession` using a binary package obtained from Guvnor using the REST API. Open the `pom.xml` file and add the following dependencies in it:

```
<dependencies>
  <dependency>
    <groupId>org.drools</groupId>
    <artifactId>knowledge-api</artifactId>
    <version>5.2.0.Final</version>
  </dependency>
  <dependency>
    <groupId>org.drools</groupId>
    <artifactId>drools-core</artifactId>
    <version>5.2.0.Final</version>
  </dependency>
</dependencies>
```

Once your project dependencies are updated then it's time to write some code. Create a `GuvnorRestApi` Java class file in the project and add the following code:

```
public class GuvnorRestApi
{
  private String guvnorURI;
  public GuvnorRestApi(String guvnorURI)
  {
  this.guvnorURI = guvnorURI;
  }
}
```

This class doesn't say too much right now, so add the following code snippet inside this class to add the needed behavior in order to communicate with Guvnor and obtain a binary package:

```
publicInputStreamgetBinaryPackage(String packageName) throws Exception
{
  URL url = new URL(guvnorURI + "/ rest/packages/" + packageName +
"/binary");
  HttpURLConnection connection = (HttpURLConnection)
  url.openConnection();
  connection.setRequestMethod("GET");
  connection.setRequestProperty("Accept",
  MediaType.APPLICATION_OCTET_STREAM);
  connection.connect();
  if (connection.getResponseCode() != 200)
  {
    throw new Exception("Bad response code: " +
    connection.getResponseCode());
  }
  if (!connection.getContentType().equalsIgnoreCase(
  MediaType.APPLICATION_OCTET_STREAM))
  {
    throw new Exception("Bad response content type: " +
    connection.getContentType());
  }
  returnconnection.getInputStream();
}
```

As you can see, the `getBinaryPackage(String packageName)` method contains the logic to obtain a binary package opening a connection with the Guvnor REST resources using an `HttpURLConnection` object.

This `HttpURLConnection` object is created using a `URL` object that contains the full URI, which in this case will be `http://localhost:8080/guvnor-5.2.0.Final-jboss-as-5.1/rest/packages/drools.cookbook/binary`.

Once the `HttpURLConnection` is created, you have to configure the request parameters before connecting to it. The REST resource should be invoked by sending a `GET` method to obtain a binary package and configuring the request media type as `application/octet-stream` using the `Accept` request property:

```
connection.setRequestMethod("GET");
connection.setRequestProperty("Accept", MediaType.APPLICATION_OCTET_
  STREAM);
```

Once the `HttpURLConnection` is configured, you only have to connect with the REST resource and check the response code and the content type of the response:

```
connection.connect();
if (connection.getResponseCode() != 200)
{
  throw new Exception("Bad response code: " +
  connection.getResponseCode());
}
if (!connection.getContentType().equalsIgnoreCase(
  MediaType.APPLICATION_OCTET_STREAM))
  {
    throw new Exception("Bad response content type: " +
    connection.getContentType());
  }
```

Finally, you have to return the response, reading the connection with the `getInputStream()` method of the `HttpURLConnection` object.

Once you write this class, you are ready to use it to interact with the REST API. Create a Java `main` method in the same class file with the following code:

```
public static void main(String[] args) throws Exception
{
  GuvnorRestApiguvnorRestApi = new
  GuvnorRestApi("http://localhost:8080/guvnor-5.2.0.Final-jboss-as-
5.1");
  InputStreambinaryPackage =guvnorRestApi
  .getBinaryPackage("defaultPackage");

  KnowledgeBuilderkbuilder = KnowledgeBuilderFactory
  .newKnowledgeBuilder();
  kbuilder.add(new InputStreamResource(binaryPackage),
  ResourceType.PKG);
  KnowledgeBase kbase = kbuilder.newKnowledgeBase();
  for (KnowledgePackagekpackage : kbase.getKnowledgePackages())
  {
    System.out.println(kpackage.getName());
    for (Rule rule : kpackage.getRules())
    {
      System.out.println("\t" + rule.getName());
    }
  }
  StatefulKnowledgeSession ksession = kbase
  .newStatefulKnowledgeSession();
}
```

The purpose of this `main` method is only to show you how to use the `GuvnorRestApi` class to interact with Guvnor. In this `main` method, you have to instantiate a `GuvnorRestApi` object with the Guvnor URI as the constructor parameter. This URI is the same that you use to access the Guvnor GUI that was deployed in a JBoss AS or another servlet container:

```
GuvnorRestApi guvnorRestApi = new GuvnorRestApi("http://
localhost:8080/guvnor- 5.2.0.Final-jboss-as-5.1");
```

Once the `GuvnorRestApi` object is instantiated, you can use the `getBinaryPackage(Str ingpackageName)` method to obtain the binary package of the package whose name used is as the method parameter. In this example, we are going to obtain the binary package of the `defaultPackage`:

```
InputStream binaryPackage =guvnorRestApi
.getBinaryPackage("defaultPackage");
```

The execution of this method will return the binary package in an `InputStream` object that you have to add into a new `KnowledgeBuilder` object as a PKG Resource:

```
KnowledgeBuilder kbuilder = KnowledgeBuilderFactory
.newKnowledgeBuilder();
kbuilder.add(new InputStreamResource(binaryPackage), ResourceType.PKG);
```

After adding all the resources in the `KnowledgeBuilder` object, you are ready to create a `KnowledgeBase` object and then a `StatefulKnowledgeSession` as you always do:

```
KnowledgeBase kbase = kbuilder.newKnowledgeBase();
StatefulKnoledgeSessionksession =kbase
   .newStatefulKnowledgeSession();
```

There's nothing remaining to do at this point, so you can start asserting facts into the `StatefulKnowledgeSession` and firing rules as you usually do.

5
Fusion: Processing Complex Events

In this chapter, we will cover the following topics:

- ▶ How to declare our facts as events
- ▶ Testing our application using a pseudo-clock
- ▶ Entry-points: What they are and how we can use them
- ▶ Setting up event stream processing mode
- ▶ Sliding windows
- ▶ Event correlations using temporal operators

Introduction

Complex Events Processing (**CEP**) is a relatively new technology that is being adopted in the market with big vendors getting more interested in it. On the other hand, we have an open source Rules Engine that can easily integrate that kind of processing in our rules production system. Drools Fusion is no more than an extension that adds event-processing capabilities to the Business Logic Integration Framework, using the same concepts of rules to define the behavior with a unified API.

In this chapter, we are going to simulate how an airport could detect incoming flights that are getting close to its air space and how to react when special events occur, such as flight communication, first contact, and so on.

How to declare our facts as events

Each event being processed by a Drools application using event processing must be declared as an event using metadata, keeping in mind that all the events are facts but not all the facts are events. This declaration has to be done because all the events need a reference to a point in time at which they were created, updated, and so on (it always depends on the business case) to be minimally considered an event.

How to do it...

In order to declare facts as events, carry out the following steps:

1. Create your domain model and identify which objects will be treated as events. In this case, we modeled a POJO that will contain the information related to an incoming flight. This flight information is associated to a period of time and is going to be used to declare it as an event:

```
package drools.cookbook.model;

import java.util.Date;

public class FlightStatus {

    private String flight;
    private Date timestamp;


    public String getFlight() {
        return flight;
    }

    public void setFlight(String flight) {
        this.flight = flight;
    }

    public Date getTimestamp() {
        return timestamp;
    }

    public void setTimestamp(Date timestamp) {
        this.timestamp = timestamp;
    }


}
```

2. Now, it is time to create a DRL rule file to add the metadata and declare it as an event:

```
package drools.cookbook;

import drools.cookbook.model.FlightStatus
import drools.cookbook.model.FlightControl

global drools.cookbook.model.FlightControl control;

declare FlightStatus
    @role(event)
    @timestamp(timestamp)
end
```

3. Once the `FlightStatus` is declared as an event, we are going to define a rule, which will register the incoming flight as soon as the first contact is received:

```
rule "First contact"
salience 100
when
    $currentFlight : FlightStatus()
    not (exists (FlightStatus(this != $currentFlight,
                flight == $currentFlight.flight)))
then
    control.addFlight($currentFlight);
    System.out.println("First contact with Flight " +
                    $currentFlight.getFlight());
end
```

4. Once the rules are defined, it is time to compile them. In this recipe, we are not going to use advanced features such as Sliding Window or Automatic Event Lifecycle Management, so the rule engine can safely execute in CLOUD mode as it normally does. This event processing mode will be discussed in the next few chapters together with the STREAM mode:

```
KnowledgeBuilder kbuilder = KnowledgeBuilderFactory
    .newKnowledgeBuilder();
kbuilder.add(new ClassPathResource("rules.drl", getClass()),
    ResourceType.DRL);

if (kbuilder.hasErrors()) {
    if (kbuilder.getErrors().size() > 0) {
        for (KnowledgeBuilderError kerror : kbuilder.getErrors())
{
            System.err.println(kerror);
        }
    }
```

```
        }

    KnowledgeBase kbase = kbuilder.newKnowledgeBase();
        kbase.addKnowledgePackages(kbuilder.getKnowledgePackages());

    StatefulKnowledgeSession ksession = kbase
        .newStatefulKnowledgeSession();
```

How it works...

The purpose of this chapter is to clarify the preliminary step needed to start using the event-correlation support added by **Drools Fusion**. This is, basically, a way to declare facts as events once they are identified in the business case. To accomplish this you only have to assign the event role using metadata, which is similar to the metadata used to declare facts.

Before we continue it's a good idea to refresh what an event is. Events are a record of a state of change in the application domain, something that has already happened and cannot be changed. Since the past can't be changed, we can say that events are immutable objects.

In this case the metadata used is `@role(fact|event)`, which can be used to declare a fact type as a regular fact or an event fact. All these event declarations must be declared inside a DRL file together with the rules:

```
import drools.cookbook.model.FlightStatus

declare FlightStatus
    @role(event)
end
```

 If there is no role associated to a fact, the default type will be a regular fact.

Once the fact is declared as an event fact, you can optionally specify the timestamp field assigned to the event, as you may remember that every event is associated to a point in time:

```
import drools.cookbook.model.FlightStatus

declare FlightStatus
    @role(event)
    @timestamp(timestamp)
end
```

 If there is no timestamp metadata present, the working memory will automatically assign one when the fact is inserted using the Session Clock.

Once all the identified events in your domain model are declared as events using the metadata, they are ready to be inserted into the working memory:

```
KnowledgeBuilder kbuilder = KnowledgeBuilderFactory
    .newKnowledgeBuilder();
kbuilder.add(new ClassPathResource("rules.drl", getClass()),
    ResourceType.DRL);

KnowledgeBase kbase = kbuilder.newKnowledgeBase(config);
    kbase.addKnowledgePackages(kbuilder.getKnowledgePackages());

StatefulKnowledgeSession ksession = kbase
    .newStatefulKnowledgeSession();
```

Once the `KnowledgeBase` is created, you are ready to create an event-processing-enabled `StatefulKnowledgeSession` object, as you normally would do. As you can see, there is no need to configure the event processing mode because in this recipe the default **CLOUD** mode is enough to accomplish our correlation requirements.

These steps are very important and always should be used to create rules using complex event processing operators, otherwise the execution is not going to behave as is expected. Once these steps are implemented, you are ready to start modeling rules using temporal operators and sliding windows (only enabling the **STREAM** event processing mode), as is going to be seen in the following chapters.

There's more...

Events can also be defined inside rules using the `declare` keyword, as was seen in the *Declaring facts in the engine* recipe of *Chapter 1, Expert: The Rule Engine*, without the need of declaration using a POJO model:

```
declare FlightStatus
    @role(event)
    @timestamp(timestamp)
    flight : String
    Date : java.util.Date
    origin : String
    destination : String
    distance : long
end
```

As always, don't forget to add this fact declaration in the first DRL rule file added to the `KnowledgeBuilder`. Otherwise the compiler isn't going to be able to find the facts needed to compile the rules and the compilation will fail.

Testing our application using a pseudo-clock

Testing the application behavior using events can be a hard task because it depends on a clock to determinate the current control of the time flow. Fortunately, Drools Fusion provides a special clock implementation that can help you deal with this scenario. In this recipe, you will see how to configure the **pseudo-clock** and how to interact with it to advance the time manually, in order to recreate the expected behavior and test your rules.

How to do it...

Carry out the following steps in order to accomplish this recipe:

1. The first step is the creation of a rule with a temporal operator. In this case, you will see a simple temporal restriction for the testing example, but this topic will be covered in depth in the forthcoming recipes:

```
rule "emergency system"
when
    $emergency : EmergencySignal() from entry-point "emergency-
channel"
    FlightStatus(flight==$emergency.flight,
                this before[0m, 10m] $emergency)
                from entry-point "flight-arrival"
then
    // Emergency in progress
    System.out.println("Emergency in progress. Flight " +
                $emergency.getFlight());
    insert (new EmergencyInCourse($emergency.flight));
end
```

2. Now that the rules have been modeled, it is time to configure the knowledge session to use a pseudo-clock instead of the regular system clock:

```
KnowledgeBaseConfiguration config = KnowledgeBaseFactory
    .newKnowledgeBaseConfiguration();
config.setOption(EventProcessingOption.STREAM);

KnowledgeBase kbase = KnowledgeBaseFactory
    .newKnowledgeBase(config);
kbase.addKnowledgePackages(kbuilder.getKnowledgePackages());

KnowledgeSessionConfiguration conf = KnowledgeBaseFactory
    .newKnowledgeSessionConfiguration();
conf.setOption(ClockTypeOption.get("pseudo"));

ksession = kbase.newStatefulKnowledgeSession(conf, null);
```

3. After the knowledge session has been configured to use the pseudo-clock you have to obtain its reference, which will be used later to simulate the time elapse.

```
SessionPseudoClock clock = ksession.getSessionClock();
```

4. With the session pseudo-clock object reference you can start to simulate the increment of time. It's done by incrementing the pseudo-clock time and specifying the time scale and the value. Next you will see some simple code that will be explained later.

```
FlighSimulation flightAA001 = new FlighSimulation("AA001",
    "San Francisco", "Los Angeles", 270);
do {
  FlightStatus flightStatus = flightAA001.update();
  if (flightStatus.getDistance() <= AIRPORT_AIR_SPACE_SCOPE) {
    WorkingMemoryEntryPoint flightArrivalEntryPoint = ksession
      .getWorkingMemoryEntryPoint("flight-arrival");
    flightArrivalEntryPoint.insert(flightStatus);
    clock.advanceTime(7, TimeUnit.MINUTES);
    EmergencySignal emergencySignal = new
      EmergencySignal("AA001", 40);
    ksession.getWorkingMemoryEntryPoint("emergency-channel")
      .insert(emergencySignal);
  } else {
    ksession.getWorkingMemoryEntryPoint("flight-control")
      .insert(flightStatus);
    clock.advanceTime(5, TimeUnit.MINUTES);
  }
} while (!flightAA001.isLanded());
```

5. Once you have added the clock incremental code to simulate the time elapsed you are ready to execute your test case.

How it works...

The pseudo-clock is an alternative to the default **real-time clock**, which internally uses the system clock to determine the current timestamp, to test the rules behavior. With this pseudo-clock it is easier to test the rules because is possible to manually control the time elapsed in your application using any of the available time scales.

To start using it, first, you have to configure the knowledge session to replace the default clock implementation with this pseudo-clock:

```
KnowledgeSessionConfiguration conf = KnowledgeBaseFactory
    .newKnowledgeSessionConfiguration();
conf.setOption(ClockTypeOption.get("pseudo"));
StatefulKnowledgeSession ksession = kbase
    .newStatefulKnowledgeSession(conf, null);
```

As you can see, first you have to obtain a `KnowledgeSessionConfiguration` object from the `KnowledgeBaseFactory` and then configure the `ClockTypeOption` with the `pseudo` parameter.

```
conf.setOption(ClockTypeOption.get("pseudo"));
```

After this you have to pass this configuration when creating the knowledge session, otherwise it is not going to have any effect.

```
StatefulKnowledgeSession ksession = kbase
    .newStatefulKnowledgeSession(conf, null);
```

The increment of time is done by specifying the time scale and the time amount as the parameters using the reference of the `SessionClock` obtained with the next line of code:

```
SessionPseudoClock clock = ksession.getSessionClock();
```

Once you have this reference, you can begin to simulate the time elapsed each time you insert a fact into the working memory or wherever you need it. For example, if you want to increment the engine clock by ten seconds you have to use the `advanceTime(long, TimeUnit)` method of the `SessionPseudoClock` object shown as follows:

```
clock.advanceTime(10, TimeUnit.SECONDS);
```

That is the only thing that you have to do to manually to simulate the elapse of time. In order to do this, you can use any of the following supported time scales:

- milliseconds
- seconds
- minutes
- hours
- days

After this explanation about how to use a `SessionPseudoClock` we can get back to the example. In it we are simulating a flight emergency of an airplane that is in the airport's airspace. This airplane sent a `FlightStatus` event to the **flight-arrival** entry-point because it was ready to land, but a few minutes later it sent an emergency signal. To test this scenario, the rule has the restriction to attend the emergency signal only if it was sent 10 or fewer minutes after the flight notified the airport of its arrival:

```
rule "emergency system"
when
    $emergency : EmergencySignal() from entry-point "emergency-
channel"
    FlightStatus(flight==$emergency.flight,
                this before[0m, 10m] $emergency)
                from entry-point "flight-arrival"
```

```
then
    // Emergency in progress
    System.out.println("Emergency in progress. Flight " +
                        $emergency.getFlight());
    insert(new EmergencyInCourse($emergency.flight));
end
```

Following the snippet code included in the steps, you can figure out that the simulation of a `FlightStatus` event is sent every 5 minutes. But when the airplane is close to the airport it sends the `FlightStatus` event by the flight-arrival entry-point:

```
WorkingMemoryEntryPoint flightArrivalEntryPoint = ksession
    .getWorkingMemoryEntryPoint("flight-arrival");
flightArrivalEntryPoint.insert(flightStatus);
    clock.advanceTime(7, TimeUnit.MINUTES);
EmergencySignal emergencySignal = new EmergencySignal("AA001", 40);
ksession.getWorkingMemoryEntryPoint("emergency-channel")
    .insert(emergencySignal);
```

After this the clock is advanced seven minutes and an `EmergencySignal` is sent through the `emergency-channel` entry-point to simulate the behavior that will activate the **emergency system** rule. Once the generated activation is fired it will insert a new `EmergencyInCourse` fact to activate the emergency system.

After this recipe you have learned or refreshed your memory on how to implement unit testing to simulate time elapsed using the `PseudoClock`.

As you have seen, this pseudo-clock implementation is great to test your complex time scenario, thanks to the easy way of controlling elapsed time.

Entry-points: What they are and how we can use them

Imagine that in your system you have a few streams where the events are transmitted, and these events can be of the same type but have to be processed in different ways without mixing them in their processing. Drools Fusion can handle this scenario by creating entry-points that can be used to integrate these streams with the rules patterns, to process the events that are going to arrive from these streams. In this recipe, you will see how to create these entry-points and how they should be used externally to insert the events.

How to do it...

Carry out the following steps in order to create entry-points in your business rules:

1. Create some rules adding entry-points in the patterns using the `from entry-point` keyword:

```
package drools.cookbook;

import drools.cookbook.model.FlightStatus
import drools.cookbook.model.FlightControl

global drools.cookbook.model.FlightControl control;

declare FlightStatus
    @role(event)
end

rule "First contact"
salience 100
when
    $currentFlight : FlightStatus() from entry-point "flight-control"
    not (exists (FlightStatus(this != $currentFlight,
        flight == $currentFlight.flight)
        from entry-point "flight-control"))
then
    control.addFlight($currentFlight);
    System.out.println("First contact with Flight " +
                    $currentFlight.getFlight());
end


rule "flight arrival"
when
    $flight : FlightStatus() from entry-point "flight-arrival"
    // Obtain resources to prepare the flight landing
then
    System.out.println("Flight " + $flight.getFlight() +
                    "arriving to " + control.getAirport() +
                    ". Sending instructions");
    // Send instructions to arriving flight
end
```

2. Compile the DRL rule file as you usually do. In this recipe, the knowledge session is also configured using a pseudo-clock to control the advance of time:

```
KnowledgeBuilder kbuilder = KnowledgeBuilderFactory
    .newKnowledgeBuilder();
kbuilder.add(new ClassPathResource("rules.drl", getClass()),
ResourceType.DRL);

if (kbuilder.hasErrors()) {
    if (kbuilder.getErrors().size() > 0) {
        for (KnowledgeBuilderError kerror : kbuilder.getErrors())
{
            System.err.println(kerror);
        }
    }
}

KnowledgeBase kbase = kbuilder.newKnowledgeBase();
kbase.addKnowledgePackages(kbuilder.getKnowledgePackages());

KnowledgeSessionConfiguration conf = KnowledgeBaseFactory
    .newKnowledgeSessionConfiguration();
conf.setOption(ClockTypeOption.get("pseudo"));

StatefulKnowledgeSession ksession = kbase
    .newStatefulKnowledgeSession(conf, null);
```

3. Once the `KnowledgeBase` has been built, you are ready to use the defined entry-points to insert your events. In this example, each time the flight status is updated, it's inserted in a different entry-point, depending on the distance to the airport:

```
FlighSimulation flightAA001 = new FlighSimulation("AA001", "San
Francisco", "Los Angeles", 270);
FlightStatus flightStatus = flightAA001.update();
if (flightStatus.getDistance() <= 50) {
    ksession.getWorkingMemoryEntryPoint("flight-arrival")
        .insert(flightStatus);
} else {
    ksession.getWorkingMemoryEntryPoint("flight-control")
        .insert(flightStatus);
}
```

4. That is all that you need to start using entry-points. Remember to check out the entry-points example provided in this book to deeply understand how this example works.

How it works...

As mentioned in the introduction, the entry-point gives a stream abstraction that allows you to plug different event streams into rule patterns in your knowledge base. These aren't the only benefits of using entry-points because they can also be used to *partition* the working memory depending on the nature of facts and are also a nice feature to reduce cross products that will degrade the pattern-matching performance.

By default, Drools properly inserts all the facts into the default entry-point named **DEFAULT**. This is transparent for the users and there is no need to reference it in the rules files. But when there is more than one entry-point defined, the compiler will identify them and create the internal structures to support them in a transparent way.

In the following **RETE** network figure, you can see how the compiler internally creates the structures to support the entry-points, where they are represented as nodes with the number **1**. This graphic represents two different rule files; the left one using multiple entry-points and the other one using only the default entry-point. In the left RETE figure, there are three entry-points for flight-arrival, flight-control, and the DEFAULT entry-point, and the other one only represents the DEFAULT entry-point:

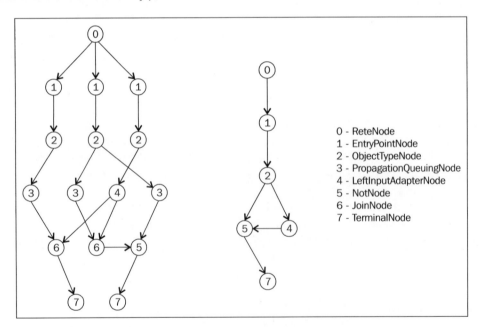

```
0 - ReteNode
1 - EntryPointNode
2 - ObjectTypeNode
3 - PropagationQueuingNode
4 - LeftInputAdapterNode
5 - NotNode
6 - JoinNode
7 - TerminalNode
```

 The complexity in the left RETE figure's network is only because the rules are more complex; the presence of more entry-points doesn't have any influence on the internal structures.

After this small introduction, we can now start defining our entry-points in the rules using the `from entry-point` operator. For example, the next rule has two patterns using the same entry-point:

```
rule "First contact"
salience 100
when
    $currentFlight : FlightStatus() from entry-point "flight-control"
    not (exists (FlightStatus(this != $currentFlight,
        flight == $currentFlight.flight)
        from entry-point "flight-control"))
then
    control.addFlight($currentFlight);
    System.out.println("First contact with Flight " +
                        $currentFlight.getFlight());
end
```

Using these entry-points in both the patterns will restrict the engine to only match with the `FlightStatus` facts that are inserted into the `flight-control` entry-point, creating a working memory partition based on the entry-point. As a consequence, any `FlightStatus` fact inserted in another working memory entry-point isn't going to be considered to match this rule.

Once the `KnowledgeBase` is compiled and a new `StatefulKnowledgeSession` is obtained, you can start to insert facts into the working memory. In order to insert facts in the entry-points, Drools provides the facility to obtain a reference to the entry-point from the knowledge session:

```
WorkingMemoryEntryPoint flightArrivalEntryPoint = ksession
    .getWorkingMemoryEntryPoint("flight-arrival");
flightArrivalEntryPoint.insert(flightStatus);
```

Also, the `StatefulKnowledgeSession` object provides a method to obtain all the defined entry-points, as can be seen in the following code snippet:

```
Collection<? extends WorkingMemoryEntryPoint> entryPoints = ksession.
getWorkingMemoryEntryPoints();
```

Instead of firing the rules each time a new fact is inserted, you can create a new thread that fires all the rules until the `StatefulKnowledgeSession` is halted. But since this method is thread blocking, it should be executed inside a new thread. Finally, to stop the thread you have to execute the `halt()` method of the `StatefulKnowledgeSession`:

```
Thread fireUntilHaltThread = new Thread() {
    @Override
    public void run() {
        ksession.fireUntilHalt();
    }
};
fireUntilHaltThread.start();
```

Ideally, these entry-points should be used with the Drools integration capabilities with another framework to avoid the manual insertion of facts, but we will see these integrations in the next few chapters.

Setting up event stream processing mode

In this recipe, you will see how to configure the knowledge base in STREAM mode and also the features that will be added.

How to do it...

This recipe consists of a simple step of assigning the STREAM mode to the configuration of a knowledge base:

```
KnowledgeBaseConfiguration config = KnowledgeBaseFactory
    .newKnowledgeBaseConfiguration();
config.setOption(EventProcessingOption.STREAM);

KnowledgeBase kbase = KnowledgeBaseFactory
    .newKnowledgeBase(config);
kbase.addKnowledgePackages(kbuilder.getKnowledgePackages());

StatefulKnowledgeSession ksession = kbase
    .newStatefulKnowledgeSession();
```

How it works...

By default, Drools internally assigns the CLOUD mode when non-event-processing mode is configured. With the CLOUD mode, which is the default mode used by Drools, all the inserted facts are treated as facts in the working memory, ignoring if some of these facts were declared as events. In this mode, there is no notion of flow of time, even when the events have an associated timestamp, and thus, the engine is not able to determinate how *old* the event is. Also, in this mode there are characteristics of the engine that cannot be implemented, such as sliding windows and automatic life-cycle management of facts.

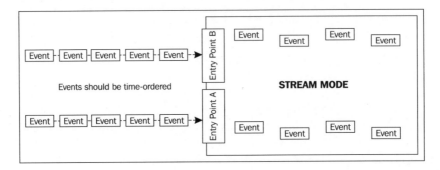

These characteristics are enabled when the knowledge base is configured in the STREAM mode, which is the right choice when the application needs to process streams of events. In this processing mode, there are other requirements to process the events in the right way, and if these aren't satisfied, there is a high probability of having unexpected results:

▶ The events should be inserted ordered in time.

▶ The stream should be synchronized using the Session Clock, or a custom synchronization mechanism.

Keeping these warnings in mind you can configure the knowledge base using the following code snippet:

```
KnowledgeBaseConfiguration config = KnowledgeBaseFactory
    .newKnowledgeBaseConfiguration();
config.setOption(EventProcessingOption.STREAM);
KnowledgeBase kbase = KnowledgeBaseFactory
    .newKnowledgeBase(config);
```

Once the knowledge base is configured and instantiated, there aren't any more configurations left and you can create the knowledge session from it as you always do.

This was a simple recipe, but is very important to keep in mind the differences of the execution and what could happen when these restrictions are ignored.

Sliding Windows

When you configure the engine to run in STREAM mode it enables extra features, and one of them is sliding windows support. Sliding windows allow us to restrict our interest to events that belong to a window that is constantly moving, using time or the number of occurrences of an event as reference. Well, that is a pretty description of what sliding windows are, but for more details you can go through this recipe.

How to do it...

Carry out the following steps to implement sliding window in your business rules:

1. Create a business rule that uses a sliding window based on time or length to calculate a value. In this case, this rule calculates the average speed of the airplane based on the last five flight statuses sent:

```
rule "flight average speed"
when
    $flight : FlightStatus() from entry-point "flight-control"
    $averageSpeed : Number(floatValue > 0) from accumulate(FlightS
tatus(flight==$flight.flight, $speed:speed) over window:length(5)
from entry-point "flight-control",
```

```
average($speed))
then
    System.out.println($flight.getFlight() + " average speed: " +
$averageSpeed);
end
```

2. Create a `StatefulKnowledgeSession` with a `KnowledgeBase` configured in STREAM mode. The knowledge session is also configured using a `SessionPseudoClock` to test the application behavior:

```
KnowledgeBaseConfiguration config = KnowledgeBaseFactory
    .newKnowledgeBaseConfiguration();
config.setOption(EventProcessingOption.STREAM);

KnowledgeBase kbase = KnowledgeBaseFactory
    .newKnowledgeBase(config);
kbase.addKnowledgePackages(kbuilder.getKnowledgePackages());

KnowledgeSessionConfiguration conf = KnowledgeBaseFactory
    .newKnowledgeSessionConfiguration();
conf.setOption(ClockTypeOption.get("pseudo"));

StatefulKnowledgeSession ksession = kbase
    .newStatefulKnowledgeSession(conf, null);
```

3. Once the `StatefulKnowledgeSession` is created, we can start to simulate the flight status event arrival to the rule engine:

```
final FlighSimulation flightAA001 = new FlighSimulation("AA001",
"San Francisco", "Los Angeles", 270);

for (int i = 0; i < 10; i++) {
    FlightStatus flightStatus = flightAA001.update();
    WorkingMemoryEntryPoint flightArrivalEntryPoint = ksession
        .getWorkingMemoryEntryPoint("flight-control");
    flightArrivalEntryPoint.insert(flightStatus);
    clock.advanceTime(5, TimeUnit.MINUTES);
    Thread.sleep(100);
}
```

How it works...

Sliding windows are an interesting way to scope a group of objects in a time interval or length that is highly coupled with the concept of *now*. Because of it the engine needs to run in STREAM mode otherwise the execution will generate unexpected results.

But, before we configure the engine, we are going to create a simple rule using sliding windows:

```
rule "flight average speed"
when
    $flight : FlightStatus() from entry-point "flight-control"
    $averageSpeed : Number(floatValue > 0) from accumulate(FlightSta
tus(flight==$flight.flight, $speed:speed) over window:length(5) from
entry-point "flight-control", average($speed))
then
    System.out.println($flight.getFlight() + " average speed: " +
                        $averageSpeed);
end
```

In this example, we are using a rule to calculate the average speed of the incoming flight using the last five `FlightStatus` events, and to achieve this, we are using the sliding windows concept. You can imagine this sliding window as a structure that will collect the last five `FlightStatus` events of the same flight each time a `FlightStatus` event is inserted into the working memory through the flight-control entry-point.

The sliding window was declared as **from accumulate** pattern, but to be clearer in the explanation this pattern is going to be split:

```
FlightStatus(flight==$flight.flight, $speed:speed) over
window:length(5) from entry-point "flight-control"
```

As you can see, the creation of a sliding window is through the `over` keyword to associate it to a pattern. But we declare the sliding window that is associated to this keyword using the `window:type(value)` keyword, where the type could be based on time or length.

In a length-based sliding window the argument is a numeric value that specifies the number of facts to be considered. But on the other hand, a time-based sliding window uses a time value formed by numeric values followed by Drools `time` keyword, which allows the creation of complex time formats to be associated to sliding windows:

- Sliding windows based on time:

```
window:time(5s)
window:time(1h10m)
```

- Sliding window based on length:

```
window:length(5)
```

Time units supported:

- ▶ **ms**: milliseconds
- ▶ **s**: seconds
- ▶ **m**: minutes
- ▶ **h**: hour
- ▶ **d**: day

After the rule creations, the engine has to be configured in the STREAM mode in the same way as was seen in the *Setting up event stream processing mode* recipe:

```
KnowledgeBaseConfiguration config = KnowledgeBaseFactory
    .newKnowledgeBaseConfiguration();
config.setOption(EventProcessingOption.STREAM);
KnowledgeBase kbase = KnowledgeBaseFactory
    .newKnowledgeBase(config);
kbase.addKnowledgePackages(kbuilder.getKnowledgePackages());
KnowledgeSessionConfiguration conf = KnowledgeBaseFactory
    .newKnowledgeSessionConfiguration();
conf.setOption(ClockTypeOption.get("pseudo"));
StatefulKnowledgeSession ksession = kbase
    .newStatefulKnowledgeSession(conf, null);
```

Once the rules are compiled, you can start inserting your facts in order to view how the sliding window behaves within the rules execution. We also configured the `StatefulKnowledgeSession` with a pseudo-clock to simulate the time elapse between the insertion of facts.

In the recipe example, we are simulating a flight between San Francisco and Los Angeles, sending information to the control tower every five minutes:

```
final FlighSimulation flightAA001 = new FlighSimulation("AA001", "San
Francisco", "Los Angeles", 270);
for (int i = 0; i < 10; i++) {
    FlightStatus flightStatus = flightAA001.update();
    WorkingMemoryEntryPoint flightArrivalEntryPoint = ksession
        .getWorkingMemoryEntryPoint("flight-control");
    flightArrivalEntryPoint.insert(flightStatus);
    clock.advanceTime(5, TimeUnit.MINUTES);
    Thread.sleep(100);
}
```

After each `FlightStatus` fact is inserted into the flight-control `WorkingMemoryEntryPoint` and the activations are fired, the **flight average speed** rule is going to display the average speed of the incoming flight.

Sliding windows are really a nice choice to control the behavior of your business model and make calculations based on its values, allowing the engine to make choices in **real time** based on event time or length.

Event correlations using temporal operators

One of the requirements of any CEP system is the ability to compare events based on their timestamp. To accomplish it, Drools implements 13 temporal operators and their negation that allow us to compare events in different ways. In this recipe you will see how to define a basic rule using one of these operators.

How to do it...

Carry out the following steps in order to accomplish this recipe:

1. Create a rule using a temporal operator to control the correlation of two independent events:

```
package drools.cookbook;

import drools.cookbook.model.FlightStatus

global drools.cookbook.helper.EmergencySystem emergencySystem;

declare FlightStatus
    @role(event)
end

rule "landing system"
when
    $flight : FlightStatus() from entry-point "flight-landing"
    FlightStatus(this!=$flight, this before[0m, 3m] $flight)
        from entry-point "flight-landing"
then
    emergencySystem.redirect($flight);
end
```

2. Compile the authored rule and create a stateful knowledge session as you usually do. As we aren't using sliding windows there is no need to configure the event processing mode. The default CLOUD mode will fit well for this rule:

```
KnowledgeBuilder kbuilder = KnowledgeBuilderFactory
    .newKnowledgeBuilder();
kbuilder.add(new ClassPathResource("rules.drl", getClass()),
```

```
                          ResourceType.DRL);

      if (kbuilder.hasErrors()) {
        if (kbuilder.getErrors().size() > 0) {
          for (KnowledgeBuilderError kerror : kbuilder.getErrors())
          {
            System.err.println(kerror);
          }
        }
      }

      KnowledgeBase kbase = kbuilder.newKnowledgeBase();

      KnowledgeSessionConfiguration conf = KnowledgeBaseFactory
          .newKnowledgeSessionConfiguration();
      conf.setOption(ClockTypeOption.get("pseudo"));

      StatefulKnowledgeSession ksession = kbase
          .newStatefulKnowledgeSession(conf, null);
```

3. Finally, once the knowledge session is created you only have to test the application behavior using the pseudo-clock to interact with the rule engine. In this example we are going to insert two different `FlightStatus` facts of flights ready to land in less than 2 minutes and the second inserted `FlightStatus` will generate an emergency to redirect the flight:

```
      SessionPseudoClock clock = ksession.getSessionClock();

      EmergencySystem emergencySystem = new EmergencySystem();
      ksession.setGlobal("emergencySystem", emergencySystem);

      FlighSimulation flightAA001 = new FlighSimulation("AA001",
          "San Francisco", "Los Angeles", 270);
      FlighSimulation flightAA002 = new FlighSimulation("AA002",
          "Dallas", "Los Angeles", 470);

      WorkingMemoryEntryPoint flightLandingEntryPoint = ksession
          .getWorkingMemoryEntryPoint("flight-landing");
      flightLandingEntryPoint.insert(flightAA001.update());
      clock.advanceTime(2, TimeUnit.MINUTES);
      ksession.fireAllRules();

      flightLandingEntryPoint.insert(flightAA002.update());
      ksession.fireAllRules();

      System.out.println("Redirected flights: " + emergencySystem
          .getRedirectedFlights().size())
```

How it works...

In this recipe we are only using one of all the available temporal operators, defined using the `before` keyword. This evaluator allows us to correlate two events and the pattern matches when the temporal distance between them belongs to the distance range declared for the operator.

For a more detailed explanation let's take the defined rule as a reference. This rule is very simple, but it is used to control the flights that will be landing, and redirect flights ready to land when there is another already landing:

```
rule "landing system"
when
    $flight : FlightStatus() from entry-point "flight-landing"
    FlightStatus(this!=$flight, this before[0m, 3m] $flight)
        from entry-point "flight-landing"
then
    emergencySystem.redirect($flight);
end
```

The pattern in which we are interested is the second one, which makes a correlation between the flight already landing and a new one that wants to land. But this new incoming flight is correlated with the first one to not allow more than one landing in a period of three minutes.

These events are correlated using the pattern constraint `this before[0m, 3m] $flight`, where both are being referenced, using the `this` keyword and the `$flight` variable, and the distance range is declared with the `[0m, 3m]` value. Being even more descriptive, the pattern used to correlate these events can be translated to a simpler equation:

```
0m <= IncomingFlight.startTimestamp - LandingFlight.endTimeStamp <= 3m
```

This is only the tip of the iceberg. There are many correlations that can be implemented using temporal operators. Explaining all of them is a task beyond this recipe. The best online reference to understand the semantics of all the temporal operators is in the official documentation, where you can find an extensive section explaining in detail how all these operators can be used in event comparisons. Check it out at `http://www.jboss.org/drools/documentation` in the Drools Fusion section.

6

Executing Drools Remotely

In this chapter, we will cover:

- ▶ Knowledge services and multiple endpoints configuration
- ▶ Deploying the Drools Server in JBoss AS 5.x
- ▶ Creating commands with XStream marshallers
- ▶ Using the REST interface to execute commands
- ▶ Testing the SOAP interface with soapUI

Introduction

One of the latest interesting features of Drools is the possibility to execute rules remotely. The Drools 5.2 release allows the creation of declarative services using Apache Camel integration to interact with knowledge sessions. Thanks to this integration, the Drools developers have provided a ready-to-use execution server, commonly known as the Drools Server, which uses all the advantages provided by Apache Camel to be integrated with the **Apache CXF** project. The Drools Server is just a WAR file that can be deployed in an application server (such as JBoss AS, Apache Tomcat, and so on) and allows it to be used by any technology that can use HTTP, through a REST interface.

In the following recipes, you will learn how to configure the Drools Server, how to create execution messages, and how to interact with it.

Knowledge services and multiple endpoints configuration

The entire Drools Server configuration is done using the **Spring Framework**, and with this integration it's possible to configure the service endpoint and knowledge sessions that will be exposed in the servlet container where this web application is deployed. In this recipe, you will see the most commonly used configuration to create these declarative services.

Getting ready

In order to start using the Drools Server, it has to be deployed in a servlet container. It works in Apache Tomcat and JBoss AS 4.x without extra configuration. However, if you want to deploy it in a JBoss AS 5.x or higher server, you should read the next recipe to know what you have to configure to make it work.

How to do it...

Carry out the following steps in order to configure a Drools Server instance in a JBoss Application Server:

1. Download the JBoss Drools 5.2.Final integration distribution file from `http://www.jboss.org/drools/downloads`.

2. Once the download finishes, decompress it and copy the `binaries/drools-camel-server-5.2.0.Final.war` file to the servlet container deployment directory. Unzip the WAR file into a folder called `drools-server`. Copy your rules files inside the `WEB-INF/classes` folder, and your domain model into the `WEB-INF/lib` or the `servlet container` libraries folder. Keep in mind that you can also configure the Drools resource bean to obtain the rules from a directory or a Guvnor instance.

3. Inside the `WEB-INF/classes` folder, you will find all the files used to configure the services. Open the default `knowledge-services.xml` file with your favorite file editor and edit the `<drools:resources/>` to add your rule file:

    ```xml
    <?xml version="1.0" encoding="UTF-8"?>

    <beans xmlns="http://www.springframework.org/schema/beans"
    xmlns:xsi="http://www.w3.org/2001/XMLSchema-instance"
    xmlns:drools="http://drools.org/schema/drools-spring"
    xsi:schemaLocation="http://www.springframework.org/schema/
    beans http://www.springframework.org/schema/beans/spring-beans-
    2.0.xsdhttp://drools.org/schema/drools-spring http://drools.org/
    schema/drools-spring-1.3.0.xsd">
    ```

```
<drools:grid-node id="node1" />

<drools:kbase id="kbase1" node="node1">
<drools:resources>
  <drools:resource  type="DRL" source="classpath:rules.drl"/>
</drools:resources>
</drools:kbase>

<drools:ksession id="ksession1" type="stateless"
kbase="kbase1" node="node1"/>

</beans>
```

4. Now that you have configured your services, you can zip the `drools-server` folder and rename it as `.war` or use the exploded folder with a `.war` file extension.

5. Start the servlet container to check that everything was properly configured.

How it works...

The Drools Server is a web application that can be deployed in any servlet container and allows the execution of knowledge bases using the REST and SOAP protocols. Internally, it uses all the features provided by integration with the Apache Camel framework to create the REST/SOAP service endpoints, to process/execute the execution messages, and so on.

The internal configurations of these services are done through a few XML files included in the WAR file. There are several files included, but the most important are the following ones:

▶ `beans.xml`: Main XML that imports `knowledge-services.xml` and `camel-server.xml`

▶ `camel-server.xml`: Configures CXF endpoints and Camel routes to expose the knowledge services

▶ `knowledge-services.xml`: Configures the knowledge bases and sessions

Before starting to modify the `knowledge-services.xml` file, you have to provide the domain model that is to be used by the server. It can simply be a JAR file that can be copied inside the servlet container libraries folder; it can also be copied inside the `WEB-INF/lib` folder of the unzipped `drools-server.war` file, or an XSD model file as was seen in *Expert: The Rule Engine* in the recipe *Declaring facts using XML* recipe of *Chapter 1*, which should be copied in the `WEB-INF/classes` folder.

The same thing happens with the rules files that are going to be used to configure the knowledge sessions, which may be provided inside the `WEB-INF/classes` folder. Obviously, they can also be authored and consumed from a `DroolsGuvnor` instance.

These files need not be copied inside the `war` file necessarily, as they can also be in another directory of your file system. This will only introduce small modifications about how the knowledge sessions are configured.

After you have decided where the domain model and the rules files are going to reside, it is time to modify the `knowledge-services.xml` file. By default, this file comes with a configuration example, which, with simple modification can be enough to meet your needs, but let's see other configuration possibilities also. In the following code, you will see a simple knowledge-service configuration file with its common configuration:

```
<beans>
<drools:grid-node id="node1" />
<drools:kbase id="kbase1" node="node1">
  <drools:resources>
    <drools:resource  type="DRL" source="classpath:rules.drl"/>
  </drools:resources>
</drools:kbase>
<drools:ksession id="ksession1" type="stateless"
kbase="kbase1" node="node1"/>
</beans>
```

As you can see, there are definitions of three beans, which are the minimum requirement:

- ► `drools:grid-node`: This bean will have the responsibility to execute the commands and will contain a reference to the knowledge session defined, which is explained in the third point here.
- ► `drools:kbase`: This bean will create a knowledge base using the configured resources.
- ► `drools:ksession`: This bean will create a stateless or stateful knowledge session using the knowledge base and grid-node beans defined.

The `drools:grid-node` doesn't need too much configuration in this scenario and the only needed property is the ID, but it's also possible to configure it as a real grid environment. The following code line illustrates this:

```
<drools:grid-node id="node1" />
```

Then the knowledge base has to be configured adding your resources and another optional extra configuration. The only required properties are the ID and grid node reference, which in this case aren't optional. This is illustrated by the following code line. It is also possible to configure other characteristics of the knowledge base (assert behavior, event processing mode, and so on); however, they aren't needed at this point. They will be explained in the *Chapter 7, Integration: How to Connect Drools*:

```
<drools:kbase id="kbase1" node="node1" />
```

This definition is going to generate an empty knowledge base, and hence we need to include some resources in it. These resources aren't limited to DRL files, it's also possible to include XSD models, BPMN2 files, DSL, DSLR, and all the resources supported by Drools.

All these resources are defined with a `<drools:resource/>` bean definition within a `<drools:resources/>` global tag.

> The `<drools:resource/>` definitions can be defined outside a `<drools:kbase/>` definition to be reused in other knowledge base definitions.

Any `<drools:resource/>` definition needs two properties to be defined:

- `type`: This can be `DRL`, `BPMN2`, `XDRL`, `DSL`, `DSLR`, `DRF`, `DTABLE`, `PKG`, `BRL`, `CHANGE_SET`, or `XSD`.

- `source`: A path to the resource file. Resources included in the same classpath have to be referenced using `classpath:` `modifier`, otherwise to point to external files, you can use `file:` `modifier`.

The following code snippet shows how the resources can be defined externally to be used in a knowledge base configuration:

```
<drools:resource id="model" type="XSD" source="classpath:model.xsd"/>
<drools:kbase id="kbase1" node="node1">
  <drools:resources>
    <drools:resource type="DRL" source="classpath:rules.drl"/>
    <drools:resource ref="model"/>
  </drools:resources>
</drools:kbase>
```

Once the knowledge base bean is configured, the only part remaining is the knowledge session configuration, which can be done using the following XML code snippet:

```
<drools:ksession id="ksession1" type="stateless"
kbase="kbase1" node="node1"/>
```

As you can see, it needs an ID, the knowledge session type (stateless or stateful), a knowledge base, and a grid node reference. This ID and the grid node ID are very important because they are used in the service endpoints to execute the command messages; by default, the `camel-server.xml` file uses the `node1` and `ksession1` names in the services' configuration, respectively, and if you change these IDs in the knowledge services' XML configuration file, they should be also changed in the `camel-server.xml` file.

Basically, in this recipe we saw how to create and configure a remote knowledge session and how to add our model definitions and rules files. Keeping these tips in mind, you can create complex configurations involving multiple knowledge sessions, which may or may not share the same knowledge base, exposed in different URIs, and so on. You can see how to do it in the *There's more* section.

There's more...

As I said before, it's possible to expose multiple knowledge sessions in different URLs, and with this approach you can create different execution endpoints to separate the business rules' execution. But before starting to configure the services, I will show a `knowledge-services.xml` example file with three knowledge sessions (with two knowledge sessions sharing the same knowledge base and grid node as shown in the following figure). In this case, there are two grid nodes because when you want to expose one or more knowledge session in different URL services, they need to be contained in different grid nodes:

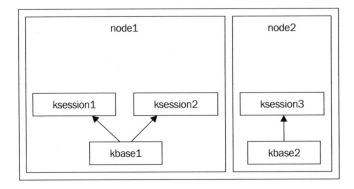

And this is how the knowledge services XML configuration file will look:

```
<beans xmlns="http://www.springframework.org/schema/beans"
xmlns:xsi="http://www.w3.org/2001/XMLSchema-instance"
xmlns:drools="http://drools.org/schema/drools-spring"
xsi:schemaLocation="http://www.springframework.org/schema/
beans http://www.springframework.org/schema/beans/spring-beans-
2.0.xsdhttp://drools.org/schema/drools-spring http://drools.org/
schema/drools-spring-1.3.0.xsd">

<drools:grid-node id="node1" />
<drools:grid-node id="node2" />
<drools:kbase id="kbase1" node="node1">
  <drools:resources>
    <drools:resource  type="DRL" source="classpath:rules.drl"/>
  </drools:resources>
```

```
</drools:kbase>

<drools:kbase id="kbase2" node="node2" />
  <drools:resources>
    <drools:resource  type="DRL" source="classpath:validation.drl"/>
  </drools:resources>
</drools:kbase>

<drools:ksession id="ksession1" type="stateless" kbase="kbase1"
node="node1"/>
<drools:ksession id="ksession2" type="stateless" kbase="kbase1"
node="node1"/>
<drools:ksession id="ksession3" type="stateless" kbase="kbase2"
node="node2"/>
</beans>
```

Once you update the knowledge services' XML configuration file, it's time to modify the `camel-server.xml` file to add the new service endpoints and the Apache Camel routes.

In this example, we want to add a new service endpoint to interact with the knowledge sessions so we have to add a new bean definition changing the bean ID and the address:

```
<cxf:rsServer id="rsValidationServer"
address="/restValidation"
serviceClass="org.drools.jax.rs.CommandExecutorImpl">
<cxf:providers>
  <bean class="org.drools.jax.rs.CommandMessageBodyReader"/>
</cxf:providers>
</cxf:rsServer>
```

If you also want access to the new knowledge service using SOAP, you can add the following bean definition to create a CXF Endpoint:

```
<cxf:cxfEndpoint id="soapValidationServer"
address="/soapValidation"
serviceName="ns:CommandExecutor"
endpointName="ns:CommandExecutorPort"
wsdlURL="soap.wsdl"
xmlns:ns="http://soap.jax.drools.org/" >
<cxf:properties>
  <entry key="dataFormat" value="MESSAGE"/>
  <entry key="defaultOperationName" value="execute"/>
</cxf:properties>
</cxf:cxfEndpoint>
```

After this, you have to add a new Camel route inside the Camel Context definition to connect the SOAP/REST services with the Drools Camel Component, as you can see in the following code:

```
<camelContext id="camel" xmlns="http://camel.apache.org/schema/
spring">
<route>
<from uri="cxfrs://bean://rsServer"/>
  <policy ref="droolsPolicy">
    <unmarshal ref="xstream" />
    <to uri="drools:node1" />
    <marshal ref="xstream" />
  </policy>
</route>
<route>
<from uri="cxf://bean://soapServer"/>
  <policy ref="droolsPolicy">
    <unmarshal ref="xstream" />
    <to uri="drools:node1" />
    <marshal ref="xstream" />
  </policy>
</route>
<route>
<from uri="cxfrs://bean://rsValidationServer"/>
  <policy ref="droolsPolicy">
    <unmarshal ref="xstream" />
    <to uri="drools:node2" />
    <marshal ref="xstream" />
  </policy>
</route>
<route>
<from uri="cxf://bean://soapValidationServer"/>
  <policy ref="droolsPolicy">
    <unmarshal ref="xstream" />
    <to uri="drools:node2" />
    <marshal ref="xstream" />
  </policy>
</route>
</camelContext>
```

One thing to keep in mind is the configuration of the policy where you can change the marshaller type for the marshalling/unmarshalling process modifying the `<unmarshal ref="xstream" />` and `<marshal ref="xstream" />` tags, and then replacing the `ref` property with a `jaxb` or `json` value:

```
<policy ref="droolsPolicy">
  <unmarshal ref="xstream" />
  <to uri="drools:node2" />
  <marshal ref="xstream" />
</policy>
```

However, this new route needs a modification in the `<to/>` tags to point to new grid nodes. As you can see, the new routes don't make references to the `ksession` as in the default configuration because the grid node has all the logic to identify and redirect the command execution to the right knowledge session.

And that's all, after the service endpoints definition and the Camel route modifications, you are ready to restart the servlet container and start sending messages to the service endpoints, as you will see in the following recipes.

Deploying the Drools Server in JBoss AS 5.x

We always like to deploy web applications in any servlet container believing that they are going to work exceptionally well. But this isn't always true, and the Drools Server doesn't make an exception because it needs extra configuration to deploy successfully in a JBoss Application Server 5.x instance, and we are going to view the details in the next recipe.

Getting ready

If you are reading this recipe, you probably have a JBoss Application Server 5.x that you want to configure, otherwise you can download it from `http://www.jboss.org/jbossas/downloads`.

How to do it...

Carry out the following steps in order to successfully install the Drools Server in a JBoss Application Server 5.x instance:

1. Download the `camel-jboss.jar` file library from `http://code.google.com/a/apache-extras.org/p/camel-extra/`. If you can't find it, read the *How it works* section to know what you have to do in order to download it.

2. Once you locate and download the `camel-jboss.jar` file, copy it into the `WEB-INF/lib` directory of your exploded `drools-camel-server-5.2.0.Final.war` directory. To explode a WAR file just rename it as `.zip`, decompress, and rename the decompressed directory as `drools-server.war`. Don't forget to remove the previously compressed WAR file.

3. Remove the `xml-apis-1.0.b2.jar` file located in the `WEB-INF/lib` directory.

4. Create a `jboss-web.xml` file in the `WEB-INF` directory with the following code to configure the classloader isolation:

```
<jboss-web>
<class-loading java2ClassLoadingCompliance="true">
  <loader-repository>drools.cookbook:archive=drools-server
   <loader-repository-config>java2ParentDelegaton=true </loader-
repository-config>
  </loader-repository>
</class-loading>
</jboss-web>
```

5. Finally, it's time to modify the `camel-server.xml` file to configure the custom class resolver needed by Apache Camel, adding the following bean definition:

```
<bean id="jbossResolver"
class="org.apache.camel.jboss.JBossPackageScanClassResolver"/>
```

6. Once these modifications are done you can safely start your JBoss AS instance.

How it works...

Since the version 5.0, the JBoss Application Server classes resolver mechanism has undergone big changes and since then Apache Camel needs an extra library to work on it. To patch this issue, the Apache Camel project offers an extra library that is located in a Google Code project hosting.

The JAR file download is pretty tricky because it isn't displayed in the downloads section and you have to browse the Maven repository using the web interface with the following URL:

```
http://code.google.com/a/apache-extras.org/p/camel-extra/source/
browse/?redir=1#svn/maven2/releases/
```

Now, navigate to the `org/apache/camel/extra/camel-jboss` folder. Once the JAR file is downloaded, it has to be copied into the `WEB-INF/lib` folder of your exploded Drools Server WAR file.

Next, you have to remove the `xml-apis-1.0.b2.jar` file located in the `WEB-INF/lib` directory to avoid issues with another XML parser's libraries included in the application server. Also, to avoid other issues with the AS classloader, you have to configure the classloader isolation creating a `jboss-web.xml` file in the `WEB/INF` directory with the content bean definition in the following step.

Lastly, you have to modify the `camel-server.xml` file to enable the custom class resolver required by Apache Camel, and to do it you only have to add the following bean definition:

```
<bean id="jbossResolver" class="org.apache.camel.jboss.
JBossPackageScanClassResolver"/>
```

There is nothing more left to do. After all these steps, you are ready to start the JBoss instance and start using the Drools Server as shown in the other recipes of this chapter.

Creating commands with XStream marshallers

The interaction with the Drools Server is made through XML commands. These XML commands can be manually written by using the marshallers and commands provided by Drools. In this recipe, you will see how to create the commands and how to marshall them using the XStream marshaller.

How to do it...

Carry out the following steps in order to learn how to interact with the Drools Server using Drools Commands:

1. Add the **XStream 1.4.1** library dependency into your project. If you are using Apache Maven you can add the following code in your `pom.xml` dependencies configuration. Otherwise, you can download the binaries from `http://xstream.codehaus.org/`.

    ```
    <dependency>
      <groupId>com.thoughtworks.xstream</groupId>
        <artifactId>xstream</artifactId>
      <version>1.4.1</version>
      </dependency>
    ```

2. Once the XStream library is added in your project dependencies, the next step is to create the Drools Commands by writing some Java code.

3. In this recipe, we are going to create a command to insert a new object instance into the remote knowledge session and then execute the rules. There are other available commands that will be explained later in the *How it works...* section:

```
Server server1 = new Server("windows-nt", 1, 2048, 2048, 3);

BatchExecutionCommandImpl batchExecutionCommand = new
BatchExecutionCommandImpl();
batchExecutionCommand.setLookup("ksession1");
InsertObjectCommand insertObjectCommand = new
InsertObjectCommand(server1);
FireAllRulesCommand fireAllRulesCommand = new
FireAllRulesCommand();
batchExecutionCommand.getCommands().add(insertObjectCommand);
batchExecutionCommand.getCommands().add(fireAllRulesCommand);
```

4. Once the commands are created, you have to obtain an XStream marshaller instance to convert them to XML:

```
XStream xStreamMarshaller = BatchExecutionHelper
.newXStreamMarshaller();
```

5. Then you have to convert the command object into XML using the XStream instance:

```
String xml = xStreamMarshaller.toXML(batchExecutionCommand);
```

6. Once you have converted the command to XML, it's ready to be sent to the REST or SOAP service endpoint.

How it works...

Drools supports three different XML command formats: JAXB, XStream, and JSON. The XML format depends on your needs and on how the Drools Server endpoints were configured, which by default come configured to use XStream XML format.

The following commands are currently supported and available in the **drools-core** module:

- ▶ BatchExecutionCommand
- ▶ InsertObjectCommand
- ▶ RetractCommand
- ▶ ModifyCommand
- ▶ GetObjectCommand
- ▶ InsertElementsCommand
- ▶ FireAllRulesCommand
- ▶ StartProcessCommand

- ▸ SignalEventCommand

- ▸ CompleteWorkItemCommand

- ▸ AbortWorkItemCommand

- ▸ QueryCommand

- ▸ SetGlobalCommand

- ▸ GetGlobalCommand

- ▸ GetObjectsCommand

All of these commands have to be wrapped in the main command, `BatchExecutionCommand`. This command contains a list of the commands that are going to be executed remotely and also has a **lookup** property to identify the remote knowledge sessions where the commands should be executed. The grid node will use this lookup property to obtain the knowledge session instance, unmarshall the XML commands, and execute them.

```
List<Command> commands = new ArrayList<Command>();
BatchExecutionCommand batchExecutionCommand = CommandFactory
.newBatchExecution(commands, "ksession1");
```

This empty command will not be useful with an empty commands list. In the previous section we added an `InsertObjectCommand` object, which will insert the `server1` object into the knowledge session:

```
Command insertObjectCommand = CommandFactory
.newInsert(server1);
```

The `newInsert()` method of the `CommandFactory` also allows us to create the `InsertObjectCommand` with other properties, which are as follows:

- ▸ `outIdentifier`: If you want to return the execution results in response, then this parameter has to be assigned with a value. The execution's result to be returned will contain the `FactHandle` generated by the object insertion.

- ▸ `returnObject`: This parameter will return the object inserted in the execution results, but only if an `outIdentifier` is specified.

- ▸ `entryPoint`: This parameter establishes the entry-point where the object has to be inserted.

Then, if we want to execute the generated activations, we have to add a `FireAllRulesCommand` object into the commands list:

```
Command fireAllRulesCommand = CommandFactory
.newFireAllRules();
```

This command also has a few properties to enable extra behavior in the rules execution:

- ▶ `max`: Establishes the maximum number of activations to be executed
- ▶ `outIdentifier`: Returns the number of activations executed into the execution results

Once all the needed commands are created, they have to be added into the wrapper `BatchExecutionCommand` object that was created together with a commands list.

```
commands.add(insertObjectCommand);
commands.add(fireAllRulesCommand);
```

At this point, you are ready to create the XML command using one of the marshallers. In this case, the XStream marshaller is chosen, so the remaining step is to obtain an XStream marshaller reference using a Drools helper class.

```
XStream xStreamMarshaller = BatchExecutionHelper
.newXStreamMarshaller();
```

After this you can convert the commands into XML using the following line of code:

```
String xml = xStreamMarshaller.toXML(batchExecutionCommand);
```

These are all of the steps needed to start the interaction with the Drools Server and send XML messages using the XStream format.

See also

For further information about all the XML commands, you can take a look at the official integration documentation available at: `http://www.jboss.org/drools/documentation`.

Using the REST interface to execute commands

In this recipe, you will see how to execute commands in the Drools Server using the **RESTful interface**. The interaction will be made using the **Apache HTTP Client**, but for more details you can continue reading through the recipe.

Getting ready

Before we interact with the Drools Server, it should be deployed into a servlet container, and of course it should be started.

How to do it...

Carry out the following steps in order to learn how to interact programmatically with the Drools Server using Java:

1. As was said before, don't forget to add the XStream 1.4.1 library dependency into your project. If you are using Apache Maven you can add the following lines in your `pom.xml` dependencies configuration. Otherwise, you can download the binaries from `http://xstream.codehaus.org/`.

   ```
   <dependency>
     <groupId>com.thoughtworks.xstream</groupId>
       <artifactId>xstream</artifactId>
     <version>1.4.1</version>
   </dependency>
   ```

2. We are going to use the **Apache HTTPClient** library to interact with the RESTful service and we need to add another dependency into the project configuration. Add the following code snippet in your `pom.xml` file or download the library from `http://www.apache.org/dist/httpcomponents/commons-httpclient/`:

   ```
   <dependency>
     <groupId>commons-httpclient</groupId>
       <artifactId>commons-httpclient</artifactId>
     <version>3.1</version>
   </dependency>
   ```

3. Add the following code where you need to interact with the Drools Server. In this step, we are going to create the commands for what we want to execute. As you can see, all the executable commands are contained in a `BatchExecutionCommand` instance:

   ```
   Server server1 = newServer("windows-nt", 1, 2048, 2048, 3);

   List<Command>commands = new ArrayList<Command>();
   BatchExecutionCommand batchExecutionCommand = CommandFactory
   .newBatchExecution(commands, "ksession1");

   Command insertObjectCommand = CommandFactory
   .newInsert(server1, "server-nt");
   Command fireAllRulesCommand = CommandFactory
   .newFireAllRules();
   commands.add(insertObjectCommand);
   commands.add(fireAllRulesCommand);
   ```

4. After creating the commands, we are going to convert them into XML using the XStream marshaller, using the following code:

```
XStream xStreamMarshaller = BatchExecutionHelper
.newXStreamMarshaller();
String xmlCommand = xStreamMarshaller
.toXML(batchExecutionCommand);
```

5. Once we have the XML command, we can start using the Apache HTTPClient instance to interact with the REST endpoints:

```
HttpClient httpClient = new HttpClient();
httpClient.getHostConfiguration().setHost("127.0.0.1", 8080);

String resourceURI = "/drools-server/kservice/rest/execute";
PostMethod postMethod = new PostMethod(resourceURI);

StringRequestEntity request = new
StringRequestEntity(xmlCommand, "text/plain", "UTF-8");
postMethod.setRequestEntity(request);
httpClient.executeMethod(postMethod);
```

6. The final step is to use JUnit for the validation of the command execution. To do this, we use the HTTP response code to validate the right execution and communication with the Drools Server, and also the returned response to validate the execution results:

```
Assert.assertEquals(200, postMethod.getStatusCode());

String response = postMethod.getResponseBodyAsString();

ExecutionResults executionResults = (ExecutionResults)
xStreamMarshaller.fromXML(response);
FactHandle factHandle = (FactHandle) executionResults.
getFactHandle("server-nt");
Assert.assertNotNull(factHandle);
```

How it works...

Drools Server, by default, comes configured with two interfaces, RESTful and SOAP, to interact with the knowledge sessions. Both interfaces are configured using the Apache CXF stack and the integration with Apache Camel, but in this recipe we are going to deal with the RESTful endpoint. Carry out the following steps in order to accomplish this:

1. Once the servlet container where the `drools-server.war` was deployed is started, you can view the available services by accessing the following URL in your web browser: `http://127.0.0.1:8080/drools-server/kservice/`. Remember to replace the server address and port number with those configured in your JBoss AS instance. This is shown in the following screenshot:

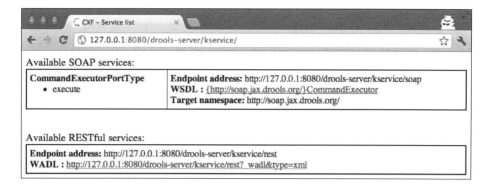

2. As you can see, the browser will display the SOAP and RESTful service details, and also their WSDL and WADL definitions. By clicking on the WADL link of the RESTful service, you will have access to the endpoint details that are displayed as follows:

```
<application>
<grammars/>
<resources base="http://127.0.0.1:8080/drools-server/kservice/
rest">
<resource path="/">
<resource path="execute">
<method name="POST">
  <request>
    <representation mediaType="text/plain"/>
  </request>
  <response>
    <representation mediaType="text/plain"/>
  </response>
</method>
</resource>
</resource>
</resources>
</application>
```

3. Reading this resources definition, we know that the resource available at the `http://127.0.0.1:8080/drools-server/kservice/rest` URL has an **execute** resource path, which consumes POST messages in *text/plain* format, pretty clear... right?

4. As we already know how to create a message, we can skip this step and start writing the code in order to interact with this RESTful service.

5. The only requirement in your project is the configuration of the **XStream** and Apache HTTPClient dependencies. If you are using Apache Maven, you can do it by adding the following dependencies in the `pom.xml` file:

```
<dependencies>
  <dependency>
    <groupId>com.thoughtworks.xstream</groupId>
    <artifactId>xstream</artifactId>
    <version>1.4.1</version>
  </dependency>
  <dependency>
    <groupId>commons-httpclient</groupId>
    <artifactId>commons-httpclient</artifactId>
    <version>3.1</version>
  </dependency>
</dependencies>
```

6. Once the dependencies are added into the project, we can finally start writing the code. Where to write it will always depend on your needs, and in this case, the code is the same that you will find in the example sources, so you will find some JUnit asserts to validate the execution response.

7. So, the next step is creating the Drools commands. In this example, we are going to insert a Server fact and fire all the generated activations by using an `InsertObjectCommand` and a `FireAllRulesCommands` object respectively. The `InsertObjectCommand` object instance is also configured to be returned into the execution results, setting the out identifier field to `"server-nt"` value:

```
Server server1 = new Server("windows-nt", 1, 2048, 2048, 3);

List<Command> commands = new ArrayList<Command>();
BatchExecutionCommand batchExecutionCommand = CommandFactory
.newBatchExecution(commands, "ksession1");
Command insertObjectCommand = CommandFactory
.newInsert(server1, "server-nt");
Command fireAllRulesCommand = CommandFactory
.newFireAllRules();
commands.add(insertObjectCommand);
commands.add(fireAllRulesCommand);
```

8. Now, it is time to convert the `BatchExecutionCommand` into XML using the next piece of code:

```
XStream xStreamMarshaller = BatchExecutionHelper
.newXStreamMarshaller();
String xmlCommand = xStreamMarshaller
.toXML(batchExecutionCommand);
```

9. Maybe you will notice that there isn't anything new until here, so this is the part where we start using the Apache HTTPClient library. All the interaction is done through an `org.apache.commons.httpclient.HttpClient` object with the IP address and the port being configured using the `getHostConfiguration().setHost` method. The IP address is obligatory but the port is optional, and only has to be configured if the port isn't the HTTP default port (80):

```
HttpClient httpClient = new HttpClient();
httpClient.getHostConfiguration().setHost("127.0.0.1", 8080);
```

10. The unique available resource consumes POST messages, so you have to create an `org.apache.commons.httpclient.methods.PostMethod` object with the resource URI as the constructor parameter:

```
String resourceURI = "/drools-server/kservice/rest/execute";
PostMethod postMethod = new PostMethod(resourceURI);
```

11. As the message type is plain text, an `org.apache.commons.httpclient. methods.StringRequestEntity` object is used to send the XML command, which also needs the content type (text/plain) and charset configuration (UTF-8). Once the `StringRequestEntity` object is created, it has to be assigned into the `postMethod` object that was previously created:

```
StringRequestEntity request = new
StringRequestEntity(xmlCommand, "text/plain", "UTF-8");
postMethod.setRequestEntity(request);
```

12. After all this code, the only remaining step is the execution of the `postMethod` using the following line of code:

```
httpClient.executeMethod(postMethod);
```

At this point the RESTful client that we are writing will connect with the Drools Server and send the message. The Drools Server will unmarshall the XML message into command objects and will execute them in the knowledge session using the `BatchExecutionCommand` lookup field. While the commands are executed, their results are added into an `ExecutionResponse` object that will be marshalled into XML once all the commands are executed and will be sent as the response body.

However, before we begin reading the response body we have to be sure that the command was properly consumed by the RESTful endpoint, using the response status code. The response status code will have associated the **HTTP Status Code** of the last response, which will have a 200 integer value (HTTP Status Code OK) if the response was successful, else it will have another value if there was something wrong. If you don't obtain a 200 HTTP status code value then there are other problems with your environment, for example, the servlet container is offline, a `war` file deployment has errors, a resource URI is malformed, and so on.

The HTTP status code of the response can be consulted using the following code:

```
if (postMethod.getStatusCode() != 200) {
    // there is something wrong in the connection/execution
}
```

If the execution was successful, then you can obtain the execution result by obtaining the response body:

```
String response = postMethod.getResponseBodyAsString();
```

The response is also in XML but it can be unmarshalled using the same XStream marshaller used to create the command to obtain an `ExecutionResults` object:

```
ExecutionResults executionResults = (ExecutionResults)
xStreamMarshaller.fromXML(response);
```

Using the `ExecutionResults` object, you can obtain the `FactHandle` generated as a result of the fact insertion. In the example, we inserted an object with a `server-nt` out identifier, and using this you can obtain the `FactHandle` that can be used later to modify or retract the fact:

```
FactHandle factHandle = (FactHandle) executionResults
.getFactHandle("server-nt");
```

Obviously, you can examine more execution results using the other available methods in the `ExecutionResults` object.

And, here is where you reach the end of the recipe. Hopefully now you will understand how to interact with the RESTful interface programmatically. As always, you can have access to all the source code that is provided in the example source code of this book.

Testing the SOAP interface with soapUI

Another alternative to test the SOAP interface is using a web services tool. In this recipe, you will see how to use the open source tool **soapUI** to do it.

Getting ready

Download a soapUI distribution compatible with your platform from `http://www.soapui.org/` or directly from `http://sourceforge.net/projects/soapui/files/soapui/`. At this moment 3.6.1 is the last stable version released.

How to do it...

Carry out the following steps to test the SOAP interface using soapUI:

1. First the `soap.wsdl` file included in the `drools-camel-server-5.2.0.Final.war` file has to be modified to bind the service to a specific address and port. Once the modification is done, you can start the servlet container where the Drools server was deployed:

```
<wsdl:service name="CommandExecutor">
  <wsdl:port binding="tns:CommandExecutorSoapBinding"
name="CommandExecutorPort">
    <soap:address location="http://127.0.0.1:8080/drools-server/
kservice/soap"/>
  </wsdl:port>
</wsdl:service>
```

2. Execute the soapUI tool using the `soapui.sh` (GNU/Linux/OSX) or `soapui.bat` (Windows) script. Once done, the following screen will appear:

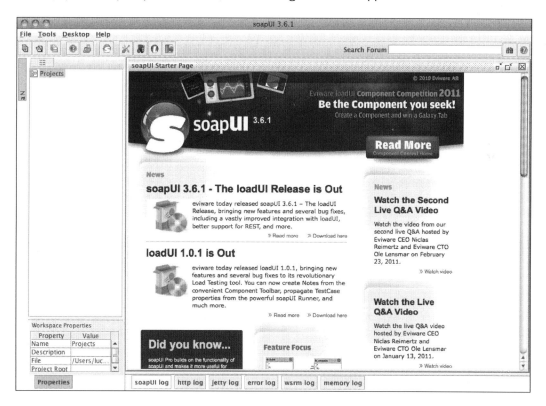

3. Select the **New soapUI Project** option from the **File** menu. Enter a **Project Name** and the WSDL URL (for example, `http://127.0.0.1:8080/drools-server/kservice/soap?wsdl`), as shown in the following screenshot:

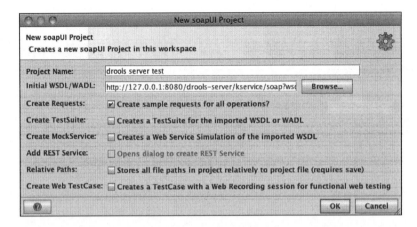

The created project will be present in the left area and will display the binding and the available operation, as shown in the following screenshot. The tool will also automatically create a SOAP request that is going to be used to send the SOAP messages, as shown in the following screenshot:

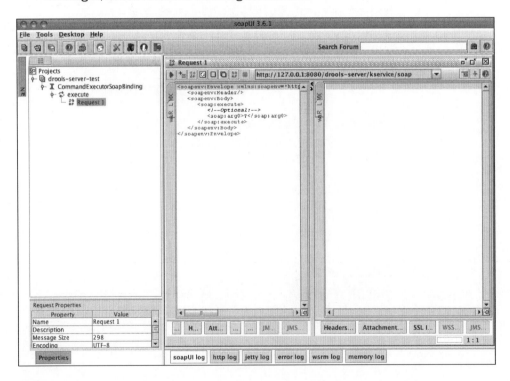

4. Now, with the soapUI project created, you have to create an XML command using the Drools marshallers. You can also do this manually if you know the XML syntax. In this example, we are using the same XML command used in the previous recipes:

```
<batch-execution lookup="ksession1">
<insert out-identifier="server-nt">
   <drools.cookbook.chapter06.Server>
      <name>windows-nt</name>
      <processors>1</processors>
      <memory>2048</memory>
      <diskSpace>2048</diskSpace>
      <virtualizations/>
      <cpuUsage>3</cpuUsage>
      <online>false</online>
   </drools.cookbook.chapter06.Server>
</insert>
<fire-all-rules/>
</batch-execution>
```

5. Paste the XML command between the `<soap:execute/>` tags of the SOAP Envelope. The XML command should be enclosed with a CDATA section so the SOAP parsers can ignore it, as shown in the following screenshot:

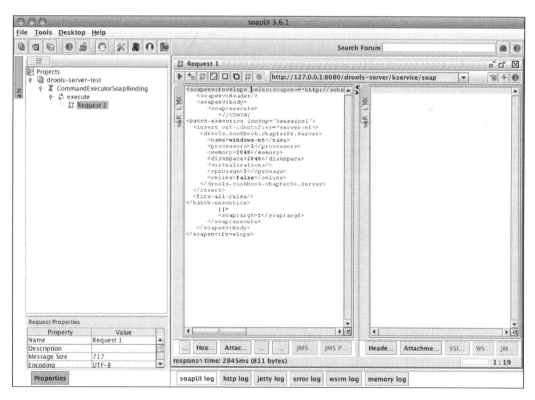

6. The last step is the submission of the request to the endpoint, which is done by clicking on the button with a green arrow. After pressing it, the SOAP response will be displayed in the right area of the request window, as shown in the following screenshot:

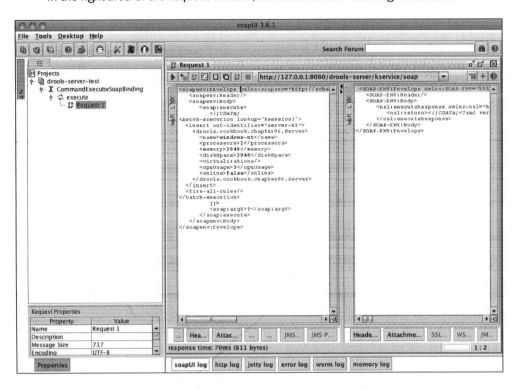

7. As you can see, the response of the Drools remote execution will also be returned inside a CDATA section and in an unindented format:

```
<SOAP-ENV:Envelope xmlns:SOAP-ENV="http://schemas.xmlsoap.org/
soap/envelope/">
<SOAP-ENV:Header/>
<SOAP-ENV:Body>
  <ns1:executeResponse xmlns:ns1="http://soap.jax.drools.org/">
      <ns1:return><![CDATA[<?xml version='1.0' encoding='UTF-
8'?><execution-results><result identifier="server-nt"><drools.
cookbook.chapter06.Server><name>windows-nt</name><processors>1</
processors><memory>2048</memory><diskSpace>2048</diskSpac
e><virtualizations/><cpuUsage>3</cpuUsage><online>false</
online></drools.cookbook.chapter06.Server></result><fact-
handle identifier="server-nt" external-form="0:-
1:117782170:117782170:2:null"/></execution-results>]]></
ns1:return>
  </ns1:executeResponse>
</SOAP-ENV:Body>
</SOAP-ENV:Envelope>
```

How it works...

soapUI is one of the most popular tools for Web Services testing, because its written in Java, and hence available for multiple platforms, and also because it can be integrated with the most popular IDE using plugins.

The first step needed before you use soapUI is the modification of the default WSDL included in the `drools-camel-server-5.2.0.Final.war` file. At the end of the file, you will find the service declaration with the port binding, where inside the `<wsdl:port />` tag you have to add the following tag without forgetting to replace the location property with your custom service location:

```
<soap:address location="http://127.0.0.1:8080/drools-server/kservice/
soap"/>
```

The following is an example of the complete configuration of the `CommandExecutor` service:

```
<wsdl:service name="CommandExecutor">
  <wsdl:port binding="tns:CommandExecutorSoapBinding"
name="CommandExecutorPort">
    <soap:address location="http://127.0.0.1:8080/drools-server/
kservice/soap"/>
  </wsdl:port>
</wsdl:service>
```

Once the `soap.wsdl` file is modified, it's safe to start the servlet container where the `drools-camel-server-5.2.0.Final.war` file is deployed.

After this, you can start using the soapUI tool to test the available service. Remember to select the **Create Requests** checkbox to automatically create the SOAP request, otherwise you will have to create it using the options. The **New soapUI Project** option from the **File** menu will display the following dialog where you have to configure the project name and the initial WSDL URI resource:

With this wizard you can also create a **TestSuite** to add multiple tests and create a really robust testing environment.

Once the project is created, you can open the generated **SOAP Request** named Request 1 and add the XML command inside the **SOAP Envelope** as you can see in the following screenshot:

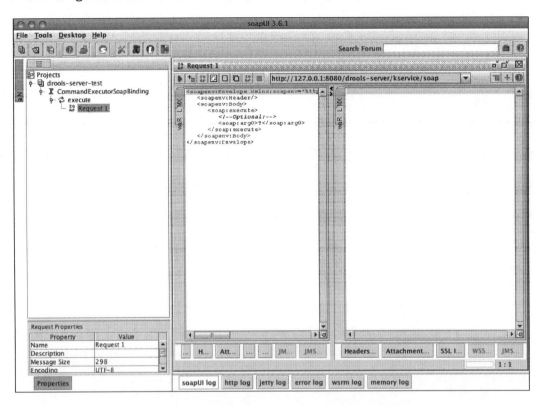

The XML command should be added inside the `<soap:execute/>` element and inside a CDATA tag to avoid issues with the SOAP parser. Otherwise the parser will try to understand the XML command and it will return an error.

 A CDATA section starts with `<![CDATA[` and ends with `]]>`

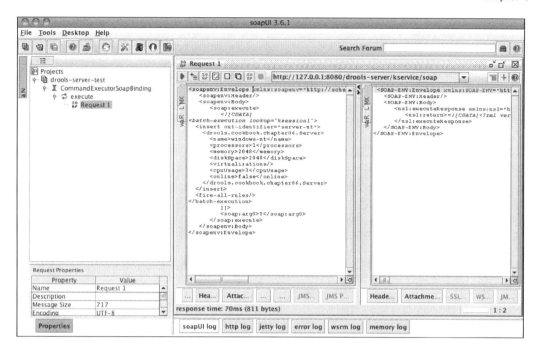

After you press the button with the green arrow to submit the SOAP request, the SOAP response will be displayed with the execution response inside the `<ns1:return/>` element and inside a CDATA section. The SOAP response will have the same format as the one displayed here:

```
<SOAP-ENV:Envelope xmlns:SOAP-ENV="http://schemas.xmlsoap.org/soap/
envelope/">
<SOAP-ENV:Header/>
<SOAP-ENV:Body>
  <ns1:executeResponse xmlns:ns1="http://soap.jax.drools.org/">
    <ns1:return><![CDATA[<?xml version='1.0' encoding='UTF-
8'?><execution-results><result identifier="server-nt"><drools.
cookbook.chapter06.Server><name>windows-nt</name><processors>1</
processors><memory>2048</memory><diskSpace>2048</diskSpace><virtu
alizations/><cpuUsage>3</cpuUsage><online>false</online></drools.
cookbook.chapter06.Server></result><fact-handle identifier="server-
nt" external-form="0:-1:117782170:117782170:2:null"/></execution-
results>]]></ns1:return>
  </ns1:executeResponse>
</SOAP-ENV:Body>
</SOAP-ENV:Envelope>
```

Maybe you figured out that the XML execution response is the same as the one returned by the RESTful interface. This is because both the interfaces share the same execution mechanism and eventually will return the response with the same format.

7

Integration: How to Connect Drools

In this chapter, we will cover:

- ▶ Setting up Drools using Spring Framework
- ▶ Configuring JPA to persist our knowledge with Spring Framework
- ▶ Integrating Apache Camel in your project
- ▶ Configuring Apache Camel with Spring Framework
- ▶ Executing Drools commands from a JMS queue

Introduction

Integration with other systems is always one of the most critical steps in development and it should be on our mind during the planning phase. *Chapter 6, Executing Drools Remotely*, covered the Drools Server, which uses a part of these integration capabilities using the Spring Framework and Apache Camel. However, in this chapter the Drools integration modules, Spring Framework and Apache Camel, will be covered explaining how they can be used independently of the Drools Server but, of course, integrated with Drools.

Setting up Drools using Spring Framework

In this recipe, you will see how to configure the Drools business rules engine using the Spring framework, using the integration module specially created to configure the Drools beans with XML.

How to do it...

Carry out the following steps in order to configure a Drools project using the Spring Framework integration:

1. Add the following dependency in your Maven project by adding this XML code snippet in the `pom.xml` file:

```
<dependency>
    <groupId>org.drools</groupId>
    <artifactId>drools-spring</artifactId>
    <version>5.2.0.Final</version>
</dependency>
```

2. Once the `drools-spring` module and the Spring Framework dependencies are added into your project, it's time to write the rules that are going to be included in the knowledge base. This recipe uses the same rule that was used in *Chapter 1*, shown as follows:

```
package drools.cookbook.chapter07

import drools.cookbook.chapter07.model.Server
import drools.cookbook.chapter07.model.Virtualization

rule "check minimum server configuration"
dialect "mvel"
when
    $server : Server(processors < 2 || memory<=1024 ||
        diskSpace<=250)
then
    System.out.println("Server \"" + $server.name +
    "\" was rejected by don't apply the minimum configuration.");
    retract($server);
end

rule "check available server for a new virtualization"
dialect "mvel"
when
    $virtualization : Virtualization($virtMemory : memory,
        $virtDiskSpace : diskSpace)
    $server : Server($memory : memory,
        $diskSpace : diskSpace, virtualizations !=null)
    Number((intValue + $virtMemory) < $memory)
        from accumulate (Virtualization($vmemory : memory)
        from $server.virtualizations, sum($vmemory))
    Number((intValue + $virtDiskSpace) < $diskSpace)
```

```
        from accumulate(Virtualization($vdiskSpace : diskSpace)
        from $server.virtualizations, sum($vdiskSpace))
then
    $server.addVirtualization($virtualization);
    retract($virtualization);
end
```

3. Then a Spring Application Context XML file has to be created to configure the Drools beans with the following code:

```xml
<?xml version="1.0" encoding="UTF-8"?>
<beans xmlns="http://www.springframework.org/schema/beans"
xmlns:xsi="http://www.w3.org/2001/XMLSchema-instance"
  xmlns:drools="http://drools.org/schema/drools-spring"
xsi:schemaLocation="
http://www.springframework.org/schema/beans
http://www.springframework.org/schema/beans/spring-beans-2.0.xsd
http://drools.org/schema/drools-spring
org/drools/container/spring/drools-spring-1.2.0.xsd
    http://camel.apache.org/schema/spring
http://camel.apache.org/schema/spring/camel-spring.xsd">

<drools:grid-node id="node1" />

<drools:resource id="resource1" type="DRL"
source="classpath:drools/cookbook/chapter07/rules.drl" />

<drools:kbase id="kbase1" node="node1">
  <drools:resources>
    <drools:resource ref="resource1" />
  </drools:resources>
</drools:kbase>

<drools:ksession id="ksession1" type="stateful"
kbase="kbase1" node="node1" />

<drools:ksession id="ksession2" type="stateless"
kbase="kbase1" node="node1" />

</beans>
```

4. After all these three steps, you are ready to load the XML file using the Spring Framework API and obtain the instantiated beans to interact with the knowledge sessions:

```
ClassPathXmlApplicationContext applicationContext = new
ClassPathXmlApplicationContext("applicationContext.xml");

applicationContext.start();

StatefulKnowledgeSession ksession1=
(StatefulKnowledgeSession)applicationContext
.getBean("ksession1");

Server debianServer = new Server("debian-1", 4, 2048,
                                 250, 0);
ksession1.insert(debianServer);
ksession1.fireAllRules();

applicationContext.stop();
```

How it works...

In order to use the Spring Framework integration in your project, first you have to add the `drools-spring` module to it. In a Maven project, you can do it by adding the following code snippet in your `pom.xml` file:

```
<dependency>
    <artifactId>org.drools</artifactId>
    <groupId>drools-spring</groupId>
    <version>5.2.0.Final</version>
</dependency>
```

This dependency will transitively include the required Spring Framework libraries in the Maven dependencies. Currently, the integration is done using the 2.5.6 version, but it should work with the newest version as well.

Now, we are going to skip the rule authoring step because it's a very common task and you really should know how to do it at this point, and we are going to move forward to the beans configuration.

As you know, the Spring Framework configuration is done through an XML file where the beans are defined and injected between them, and to make Drools declaration easy the integration module provides a schema and custom parsers. Before starting the bean configuration, the schema must be added into the XML namespace declaration, otherwise the Spring XML Bean Definition Reader is not going to recognize the Drools tags and some exceptions will be thrown. In the following code lines, you can see the namespace declarations that are needed before you start writing the bean definitions:

```
<?xml version="1.0" encoding="UTF-8"?>
<beans xmlns="http://www.springframework.org/schema/beans"
xmlns:xsi="http://www.w3.org/2001/XMLSchema-instance"
xmlns:drools="http://drools.org/schema/drools-spring"
xsi:schemaLocation="
http://www.springframework.org/schema/beans
     http://www.springframework.org/schema/beans/spring-beans-2.0.xsd
http://drools.org/schema/drools-spring
org/drools/container/spring/drools-spring-1.2.0.xsd
http://camel.apache.org/schema/spring
http://camel.apache.org/schema/spring/camel-spring.xsd">

<!-- define your beans here -->

</beans>
```

> If you have read *Chapter 6*, *Executing Drools Remotely*, you should know that all the most important Drools bean tags have already been covered in the recipes of that chapter. So, for a quick introduction we are going to skip those concepts and provide a general overview of the configuration used in this recipe.

After this, the drools beans can be added inside the XML configuration file using the friendly `<drools: />` tags:

```
<?xml version="1.0" encoding="UTF-8"?>
<beans xmlns="http://www.springframework.org/schema/beans"
  xmlns:xsi="http://www.w3.org/2001/XMLSchema-instance"
  xmlns:drools="http://drools.org/schema/drools-spring"
xsi:schemaLocation="
    http://www.springframework.org/schema/beans
    http://www.springframework.org/schema/beans/spring-beans-2.0.xsd
    http://drools.org/schema/drools-spring
    org/drools/container/spring/drools-spring-1.2.0.xsd
    http://camel.apache.org/schema/spring
    http://camel.apache.org/schema/spring/camel-spring.xsd">
```

```
<drools:grid-node id="node1" />

<drools:resource id="resource1" type="DRL"
      source="classpath:drools/cookbook/chapter07/rules.drl" />

<drools:kbase id="kbase1" node="node1">
  <drools:resources>
    <drools:resource ref="resource1" />
  </drools:resources>
</drools:kbase>

<drools:ksession id="ksession1" type="stateful"
kbase="kbase1" node="node1" />

</beans>
```

As you can see, there is only one stateful knowledge session bean configured by using the `<drools:ksession />` tag with a `ksession1` ID. This `ksession1` bean was injected with a knowledge base and a grid node so that the Drools Spring beans factories, which are provided by the integration module, can instantiate it.

Once the drools beans are configured, it's time to instantiate them using the Spring Framework API, as you usually do:

```
public static void main(String[] args) {

    ClassPathXmlApplicationContext applicationContext = new ClassPathX
mlApplicationContext("applicationContext.xml");
applicationContext.start();

    StatefulKnowledgeSession ksession1 = (StatefulKnowledgeSession)
applicationContext.getBean("ksession1");

Server debianServer = new Server("debian-1", 4, 2048, 250, 0);
ksession1.insert(debianServer);
ksession1.fireAllRules();

applicationContext.stop();
}
```

In the Java `main` method, a `ClassPathXmlApplicationContext` object instance is used to load the bean definitions, and once they are successfully instantiated they are available to be obtained using the `getBean(beanId)` method. At this point, the Drools beans are instantiated and you can start interacting with them as usual by just obtaining their references.

As you saw in this recipe, the Spring framework integration provided by Drools is pretty straightforward and allows the creation of a complete integration, thanks to its custom tags and simple configuration.

See also

For more information about the Drools bean definitions, you can read the *Knowledge services and multiple endpoints configuration* recipe included in *Chapter 6* where these definitions are explained in detail. Also, don't forget to read the *Spring Integration* chapter in the official documentation available at `http://www.jboss.org/drools/documentation`.

Configuring JPA to persist our knowledge with Spring Framework

In the *Chapter 1, Expert: The Rule Engine*, we saw how knowledge can be persisted using different approaches, and among them one method was using JPA persistence. The JPA persistence module can also be configured using the Spring module integration, which you will see in this recipe.

How to do it...

Carry out the following steps in order to configure the Drools JPA persistence using the Spring module integration:

1. In your Maven project, add the following dependencies in the `pom.xml` file to use JPA persistence using the Spring Framework:

```
<dependency>
  <groupId>org.drools</groupId>
  <artifactId>drools-spring</artifactId>
  <version>5.2.0.Final</version>
</dependency>
<dependency>
  <groupId>org.drools</groupId>
  <artifactId>drools-persistence-jpa</artifactId>
  <version>5.2.0.Final</version>
</dependency>
<dependency>
  <groupId>org.springframework</groupId>
```

```
  <artifactId>spring-orm</artifactId>
  <version>2.5.6</version>
</dependency>
<dependency>
  <groupId>org.springframework</groupId>
<artifactId>spring-jdbc</artifactId>
  <version>2.5.6</version>
</dependency>
<dependency>
  <groupId>org.jbpm</groupId>
  <artifactId>jbpm-persistence-jpa</artifactId>
  <version>5.1.0.Final</version>
</dependency>
```

2. Implement the `java.io.Serializable` interface to the objects of your domain model that will be persisted.

3. Create a `persistence.xml` file inside the `resources/META-INF` folder to configure the persistence unit. In this recipe, we will use an embedded H2 database for testing purposes, but you can configure it for any relational database engine:

```
<?xml version="1.0" encoding="UTF-8"?>
<persistence version="1.0" xmlns="http://java.sun.com/xml/ns/
persistence"
xmlns:orm="http://java.sun.com/xml/ns/persistence/
orm"xmlns:xsi="http://www.w3.org/2001/XMLSchema-instance"

xsi:schemaLocation="http://java.sun.com/xml/ns/persistence http://
java.sun.com/xml/ns/persistence/persistence_1_0.xsd
http://java.sun.com/xml/ns/persistence/orm http://java.sun.com/
xml/ns/persistence/orm_1_0.xsd">

<persistence-unit name="drools.cookbook.spring.jpa" transaction-
type="RESOURCE_LOCAL">
  <provider>org.hibernate.ejb.HibernatePersistence</provider>
  <class>org.drools.persistence.info.SessionInfo</class>

  <properties>
    <property name="hibernate.dialect"
value="org.hibernate.dialect.H2Dialect" />
    <property name="hibernate.max_fetch_depth" value="3" />
    <property name="hibernate.hbm2ddl.auto" value="create" />
    <property name="hibernate.show_sql" value="false" />
  </properties>
</persistence-unit>
</persistence>
```

4. Now, we have to create an XML file named `applicationContext.xml` in the `resources` folder, in which we are going to define the beans needed to configure the JPA persistence and the Drools beans:

```xml
<?xml version="1.0" encoding="UTF-8"?>
<beans xmlns="http://www.springframework.org/schema/
beans" xmlns:xsi="http://www.w3.org/2001/XMLSchema-
instance"xmlns:drools="http://drools.org/schema/drools-spring"

xsi:schemaLocation="http://www.springframework.org/schema/
beans http://www.springframework.org/schema/beans/spring-
beans-2.0.xsdhttp://drools.org/schema/drools-spring org/drools/
container/spring/drools-spring-1.2.0.xsd
http://camel.apache.org/schema/spring http://camel.apache.org/
schema/spring/camel-spring.xsd">

<bean id="dataSource" class="org.springframework.jdbc.datasource.
DriverManagerDataSource">
    <property name="driverClassName" value="org.h2.Driver" />
    <property name="url" value="jdbc:h2:tcp://localhost/Drools" />
    <property name="username" value="sa" />
    <property name="password" value="" />
</bean>

<bean id="entityManagerFactory" class="org.springframework.orm.
jpa.LocalContainerEntityManagerFactoryBean">
    <property name="dataSource" ref="dataSource" />
    <property name="persistenceUnitName" value="drools.cookbook.
spring.jpa" />
</bean>

<bean id="txManager" class="org.springframework.orm.jpa.
JpaTransactionManager">
    <property name="entityManagerFactory"
ref="entityManagerFactory" />
</bean>

<drools:grid-node id="node1" />

<drools:kstore id="kstore1" />

<drools:resource id="resource1" type="DRL"
source="classpath:drools/cookbook/chapter07/rules.drl" />
```

```xml
<drools:kbase id="kbase1" node="node1">
  <drools:resources>
    <drools:resource ref="resource1" />
  </drools:resources>
</drools:kbase>

<drools:ksession id="ksession1" type="stateful"
kbase="kbase1" node="node1">
  <drools:configuration>
    <drools:jpa-persistence>
      <drools:transaction-manager ref="txManager" />
      <drools:entity-manager-factory
ref="entityManagerFactory" />
    </drools:jpa-persistence>
  </drools:configuration>
</drools:ksession>

</beans>
```

5. Finally, we have to write the following code in a new Java class file, or in an existing one, in order to interact with the `Stateful` knowledge session and persist this state into the H2 database without further actions:

```java
public void startApplicationContext()
{
  ClassPathXmlApplicationContext applicationContext
    =newClassPathXmlApplicationContext("/applicationContext.xml");

  applicationContext.start();

  StatefulKnowledgeSession ksession1 = (StatefulKnowledgeSession)
    applicationContext.getBean("ksession1");
  int sessionId = ksession1.getId();

  Server debianServer = new Server("debianServer",
    4, 2048, 1222, 0);

  ksession1.insert(debianServer);
  ksession1.fireAllRules();

  ksession1.dispose();

  Environment env = KnowledgeBaseFactory.newEnvironment();

  env.set(EnvironmentName.ENTITY_MANAGER_FACTORY,
```

```
applicationContext.getBean("entityManagerFactory"));

    env.set(EnvironmentName.TRANSACTION_MANAGER,
    applicationContext.getBean("txManager"));

    Virtualization virtualization = new Virtualization(
    "dev","debian", 512, 30);

    KnowledgeStoreService kstore =    (KnowledgeStoreService)
      applicationContext.getBean("kstore1");
    KnowledgeBase kbase1 =    (KnowledgeBase)applicationContext.
      getBean("kbase1");

    ksession1 = kstore
      .loadStatefulKnowledgeSession(sessionId, kbase1, null, env);

    ksession1.insert(virtualization);
    ksession1.fireAllRules();

    applicationContext.stop();
}
```

How it works...

Before we start declaring the beans that are needed to persist the knowledge using JPA, we have to add some dependencies into our project configuration, especially the ones used by the Spring Framework. These dependencies were already described in the first step of the previous section, so we can safely continue with the remaining steps.

Once the dependencies are added into the project, we have to implement the `java.io.Serializable` interface in the classes of our domain model that will be persisted.

After this, we have to create a persistence unit configuration by using the default `persistence.xml` file located in the `resources/META-INF` directory of our project. This persistence unit is named `drools.cookbook.spring.jpa` and uses the Hibernate JPA implementation. Also, it is configured to use an H2 Java database, but in your real environment, you should supply the appropriate configuration. Next, you will see the persistence unit example, with the annotated `SessionInfo` entity that will be used to store the session data, which is ready to be used with Drools:

```
<?xml version="1.0" encoding="UTF-8"?>
<persistence version="1.0" xmlns="http://java.sun.com/xml/ns/
persistence"
xmlns:orm="http://java.sun.com/xml/ns/persistence/orm"
xmlns:xsi="http://www.w3.org/2001/XMLSchema-instance"
```

```
xsi:schemaLocation="http://java.sun.com/xml/ns/persistence http://
java.sun.com/xml/ns/persistence/persistence_1_0.xsd
http://java.sun.com/xml/ns/persistence/orm http://java.sun.com/xml/ns/
persistence/orm_1_0.xsd">

<persistence-unit name="drools.cookbook.spring.jpa" transaction-
type="RESOURCE_LOCAL">
<provider>org.hibernate.ejb.HibernatePersistence</provider>
<class>org.drools.persistence.info.SessionInfo</class>

   <properties>
     <property name="hibernate.dialect"
                 value="org.hibernate.dialect.H2Dialect" />
     <property name="hibernate.max_fetch_depth"
                 value="3" />
     <property name="hibernate.hbm2ddl.auto"
                 value="create" />
     <property name="hibernate.show_sql" value="false" />
   </properties>
</persistence-unit>
</persistence>
```

Now, we are ready to declare the beans that are needed to enable the JPA persistence with an XML file, where the most important section is the declaration of the Spring `DriverManagerDataSource` and `LocalContainerEntityManagerFactoryBean` beans, which are very descriptive and can be configured with the parameters of your database engine. Also, one of the most important declarations is the `KnowledgeStoreService` bean, using the `<drools:kstore />` tag, that will be primarily used to load the persisted knowledge session:

```
<?xml version="1.0" encoding="UTF-8"?>
<beans xmlns="http://www.springframework.org/schema/
beans" xmlns:xsi="http://www.w3.org/2001/XMLSchema-instance"
xmlns:drools="http://drools.org/schema/drools-spring"

xsi:schemaLocation="http://www.springframework.org/schema/beans
http://www.springframework.org/schema/beans/spring-beans-2.0.xsd
http://drools.org/schema/drools-spring org/drools/container/spring/
drools-spring-1.2.0.xsd
http://camel.apache.org/schema/spring http://camel.apache.org/schema/
spring/camel-spring.xsd">

<bean id="dataSource" class="org.springframework.jdbc.datasource.
DriverManagerDataSource">
```

```xml
    <property name="driverClassName"value="org.h2.Driver" />
      <property name="url"value="jdbc:h2:tcp://localhost/Drools" />
      <property name="username" value="sa" />
      <property name="password" value="" />
    </bean>
    <bean id="entityManagerFactory" class="org.springframework.orm.jpa.
    LocalContainerEntityManagerFactoryBean">
      <property name="dataSource" ref="dataSource" />
      <property name="persistenceUnitName"
    value="drools.cookbook.spring.jpa" />
    </bean>
    <bean id="txManager" class="org.springframework.orm.jpa.
    JpaTransactionManager">
      <property name="entityManagerFactory" ref="entityManagerFactory" />
    </bean>

    <drools:grid-node id="node1" />
    <drools:kstore id="kstore1" />
    <drools:resource id="resource1" type="DRL" source="classpath:drools/
    cookbook/chapter07/rules.drl" />
    <drools:kbase id="kbase1" node="node1">
      <drools:resources>
        <drools:resource ref="resource1" />
      </drools:resources>
    </drools:kbase>
    <drools:ksession id="ksession1" type="stateful"
    kbase="kbase1" node="node1">
      <drools:configuration>
        <drools:jpa-persistence>
          <drools:transaction-manager ref="txManager" />
          <drools:entity-manager-factory
    ref="entityManagerFactory" />
        </drools:jpa-persistence>
      </drools:configuration>
    </drools:ksession>

    </beans>
```

After the bean definitions, we can start writing the Java code needed to initialize the Spring Framework application context and interact with the defined beans. After loading the application context by using a `ClassPathXmlApplicationContext` object, we have to obtain the stateful knowledge session to insert the facts into the working memory, and also obtain the ID of the knowledge session to recover it later:

```
ClassPathXmlApplicationContext applicationContext = new
ClassPathXmlApplicationContext("/applicationContext.xml");
applicationContext.start();

StatefulKnowledgeSession ksession1 = (StatefulKnowledgeSession)
applicationContext.getBean("ksession1");

int sessionId = ksession1.getId();
Server debianServer = new Server("debianServer", 4, 2048,
                                 1222, 0);
ksession1.insert(debianServer);
ksession1.fireAllRules();

ksession1.dispose();
```

Once we are done interacting with the knowledge session and inserting facts, firing the rules, and so on, these can be disposed. They can be restored later using the `KnowledgeStoreService` bean, but we have to create a new `org.drools.runtime.Environment` object to set the `EntityManager` and `TransactionManager` used in the persistence process before trying to load the persisted knowledge session. The `org.drools.runtime.Environment` object can be created as follows:

```
Environment env = KnowledgeBaseFactory.newEnvironment();
env.set(EnvironmentName.ENTITY_MANAGER_FACTORY,
applicationContext.getBean("entityManagerFactory"));
env.set(EnvironmentName.TRANSACTION_MANAGER,
applicationContext.getBean("txManager"));

Virtualization virtualization = new Virtualization("dev",
    "debian", 512, 30);
```

Finally, with the `Environment` object created, we can obtain the `KnowledgeStoreService` bean together with the `KnowledgeSession` bean and the `StatefulKnowledgeSession` ID to load the stored state and start to interact with it as we do usually:

```
KnowledgeStoreService kstore = (KnowledgeStoreService)
applicationContext.getBean("kstore1");
KnowledgeBase kbase1 = (KnowledgeBase) applicationContext.
getBean("kbase1");
```

```
ksession1 = kstore.loadStatefulKnowledgeSession(sessionId, kbase1,
null, env);

ksession1.insert(virtualization);
ksession1.fireAllRules();

applicationContext.stop();
```

As you saw in this recipe, the knowledge session persistence is totally transparent to the user and automatic without any extra steps to save the state. By following these steps
or any other vendor's JPA
knowledge session using the

n your project

Drools with the **Apache Camel**
e and execute Drools commands. The
possible the implementation of more
ady know from the previous recipes,
g command objects or their XML
ils you can read this recipe.

Camel Framework can be integrated

u have to add the `drools-camel`
d using Apache Maven, as is
ependencies by adding the following

```
>
```

les and create the knowledge
rules created in the first recipe
we can continue moving forward.

3. After this, you are ready to start implementing the integration, firstly, by creating a Stateful knowledge session with the previously defined rules. Create a `CamelIntegration` class and get ready to write the code, as follows:

```
private StatefulKnowledgeSession createKnowledgeSession() {

    KnowledgeBuilder kbuilder = KnowledgeBuilderFactory
    .newKnowledgeBuilder();
    kbuilder.add(new ClassPathResource("rules.drl",
    getClass()), ResourceType.DRL);

    if (kbuilder.hasErrors()) {
        if (kbuilder.getErrors().size() > 0) {
            for (KnowledgeBuilderError kerror : kbuilder.getErrors()) {
                System.err.println(kerror);
            }
        }
    }
    KnowledgeBase kbase = kbuilder.newKnowledgeBase();
        return kbase.newStatefulKnowledgeSession();
}
```

4. In this step, you have to create an `org.drools.grid.GridNode` object and assign it to a JNDI context, which will be used in the next step to create a `Camelcontext` object:

```
private Context createContext(StatefulKnowledgeSession ksession) {
        GridImpl grid = new GridImpl();
        grid.addService(WhitePages.class, new WhitePagesImpl());
        GridNode node = grid.createGridNode("node");
        Context context = new JndiContext();
        context.bind("node", node);
        node.set("ksession1", ksession);
        return context;
}
```

5. At this point, you are ready to create an `org.apache.camel.CamelContext` object and define the route that will be used to consume the Drools commands:

```
private CamelContextCamelContext createCamelContext(Context
context) {
CamelContext camelContext = new DefaultCamelContext(context);
        RouteBuilder rb = new RouteBuilder() {
            public void configure() throws Exception {
```

```
ksession1 = kstore.loadStatefulKnowledgeSession(sessionId, kbase1,
null, env);

ksession1.insert(virtualization);
ksession1.fireAllRules();

applicationContext.stop();
```

As you saw in this recipe, the knowledge session persistence is totally transparent to the user and automatic without any extra steps to save the state. By following these steps you can easily integrate JPA persistence using Hibernate, or any other vendor's JPA implementation, in order to save the current state of the knowledge session using the Spring Framework Integration.

Integrating Apache Camel in your project

This recipe will explain how to programmatically integrate Drools with the **Apache Camel framework** to define execution routes, which will consume and execute Drools commands. The advantage of this integration is that Apache Camel makes possible the implementation of more advanced enterprise integration patterns. As you may already know from the previous recipes, the interaction with knowledge sessions is done by sending command objects or their XML representation to defined routes. However, for further details you can read this recipe.

How to do it...

In the following steps, you will see how easily the Apache Camel Framework can be integrated with JBoss Drools:

1. In order to use the Apache Camel integration, you have to add the `drools-camel` module to your project. If your project is managed using Apache Maven, as is recommended, then you can add the required dependencies by adding the following snippet code in the `pom.xml` file:

```
<dependency>
  <groupId>org.drools</groupId>
  <artifactId>drools-camel</artifactId>
  <version>5.2.0.Final</version>
</dependency>
```

2. As usual, you need to create a DRL file to add rules and create the knowledge session. However, we are going to use the same rules created in the first recipe (*Setting up Drools using Spring Framework*), and we can continue moving forward.

3. After this, you are ready to start implementing the integration, firstly, by creating a Stateful knowledge session with the previously defined rules. Create a `CamelIntegration` class and get ready to write the code, as follows:

```
private StatefulKnowledgeSession createKnowledgeSession() {

KnowledgeBuilder kbuilder = KnowledgeBuilderFactory
.newKnowledgeBuilder();
kbuilder.add(new ClassPathResource("rules.drl",
getClass()), ResourceType.DRL);

if (kbuilder.hasErrors()) {
    if (kbuilder.getErrors().size() > 0) {
        for (KnowledgeBuilderError kerror : kbuilder.getErrors()) {
            System.err.println(kerror);
        }
    }
}
KnowledgeBase kbase = kbuilder.newKnowledgeBase();
    return kbase.newStatefulKnowledgeSession();
}
```

4. In this step, you have to create an `org.drools.grid.GridNode` object and assign it to a JNDI context, which will be used in the next step to create a `Camelcontext` object:

```
private Context createContext(StatefulKnowledgeSession ksession) {
    GridImpl grid = new GridImpl();
    grid.addService(WhitePages.class, new WhitePagesImpl());
    GridNode node = grid.createGridNode("node");
    Context context = new JndiContext();
    context.bind("node", node);
    node.set("ksession1", ksession);
    return context;
}
```

5. At this point, you are ready to create an `org.apache.camel.CamelContext` object and define the route that will be used to consume the Drools commands:

```
private CamelContextCamelContext createCamelContext(Context
context) {
CamelContext camelContext = new DefaultCamelContext(context);
    RouteBuilder rb = new RouteBuilder() {
        public void configure() throws Exception {
```

```
                from("direct:test-with-session")
                .to("drools://node/ksession1");
            }
        };
        camelContext.addRoutes(rb);
    }
```

6. Finally, after the routes are created the `CamelContext` is ready to consume the Drools commands to interact with the routes defined:

```
Server debianServer = new Server("debian", 2, 2048,
 2048, 0);
Server winServer = new Server("win", 2, 1024, 250, 0);

Virtualization virtualization = new Virtualization("dev",
"debian", 512, 30);

InsertObjectCommand insertServerCommand = (InsertObjectCommand)
CommandFactory.newInsert(debianServer, "debian-server");

InsertObjectCommand insertBadServerCommand = (InsertObjectCommand)
CommandFactory.newInsert(winServer, "win-server");

InsertObjectCommand insertVirtualizationCommand =
(InsertObjectCommand) CommandFactory
.newInsert(virtualization, "dev-virtualization");

FireAllRulesCommand fireAllRulesCommand = (FireAllRulesCommand)
CommandFactory.newFireAllRules("executed-rules");

List<Command> commands = new ArrayList<Command>();
commands.add(insertServerCommand);
commands.add(insertBadServerCommand);
commands.add(insertVirtualizationCommand);
commands.add(fireAllRulesCommand);
BatchExecutionCommand batchExecutionCommand =
CommandFactory.newBatchExecution(commands, "ksession1");

StatefulKnowledgeSession ksession =
createKnowledgeSession();
Context context = createContext(ksession);
CamelContext camelContext = createCamelContext(context);
```

```
camelContext.start();

ProducerTemplate template = camelContext
.createProducerTemplate();
ExecutionResults response = (ExecutionResults) template.
requestBody("direct:test-with-session", batchExecutionCommand);

DefaultFactHandle handle = (DefaultFactHandle)
response.getFactHandle("debian-server"));

Long executedRules = response.getValue("executed-rules");
camelContext.stop();
```

How it works...

The Apache Camel integration allows us to interact with a Drools stateless or stateful knowledge session through a pipeline, transforming the XML commands into executable commands, and executing each of them. It is the evolution of the old `drools-pipeline` module that is not available anymore. The advantage of this integration is that now it is possible to implement most of the available **Enterprise Integration Patterns** to solve a specific design problem with an elegant solution.

 A list of the Enterprise Integration Patterns supported by Apache Camel is available at `http://camel.apache.org/ enterprise-integration-patterns.html`.

With this integration, you can also use any of the available **Apache Camel Components** in the endpoints declaration to create declarative services. You can find these Camel Components at `http://camel.apache.org/component.html`. For example, you can consume messages from a JMS Queue/Topic, send them to the Drools Component to execute them, and then send the execution results to another system using **Apache MINA**. As you can see, this brings a more powerful interoperability mechanism to integrate Drools with other systems. After this introduction, we can go forward through the recipe steps.

First, you have to add the `drools-camel` library to your project. In this book we recommend the use of Apache Maven to manage the projects. If you are following this advice then you can modify the `pom.xml` file and add the following dependency in the dependencies declaration section:

```
<dependency>
  <groupId>org.drools</groupId>
  <artifactId>drools-camel</artifactId>
  <version>5.2.0.Final</version>
</dependency>
```

This dependency will include the 2.4.0 version of Apache Camel, among other dependencies, which was optimized by the Apache Camel developers to provide a complete integration.

At this point, we can skip the rules authoring and the knowledge session creation steps, and move on to the most important ones.

The integration is coupled with another Drools module called **drools-grid** that allows an interaction with Drools knowledge sessions, independent of the JVM location. In this case, it is primarily used to execute the commands locally. This module is a transitive dependency of the `drools-camel` module, so you don't have to worry about this dependency.

At this point, you have to create an `org.drools.grid.impl.GridImpl` object instance and add to it a `WhitePages` service, which is a directory used to register all the available services. Using this `GridImpl` object, you have to create a `GridNode` that will have the responsibility to find the registered knowledge sessions and execute the commands on it with the previous registration of the knowledge session in the `GridNode`. The only step remaining is the creation of a `JndiContext` object that will be used later, and the binding of the `GridNode` on it:

```
GridImpl grid = new GridImpl();
grid.addService(WhitePages.class, new WhitePagesImpl());
GridNode node = grid.createGridNode("node");
Context context = new JndiContext();
context.bind("node", node);
node.set("ksession1", ksession);
```

Now, we can create a `CamelContext` object using the previously created `JndiContext`. As we are programmatically configuring Apache Camel, a `DefaultCamelContext` is going to be used, but if you wish to use Spring Framework or OSGi, then there are appropriate `CamelContext` implementations provided by Camel for these.

Now, this is the part where you can define the routes, which is one of the most powerful features of this integration because of its very large library of components provided by Apache Camel to build pipelines. The routes are created by using a `RouteBuilder` object and adding the route definition using the Camel Java DSL `from()` and `to()` definitions. Once the routes are defined they must be added in the `CamelContext` object instance and the `CamelContext` must be started, otherwise the routes aren't going to be available. The following code snippet shows how to declare a simple route using a `RouteBuilder` object and add it to the `CamelContext` before getting started:

```
CamelContext camelContext = new
DefaultCamelContext(context);
RouteBuilder rb = new RouteBuilder() {
    public void configure() throws Exception {
        from("direct:test-with-session")
        .to("drools://node/ksession1");
```

```
        }
    };
    camelContext.addRoutes(rb);
    camelContext.start();
```

In the previous route definition, we were consuming messages from a *direct endpoint* and sending them to a *Drools endpoint*, which has the following syntax:

```
drools://{1}/{2}
```

where the parameters are as follows:

- ▶ {1}: The Grid Node identifier that was registered in the `CamelContext`
- ▶ {2}: The identifier of the knowledge session registered in the Grid node with identifier {1}

> The knowledge session identifier is optional if it is supplied in the `BatchExecutionCommand` message. When this identifier is not configured the Grid node will obtain the knowledge session using its internal directory.

This route is very simple, but routes can be made more complex by adding **Enterprise Integration Patterns** (**EIP**), such as **Message Filter** or **Content Based Router**, which can be implemented using `filter()` and `choice()` predicates.

- ▶ Message Filter example:

```
RouteBuilder messageFilter = new RouteBuilder() {
    public void configure() throws Exception {
        from("direct:test-with-session")
            .filter(header("priority").isNotEqualsTo("high"))
            .to("drools://node/ksession1");
    }
};
```

- ▶ Content Based Router example:

```
RouteBuilder contentBasedRouter = new RouteBuilder() {
    public void configure() throws Exception {
        from("direct:test-with-session")
            .choice()
            When(or(header("priority").isEqualsTo("low"),
            header("priority").isEqualsTo("medium")))
            .to("drools://node/ksession1");
            when(header("priority").isEqualsTo("high"))
            .to("drools://node/ksession2");
            }
};
```

> Take a look at `http://camel.apache.org/routes.html` to learn how to create more complex routes. Also, to know more about the available predicates, you can find useful information at `http://camel.apache.org/predicate.html`.

Now, that the routes are started, you are ready to create the Drools commands and send them to `CamelContext` object:

```
List<Command> commands = new ArrayList<Command>();
commands.add(insertServerCommand);
commands.add(insertBadServerCommand);
commands.add(insertVirtualizationCommand);
commands.add(fireAllRulesCommand);
BatchExecutionCommand batchExecutionCommand = CommandFactory
.newBatchExecution(commands, "ksession1");
```

The interaction with `CamelContext` object is realized by obtaining a `ProducerTemplate` object instance from it and sending the `BatchExecutionCommand` to the input endpoint by using the `requestBody()` method, as shown in the following code:

```
ProducerTemplate template = camelContext
.createProducerTemplate();
ExecutionResults response = (ExecutionResults) template
.requestBody("direct:test-with-session", batchExecutionCommand);
```

> Headers objects can be sent together with the `BatchExecutionCommand` by using the `requestBodyAndHeader()` method.

The `BatchExecutionCommand` instance will be delivered from the direct endpoint to the Drools endpoint by Apache Camel, where the registered `GridNode` will unmarshall/marshall the message if necessary, execute it, and return the results in an `ExecutionResults` object. With this object, you can access the different types of returned results, which will depend on the commands sent. You can see this in the following code snippet:

```
DefaultFactHandle handle = (DefaultFactHandle)response
.getFactHandle("debian-server"));
Long executedRules = response.getValue("executed-rules");
```

In this recipe, you saw how to create a complete integration of Drools with Apache Camel with its most used features. In a later recipe, you will see how to integrate it with a JMS queue to develop a complex integration.

► Refer to the *Creating commands with XStream marshallers* recipe of *Chapter 6, Executing Drools Remotely*

Configuring Apache Camel with Spring Framework

The Apache Camel framework also provides a module to configure it using the Spring Framework. In this recipe, you will see how we can declare Apache Camel and Drools beans using the Spring integration.

How to do it...

Carry out the following steps in order to create a declarative integration between Apache Camel, JBoss Drools, and the Spring Framework. Don't forget to check the provided examples for further details.

1. In your Apache Maven project, add the following dependency in the pom.xml file. If you don't include the extra needed dependencies, such as drools-spring, camel-spring, and so on, they will be transitively included:

   ```
   <dependency>
     <groupId>org.drools</groupId>
     <artifactId>drools-camel</groupId>
     <version>5.2.0.Final</version>
   </dependency>
   ```

2. In this step, we should create the rules files, but in this recipe we are again going to use the same rules created in the first recipe of this chapter (*Setting up Drools using Spring Framework*).

3. Create an XML file with the following Spring Framework application context declaration, where the Drools beans and the Apache Camel beans are going to be defined:

   ```
   <beans xmlns="http://www.springframework.org/schema/beans"
   xmlns:xsi="http://www.w3.org/2001/XMLSchema-instance"
     xmlns:drools="http://drools.org/schema/drools-spring"
   xmlns:camel="http://camel.apache.org/schema/spring"
   xsi:schemaLocation="http://www.springframework.org/schema/
   beans http://www.springframework.org/schema/beans/spring-beans.
   xsdhttp://camel.apache.org/schema/spring http://camel.apache.org/
   schema/spring/camel-spring.xsdhttp://drools.org/schema/drools-
   spring org/drools/container/spring/drools-spring-1.2.0.xsd">

     <bean id="droolsPolicy"
   ```

```
class="org.drools.camel.component.DroolsPolicy" />

<drools:grid-node id="node1" />

<drools:resource id="resource1" type="DRL"
source="classpath:drools/cookbook/chapter07/rules.drl" />

<drools:kbase id="kbase1" node="node1">
  <drools:resources>
    <drools:resource ref="resource1" />
  </drools:resources>
</drools:kbase>

<drools:ksession id="ksession1" type="stateful"
kbase="kbase1" node="node1" />

<camel:camelContext id="camelContext">
  <camel:route>
    <camel:from uri="direct:test-with-session" />
    <camel:policy ref="droolsPolicy">
      <camel:unmarshal ref="xstream" />
      <camel:to uri="drools:node1/ksession1" />
      <camel:marshal ref="xstream" />
    </camel:policy>
  </camel:route>
</camel:camelContext>
</beans>
```

4. Finally, we are ready to create a `DroolsCamelSpringIntegration` class file, in order to write the Java code to start the application context, create the Drools commands, and send it to the `CamelContext`:

```
public class DroolsCamelSpringIntegration {

    private String fileName = "/applicationContext.xml";
    private ClassPathXmlApplicationContext applicationContext;

    public DroolsCamelSpringIntegration() {
        startApplicationContext();
    }

private void startApplicationContext() {
  ClassPathXmlApplicationContext applicationContext = new ClassPat
  hXmlApplicationContext(fileName);
  applicationContext.start();
```

```
    }

    private ProducerTemplate getProducerTemplate() {
    CamelContext camelContext = (CamelContext)
    applicationContext.getBean("camelContext");
        return camelContext.createProducerTemplate();
    }

    public static void main() {
Server debianServer = new Server("debian", 2, 2048,
 2048, 0);
Virtualization virtualization = new Virtualization(
"dev", "debian", 512, 30);

InsertObjectCommand insertServerCommand = (InsertObjectCommand)
CommandFactory
.newInsert(debianServer,"debian-server",
true, "DEFAULT");

InsertObjectCommand insertBadServerCommand = (InsertObjectCommand)
CommandFactory
.newInsert(winServer,"win-server",
true, "DEFAULT");

InsertObjectCommand insertVirtualizationCommand =
(InsertObjectCommand) CommandFactory
.newInsert(virtualization, "dev-virtualization", true, "DEFAULT");

FireAllRulesCommand fireAllRulesCommand = (FireAllRulesCommand)
CommandFactory
.newFireAllRules("executed-rules");

List<Command> commands = new ArrayList<Command>();
commands.add(insertServerCommand);
commands.add(insertBadServerCommand);
commands.add(insertVirtualizationCommand);
commands.add(fireAllRulesCommand);
BatchExecutionCommand batchExecutionCommand = CommandFactory.
newBatchExecution(commands, "ksession1");

String xmlCommand = BatchExecutionHelper
.newXStreamMarshaller()
.toXML(batchExecutionCommand);
```

```
        DroolsCamelSprinIntegration dcsi =
            new DroolsCamelSpringIntegration();
    ProducerTemplate producerTemplate = dcsi.getProducerTemplate();
    String outXml = new String((byte[]) producerTemplate.
    requestBody("direct:test-with-session", xmlCommand));

    ExecutionResults result = (ExecutionResults)
    BatchExecutionHelper.newXStreamMarshaller().fromXML(outXml);

        DefaultFactHandle factHandle =
    (DefaultFactHandle)result.getFactHandle("debian-server");

        dcsi.stop();
    }

    public void stop() {
    applicationContext.stop();
    }
}
```

How it works...

Apache Camel can also be integrated with the Spring Framework in an easy way. Taking advantage of this, we are going to define the integration between Drools and Apache Camel in a declarative way.

First you have to add the `drools-camel` dependency in your project:

```
<dependency>
  <groupId>org.drools</groupId>
  <artifactId>drools-camel</groupId>
  <version>5.2.0.Final</version>
</dependency>
```

After we add this dependency, more dependencies are going to be transitively added, where some of the most important ones are:

▶ **drools-spring**: Spring Framework integration for JBoss Drools

▶ **drools-grid**: Remote execution support for Drools

▶ **camel-spring**: Spring Framework integration for Apache Camel

Once the project has all the necessary dependencies, we can start to write the bean declarations in the XML file. This Spring Framework application context file needs to have the namespaces and schema declaration for both Drools and Camel modules, as we can see in the following code snippet:

```
<beans xmlns="http://www.springframework.org/schema/beans"
  xmlns:xsi="http://www.w3.org/2001/XMLSchema-instance"
  xmlns:drools="http://drools.org/schema/drools-spring"
  xmlns:camel="http://camel.apache.org/schema/spring"
xsi:schemaLocation="http://www.springframework.org/schema/beans
http://www.springframework.org/schema/beans/spring-beans.xsd http://
camel.apache.org/schema/spring http://camel.apache.org/schema/spring/
camel-spring.xsd http://drools.org/schema/drools-spring  org/drools/
container/spring/drools-spring-1.2.0.xsd">
<!--beans declaration -->
</beans>
```

In this recipe, we are going to send the Drools commands in XML format, so we need to define a Drools Camel policy object that will be used later in the Camel routes declaration:

```
<bean id="droolsPolicy"class="org.drools.camel.component.
DroolsPolicy" />
```

Then, we will have to declare the Drools beans definitions, as we saw in the previous recipes of this chapter. This is a very simple definition where a stateful knowledge session is created by using a knowledge base with only one DRL resource file:

```
<drools:grid-node id="node1" />
<drools:resource id="resource1" type="DRL"
  source="classpath:drools/cookbook/chapter07/rules.drl" />
<drools:kbase id="kbase1" node="node1">
  <drools:resources>
    <drools:resource ref="resource1" />
  </drools:resources>
</drools:kbase>
<drools:ksession id="ksession1" type="stateful" kbase="kbase1"
node="node1" />
```

Once the Drools beans are defined, we are ready to define the Apache Camel context and the routes using XML instead of the Java DSL used in the previous recipe. In the from() declaration we are still using a direct endpoint to directly send the messages to the next endpoint without any message processing. However, in the Drools endpoint declaration, we are wrapping the <camel:to /> declaration with a Drools Camel Policy to add XStream unmarshall/marshall commands processing:

```
<camel:camelContext id="camelContext">
<camel:route>
```

```
<camel:from uri="direct:test-with-session" />
    <camel:policy ref="droolsPolicy">
      <camel:unmarshal ref="xstream" />
      <camel:to uri="drools:node1/ksession1" />
      <camel:marshal ref="xstream" />
    </camel:policy>
  </camel:route>
</camel:camelContext>
```

 The Drools policy object is used to augment the node declarations in order to modify the defined routes by adding the marshalling and unmarshalling of the commands and the execution results object.

If you want to use other marshallers such as **JAXB** or **JSON**, you can easily change the `<camel:marshall />` and `<camel:unmarshall>` tag value to JAXB or JSON, without forgetting to marshall the commands by using a **JAXB Context** or **JSON marshaller**.

Once all the beans are defined, we can start writing Java code to load the Spring Framework application context and create the commands.

The first step is the creation and initialization of the `ApplicationContext` as you can see in the following code snippet:

```
ClassPathXmlApplicationContext  applicationContext = new
ClassPathXmlApplicationContext("/applicationContext.xml");
applicationContext.start();
```

Once the Application context starts, we can start interacting with the Apache Camel routes, but first we have to create the Drools commands that are going to be executed later. In this case, we are creating two commands, an `InsertObjectCommand` and a `FireAllRulesCommand` command, to insert an object and then execute the generated activations:

```
Server debianServer = new Server("debian", 2, 2048, 2048, 0);
Virtualization virtualization = new Virtualization("dev", "debian",
512, 30);

InsertObjectCommand insertServerCommand = (InsertObjectCommand)
CommandFactory
.newInsert(debianServer,"debian-server", true, "DEFAULT");

InsertObjectCommand insertBadServerCommand = (InsertObjectCommand)
CommandFactory
.newInsert(winServer,"win-server",true, "DEFAULT");
```

```
InsertObjectCommand insertVirtualizationCommand =
(InsertObjectCommand) CommandFactory
.newInsert(virtualization, "dev-virtualization", true, "DEFAULT");

FireAllRulesCommand fireAllRulesCommand = (FireAllRulesCommand)
CommandFactory.newFireAllRules("executed-rules");

List<Command> commands = new ArrayList<Command>();
commands.add(insertServerCommand);
commands.add(insertBadServerCommand);
commands.add(insertVirtualizationCommand);
commands.add(fireAllRulesCommand);
BatchExecutionCommand batchExecutionCommand = CommandFactory
.newBatchExecution(commands, "ksession1");
```

With the Drools commands created, we can obtain an `XStream` marshaller using the `BatchExecutionHelper` object to convert them to XML:

```
String xmlCommand = BatchExecutionHelper.newXStreamMarshaller()
.toXML(batchExecutionCommand);
```

Then we have to obtain the `camelContext` declared bean to be able to create a `ProducerTemplate` object, which will be used to send the XML command:

```
CamelContext camelContext = (CamelContext) applicationContext
.getBean("camelContext");
ProducerTemplate producerTemplate = camelContext
.createProducerTemplate();
```

Next, we have to obtain the `camelContext` bean to be able to create a `ProducerTemplate` object, which will be used to send the XML command. The `requestBody()` method of `ProducerTemplate` is invoked with two parameters to define the endpoint URI destination and the message to be sent, and this method will return the XML response in a `byte[]` that must be converted to a String:

```
String outXml = new String((byte[]) producerTemplate
.requestBody("direct:test-with-session", xmlCommand));
```

Again, using an `XStream` marshaller, we can convert the XML response in an object representation for an easy interpretation of the execution, from where we can obtain the `FactHandle` of the inserted objects and other execution results:

```
ExecutionResults result = (ExecutionResults)BatchExecutionHelper
.newXStreamMarshaller().fromXML(outXml);
DefaultFactHandle factHandle = (DefaultFactHandle)result
.getFactHandle("debian-server");
```

Once we are ready with the execution, we can finally stop the application context in order to stop the routes and release the resources, using the following line of code:

```
applicationContext.stop();
```

In this recipe, we took advantage of the Spring Framework integration on both frameworks, JBoss Drools, and Apache Camel, to create a complete declarative **frameworks integration system**. For more general details about the integration with another framework you can take a look at the following recipe.

See also

▶   Refer to the *Integrating Apache Camel in your project* recipe in this chapter.

Executing Drools commands from a JMS queue

ActiveMQ is one of the most popular open source message brokers used in the enterprise layer. In this integration with Drools it will be used as a system to store and consume commands from a JMS queue to create an asynchronous execution system.

Getting ready

Download an ActiveMQ distribution compatible with your OS from `http://activemq.apache.org` and then unzip it. In this recipe, we will be using the 5.4.3 version, which is the latest stable release with JVM 1.5 support, but you can use a newer version also.

How to do it...

After downloading the ActiveMQ distribution, you are ready to carry out the following steps in order to create this advanced integration that you can use as a starting point to create advanced enterprise integration patterns:

1.   Start the ActiveMQ message broker using the `activemq` executable file located in the `bin` directory of the distribution or executing java -jar `run.jar` start from the command line.. After this, you can test the correct initialization of the message broker by pointing your web browser to `http://localhost:8161/admin`.

>   For further information about the installation and initial configuration I would encourage you to read the official ActiveMQ documentation at `http://activemq.apache.org/version-5-getting-started.html`.

2. Once the message broker is correctly initialized, it's time to add the required dependencies in the `pom.xml` file of your Apache Maven project:

```xml
<dependency>
   <groupId>org.drools</groupId>
   <artifactId>drools-camel</artifactId>
   <version>5.2.0.Final</version>
</dependency>
<dependency>
   <groupId>org.apache.camel</groupId>
   <artifactId>camel-jms</artifactId>
   <version>2.4.0</version>
</dependency>
<dependency>
   <groupId>org.apache.xbean</groupId>
   <artifactId>xbean-spring</artifactId>
   <version>3.7</version>
</dependency>
<dependency>
   <groupId>org.apache.activemq</groupId>
   <artifactId>activemq-core</artifactId>
   <version>5.4.3</version>
</dependency>
<dependency>
   <groupId>org.apache.activemq</groupId>
   <artifactId>activemq-camel</artifactId>
   <version>5.4.3</version>
</dependency>
```

3. After adding the dependencies, the first thing that you can do in your Java project is to configure the Spring application context where the ActiveMQ, Jboss Drools, and Apache Camel beans are going to be defined:

```xml
<beans xmlns="http://www.springframework.org/schema/beans"
xmlns:xsi="http://www.w3.org/2001/XMLSchema-instance"
xmlns:amq="http://activemq.apache.org/schema/core"
xmlns:jms="http://www.springframework.org/schema/jms"
xmlns:drools="http://drools.org/schema/drools-spring"
   xsi:schemaLocation="http://www.springframework.org/schema/
beans http://www.springframework.org/schema/beans/spring-
beans.xsdhttp://www.springframework.org/schema/jms http://www.
springframework.org/schema/jms/spring-jms-2.5.xsd
                        http://activemq.apache.org/schema/core
http://activemq.apache.org/schema/core/activemq-core.xsd
http://camel.apache.org/schema/spring
http://camel.apache.org/schema/spring/camel-spring.xsd
```

```
http://drools.org/schema/drools-spring
org/drools/container/spring/drools-spring-1.2.0.xsd">

<amq:connectionFactory id="amqConnectionFactory"
brokerURL="tcp://localhost:61616" />

<bean class="org.springframework.jms.connection.CachingConnectionF
actory"id="connectionFactory">
  <constructor-arg ref="amqConnectionFactory" />
  <property name="sessionCacheSize" value="100" />
</bean>

<bean class="org.springframework.jms.core.JmsTemplate"
id="jmsTemplate">
  <constructor-arg ref="connectionFactory" />
</bean>

<bean
class="drools.cookbook.chapter07.jms.JMSQueueProducer"
id="queueProducer">
  <property name="jmsTemplate" ref="jmsTemplate" />
  <property name="queueName" value="commandsQueue" />
</bean>

<bean id="droolsPolicy"
class="org.drools.camel.component.DroolsPolicy" />

<drools:grid-node id="node1" />

<drools:resource id="resource1" type="DRL"
source="classpath:drools/cookbook/chapter07/rules.drl" />

<drools:kbase id="kbase1" node="node1">
  <drools:resources>
    <drools:resource ref="resource1" />
  </drools:resources>
</drools:kbase>

<drools:ksession id="ksession1" type="stateful"
kbase="kbase1" node="node1" />

<camelContext id="camelContext"
xmlns="http://camel.apache.org/schema/spring">
  <route>
```

```
<from uri="activemq:queue:commandsQueue" />
  <policy ref="droolsPolicy">
    <unmarshal ref="xstream" />
    <to uri="drools:node1/ksession1" />
    <marshal ref="xstream" />
  </policy>
</route>
</camelContext>

</beans>
```

4. At this point, you need to create the rules that are added into the knowledge base using the Drools Spring integration beans. Again, to simplify this recipe, we are going to use the same rules that we created in the first recipe (*Setting up Drools using Spring Framework*).

5. Finally, we are going to initialize the ApplicationContext and create the Drools commands that will be converted to XML. This XML command representation will be sent to the ActiveMQ instance through a JMSQueueProducer service that was previously configured in the Spring Framework configuration file. Once the XML command is sent, it will be consumed by the ActiveMQ Camel endpoint and redirected to the Drools endpoint, which will execute it, finalizing the execution cycle:

```
ClassPathXmlApplicationContext applicationContext = new
ClassPathXmlApplicationContext("/camel-amq.xml");
applicationContext.start();

Server debianServer = new Server("debian", 2, 1024, 250, 0);

InsertObjectCommand insertServerCommand = (InsertObjectCommand)
CommandFactory
.newInsert(debianServer,"debian-server", true, "DEFAULT");

InsertObjectCommand insertBadServerCommand = (InsertObjectCommand)
CommandFactory
.newInsert(winServer,"win-server", true, "DEFAULT");

InsertObjectCommand insertVirtualizationCommand =
(InsertObjectCommand) CommandFactory
.newInsert(virtualization, "dev-virtualization",true, "DEFAULT");

FireAllRulesCommand fireAllRulesCommand = (FireAllRulesCommand)
CommandFactory.newFireAllRules("executed-rules");

List<Command> commands = new ArrayList<Command>();
commands.add(insertServerCommand);
commands.add(insertBadServerCommand);
commands.add(insertVirtualizationCommand);
commands.add(fireAllRulesCommand);
```

```
BatchExecutionCommand batchExecutionCommand = CommandFactory.
newBatchExecution(commands, "ksession1");

String xmlCommand = BatchExecutionHelper
.newXStreamMarshaller().toXML(batchExecutionCommand);

JMSQueueProducer queueProducer = (JMSQueueProducer)
applicationContext.getBean("queueProducer");
queueProducer.send(xmlCommand);

Thread.sleep(2000);

applicationContext.stop();
```

How it works...

In this recipe, we used ActiveMQ as the message broker just because Apache Camel gives us a full integration with it. The first step was about downloading a distribution compatible with your OS and starting it from a terminal by executing the `activemq` executable file (which can be found inside the `bin` directory or executing java -jar `run.jar` start from the command line).

After the command execution, you can verify the correct initialization with your web browser by pointing it to `http://localhost:8161/admin` shown in the following screenshot to provide access to a web application that is used to view the ActiveMQ resources status and administer them:

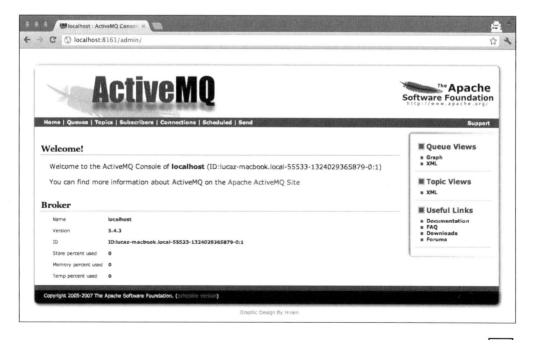

Once the ActiveMQ instance is correctly initialized, you can add the required dependencies, which were already enumerated in the first step, in the `pom.xml` file of your Apache Maven project.

 Remember that is always a good practice to include other Drools core modules, such as `knowledge-api`, `drools-compiler`, and `drools-core` in your project configuration.

Before we start configuring the Spring Framework application context, we need to create a helper class that will be used to send the message to the ActiveMQ instance. As we are going to use the Spring JMS framework, which will simplify the use of the JMS API for us, this class will contain a `SpringJmsTemplate` object that will be used to send the messages. This class is really simple, as you can see from the following code:

```
package drools.cookbook.chapter07.jms;

import org.springframework.jms.core.JmsTemplate;

public class JMSQueueProducer {

    private String queueName;
    private JmsTemplate jmsTemplate;

    public void send(String message) {
        jmsTemplate.convertAndSend(queueName, message);
    }

    public void setJmsTemplate(JmsTemplate jmsTemplate) {
        this.jmsTemplate = jmsTemplate;
    }

    public JmsTemplate getJmsTemplate() {
        return jmsTemplate;
    }

    public void setQueueName(String queueName) {
        this.queueName = queueName;
    }

    public String getQueueName() {
        return queueName;
    }

}
```

After this, we are ready to configure the Spring Framework application context by writing a lot of XML declarations. We do this by creating an XML file with the following initial context and the required namespaces for this example:

```
<beans xmlns="http://www.springframework.org/schema/beans"
       xmlns:xsi="http://www.w3.org/2001/XMLSchema-instance"
       xmlns:amq="http://activemq.apache.org/schema/core"
       xmlns:jms="http://www.springframework.org/schema/jms"
       xmlns:drools="http://drools.org/schema/drools-spring"
       xsi:schemaLocation="http://www.springframework.org/schema/
beans http://www.springframework.org/schema/beans/spring-beans.xsd
http://www.springframework.org/schema/jms http://www.springframework.
org/schema/jms/spring-jms-2.5.xsd http://activemq.apache.org/schema/
core http://activemq.apache.org/schema/core/activemq-core.xsd http://
camel.apache.org/schema/spring http://camel.apache.org/schema/spring/
camel-spring.xsd http://drools.org/schema/drools-spring org/drools/
container/spring/drools-spring-1.2.0.xsd">
<!-- beans declarations -->
</beans>
```

Now, we are going to start the configuration of the connection with the ActiveMQ instance, keeping in mind that all the following bean declarations must be added inside the previously created XML file. To configure it we have to supply the message broker URL connection and also configure the connection factory cache as follows:

```
<amq:connectionFactory id="amqConnectionFactory"
brokerURL="tcp://localhost:61616" />

<bean class="org.springframework.jms.connection.CachingConnectionFacto
ry"id="connectionFactory">
  <constructor-arg ref="amqConnectionFactory" />
  <property name="sessionCacheSize" value="100" />
</bean>
```

The ActiveMQ default connection port is **61616** and it can be changed by editing the `<transportConnectors/>` configuration of the `<broker/>` bean declaration in the `conf/activemq.conf` file.

Then we have to declare the `JmsTemplate` bean by using the `connectionFactory` bean:

```
<bean class="org.springframework.jms.core.JmsTemplate"
id="jmsTemplate">
  <constructor-arg ref="connectionFactory" />
</bean>
```

After this declaration, we need to declare the helper bean that is used to send the messages. In the declaration of this bean, it is necessary to assign it the `queueName` property—the name of the JMS queue to be used to consume the messages:

```
<bean class="drools.cookbook.chapter07.jms.JMSQueueProducer"
id="queueProducer">
  <property name="jmsTemplate" ref="jmsTemplate" />
  <property name="queueName" value="commandsQueue" />
</bean>
```

Now, it is time to configure the Drools Spring beans, as you may already know after reading the previous recipe:

```
<bean id="droolsPolicy"
class="org.drools.camel.component.DroolsPolicy" />

<drools:grid-node id="node1" />

<drools:resource id="resource1" type="DRL"
source="classpath:drools/cookbook/chapter07/rules.drl" />

<drools:kbase id="kbase1" node="node1">
  <drools:resources>
    <drools:resource ref="resource1" />
  </drools:resources>
</drools:kbase>

<drools:ksession id="ksession1" type="stateful"
kbase="kbase1" node="node1" />
```

As only the last declaration is left, we are going to declare an Apache Camel Context with a route starting with an ActiveMQ endpoint and ending in a Drools endpoint, where the ActiveMQ endpoint is configured using the following endpoint URI nomenclature:

```
activemq:[queue:|topic:]destinationName.
```

The Drools endpoint is also wrapped with a Drools policy to add the `XStream` marshalling/ unmarshalling capabilities:

```
<camelContext id="camelContext"
              xmlns="http://camel.apache.org/schema/spring">
  <route>
    <from uri="activemq:queue:commandsQueue" />
    <policy ref="droolsPolicy">
      <unmarshal ref="xstream" />
      <to uri="drools:node1/ksession1" />
      <marshal ref="xstream" />
    </policy>
  </route>
</camelContext>
```

Finally, we are ready to write the code to interact with all this integration. This is pretty simple. Just load the Spring Framework application context XML file by using a `ClassPathXmlApplicationContext` object, create the Drools commands, and convert them into `XStream` XML by using `BatchExecutionHelper`. Probably, you already know how to do it after reading the recipes in this chapter, so we are going to skip the explanation.

After the Drools commands are marshalled, we are ready to obtain an object reference of the `queueProducer` bean and send the XML command to the JMS Queue using the following code snippet:

```
JMSQueueProducer queueProducer = (JMSQueueProducer)
applicationContext.getBean("queueProducer");
queueProducer.send(xmlCommand);
```

Once the XML command message is sent, it will be stored in an ActiveMQ JMS queue named commandsQueue and it will be ready to be consumed. The ActiveMQ Camel endpoint defined in the Camel route is subscribed to this JMS Queue. It will then consume the message to redirect it to the Drools endpoint, which will unmarshall the message, execute it, and marshall the execution results to complete the execution cycle.

See also

▶ Refer to the _Integrating Apache Camel in your project application_ recipe
▶ Refer to the _Configuring Apache Camel with Spring Framework_ recipe

8
Planner: Optimizing Your Automated Planning

In this chapter, we will cover:

- ▶ Solving a resource assignment problem
- ▶ Using a Simulated Annealing acceptor
- ▶ Terminating the Solver
- ▶ Creating a basic benchmarker

Introduction

Drools Planner is a Drools module used to optimize automated planning problems combining search algorithms with the core of the rule engine. It can be used to solve a lot of different use cases such as scheduling, routing, timetables and more. One of the characteristics is the calculation of the solution score using the rule engine; it means that you define your problem constraints implementing business rules and assigning a score to each one, making it easy to implement and scale.

Also, it supports several search algorithms that can be easily implemented just by adding new content into the configuration file, which will boost the search for the best solution among all the possible solutions.

In the following recipes, you will see how to implement a typical resource assignment problem with the necessary configuration and also how to configure a simulated annealing acceptor.

Solving a resource assignment problem

In this recipe, you will see how to solve a resource assignment problem using the commonly used **Tabu search acceptor**. Don't worry if you don't know what the Tabu search acceptor is and how to use it, because it will be explained in this recipe. The scenario of this recipe is really simple. Imagine you have a company that provides technicians with different skills to other companies based on the skills, location, and availability of the technicians, and you want to automatically choose the best technician for every request. With this image in your mind, you can read ahead to understand how to use Planner to solve this scenario.

How to do it...

Carry out the following steps in order to complete this recipe:

1. Create a new Java project using Apache Maven and add the following dependency in the pom.xml file:

```
<dependencies>
  <dependency>
    <groupId>org.drools.planner</groupId>
    <artifactId>drools-planner-core</artifactId>
    <version>5.3.0.Final</version>
  </dependency>
</dependencies>
```

2. In this recipe, we are going to simulate the resource assignment of technicians with different skills to a service request. So, first we need to create our domain model. In order to create it, we have to create a Java package named drools.cookbook.chapter08.domain and create a Skill enum type with the following content:

```
package drools.cookbook.chapter08.domain;

public enum Skill {

    JAVA, SCALA, REST, DROOLS, HADOOP;

}
```

3. Now, you need to create a Location enum type in the same package with the following definition:

```
package drools.cookbook.chapter08.domain;

public enum Location {

    SAN_DIEGO, MONTANA, NY, NORTH_CAROLINA, WASHINGTON_DC

}
```

4. Also, in the same package, create a `TrainingLevel` enum type with the following content:

```
package drools.cookbook.chapter08.domain;

public enum TrainingLevel {

    SENIOR("sr"), SEMISENIOR("ssr"),
    JUNIOR("jr"), TRAINEE("tr");

    private String abreviation;

    private TrainingLevel(String abreviation) {
        this.abreviation = abreviation;
    }

    public String getAbreviation() {
        return this.abreviation;
    }

}
```

5. Create a new `Technician` Java class with the following content. As you can see, this class has a constructor to clone it and also overrides the `hashCode()` and `equals()` methods. Drools Planner needs these methods to be overridden; however, we will discuss it later:

```
package drools.cookbook.chapter08.domain;

import java.util.Arrays;
import java.util.Collections;
import java.util.Set;

public class Technician {

    private Location location;
    private TrainingLevel trainingLevel;
    private boolean busy;
    private Set<Skill> skills;

    public Technician() {}

    public Technician(Location location,
                      TrainingLevel training,
                      boolean busy, Set<Skill> skills) {
        this.location = location;
```

```
                                    this.trainingLevel = training;
                                    this.busy = busy;
                                    this.skills = skills;
        }

        public Technician(Technician technician) {
            this(technician.location,
                technician.trainingLevel,
                technician.busy,
                (technician.skills.isEmpty()) ?
                Collections.<Skill> emptySet() :
                technician.skills);
        }

        public Location getLocation() {
            return location;
        }

        public TrainingLevel getTrainingLevel() {
            return trainingLevel;
        }

        public boolean isBusy() {
            return busy;
        }

        public Set<Skill> getSkills() {
            return skills;
        }

        @Override
        public String toString() {
        // don't forget to implement the toString method
        }

        @Override
        public int hashCode() {
        // don't forget to implement the hashCode method
        }

        @Override
        public boolean equals(Object obj) {
        // don't forget to implement the equals method
        }
    }
```

6. The last domain class is the `ServiceRequest` file, which will specify the required skills and the desired location of the requested technician. This class must be annotated with a `@PlanningEntity` annotation; however, we will discuss it later:

```java
package drools.cookbook.chapter08.domain;

import java.util.Arrays;
import java.util.EnumSet;
import java.util.Set;
import org.drools.planner.api.domain.entity.PlanningEntity;
import org.drools.planner.api.domain.variable.PlanningVariable;
import org.drools.planner.api.domain.variable.ValueRangeUndefined;

@PlanningEntity
public class ServiceRequest {

    private Location location;
    private Set<Skill> neededSkills;
    private Technician technician;

    public ServiceRequest() {}

    public ServiceRequest(Location location, Set<Skill>
neededSkills) {
        this.location = location;
        this.neededSkills = neededSkills;
    }

    public ServiceRequest(ServiceRequest serviceRequest) {
        this(serviceRequest.location, EnumSet.
copyOf(serviceRequest.neededSkills));
        if (serviceRequest.technician != null) {
            setTechnician(new Technician(serviceRequest.
technician));
        }
    }

    public Location getLocation() {
        return this.location;
    }

    @PlanningVariable
    @ValueRangeFromSolutionProperty(propertyName =
        "serviceRequests")
    public Technician getTechnician() {
```

```
        return technician;
    }

    public void setTechnician(Technician technician) {
        this.technician = technician;
    }

    public Set<Skill> getNeededSkills() {
        return neededSkills;
    }

    @Override
    public String toString() {
    // don't forget to implement the toString method
    }

    @Override
    public int hashCode() {
    // don't forget to implement the hashCode method
    }

    @Override
    public boolean equals(Object obj) {
    // don't forget to implement the equals method
    }
}
```

7. With the domain model defined, we can start creating the classes needed by Drools
    Planner. First, create a new Java package named `drools.cookbook.chapter08.`
    `planner` and create a new `TechnicianMove` class, which must implement the
    `org.drools.planner.core.move.Move` interface, and generate the changes
    between different solutions.

 All the related code and configuration is available and fully
explained in the *How it works...* section.

8. Next, we have to generate the moves in order to evolve the current solution using a
    `MoveFactory` object.

9. Create a new Java class named `SelectNextTechnician` and extend the `org.`
    `drools.planner.core.move.factory.CachedMoveFactory` abstract class
    provided by Drools Planner.

10. Write the `Solution` implementation using a `SimpleScore` configuration, in this case. We will explain the Score and discuss its implementation in the *How it works...* section.

11. At this point, we must create a few rules using constraints to calculate the score. In this recipe, four rules constraints were defined to calculate the solution score. Create a new `serviceRequestScoreRules.drl` file in the `main/resources` folder of the project and add the rules explained in the *How it works...* section.

12. Create a solver configuration file with the selector, acceptor, forager, score rules, and extra configurations. All these concepts will be explained later, but for now just create a new file named `ServiceRequestSolverConfig.xml` in the `main/resources` folder of the project with the content available in the *How it works...* section.

13. Finally, we are ready to write the code where all the previous steps are used to enable the Drool Planner to choose the best solution. Create a Java class named `BestAvailableTechnician` and add the following code to it. Once you write it, you are ready to execute it to obtain the solution:

```
package drools.cookbook.chapter08;

import java.util.ArrayList;
import java.util.Collections;
import java.util.EnumSet;
import java.util.List;

import org.drools.planner.config.XmlSolverConfigurer;
import org.drools.planner.core.Solver;

import drools.cookbook.chapter08.domain.Location;
import drools.cookbook.chapter08.domain.ServiceRequest;
import drools.cookbook.chapter08.domain.Skill;
import drools.cookbook.chapter08.domain.Technician;
import drools.cookbook.chapter08.domain.TrainingLevel;
import drools.cookbook.chapter08.planner.TechniciansSolution;

public class BestAvailableTechnician {

    public static void main(String[] args) {
        // technicians
        List<Technician> technicians = new
            ArrayList<Technician>();
        technicians.add(new Technician(
            Location.WASHINGTON_DC, TrainingLevel.JUNIOR,
            false, Collections.<Skill> emptySet()));
        technicians.add(new Technician(Location.MONTANA,
```

```java
            TrainingLevel.SEMISENIOR, false,
            EnumSet.of(Skill.HADOOP)));
        technicians.add(new Technician(Location.NY,
            TrainingLevel.SENIOR, true,
            EnumSet.of(Skill.JAVA, Skill.DROOLS)));
        technicians.add(new Technician(
            Location.NORTH_CAROLINA, TrainingLevel.SENIOR,
            true, EnumSet.of(Skill.JAVA)));
        technicians.add(new Technician(Location.NY,
            TrainingLevel.SEMISENIOR, false,
            EnumSet.of(Skill.JAVA, Skill.REST)));
        technicians.add(new Technician(Location.SAN_DIEGO,
            TrainingLevel.SENIOR, false,
            EnumSet.of(Skill.SCALA)));
        // requested service
        List<ServiceRequest> requests = new
            ArrayList<ServiceRequest>();
            requests.add(new ServiceRequest(
            Location.SAN_DIEGO,
            EnumSet.of(Skill.JAVA)));

        XmlSolverConfigurer configurer = new
            XmlSolverConfigurer();
        configurer.
            configure("/ServiceRequestSolverConfig.xml");
        Solver solver = configurer.buildSolver();

        for (ServiceRequest serviceRequest : requests) {
            serviceRequest
                .setTechnician(technicians.get(0));
        }
        TechniciansSolution initialSolution = new
            TechniciansSolution(technicians, requests);

        solver.setStartingSolution(initialSolution);
        solver.solve();
        TechniciansSolution finalSolution =
            (TechniciansSolution) solver.getBestSolution();

        Technician selectedTechnician = finalSolution
            .getServiceRequests().get(0).getTechnician();
        System.out.println("Selected technician: " +
            selectedTechnician);
    }

}
```

How it works...

If you followed the **steps in the** *How to do it...* **section**, you probably will know the Drools Planner requirements to solve automated planning problems. First, create a new Java project using Apache Maven and add the Drools Planner core dependency in the `pom.xml` file as shown in the following code. Remember that there's no need to include the Drools core dependencies because they will be automatically included as transitive dependencies:

```
<dependencies>
  <dependency>
    <groupId>org.drools.planner</groupId>
    <artifactId>drools-planner-core</artifactId>
    <version>5.3.0.Final</version>
  </dependency>
</dependencies>
```

Once the dependencies are added into the project, we can move on to the next step. In the *How to do it...* section, we created the domain model (shown in the following figure), beginning from the second step till the sixth step. However, we are going to skip these steps in order to avoid the repeatation of the code:

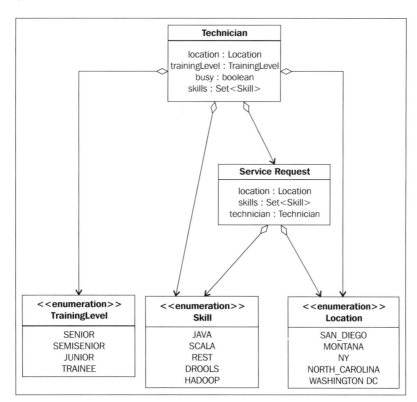

The only thing to keep in mind is the `ServiceRequest` entity class that was annotated with the `@PlanningEntity` annotation. What is a planning entity? It's a POJO that changes during the solving phase. In this example, only the `ServiceRequest` property's values will change during the execution of the planning steps, but some use cases can have multiple planning entities, raising the implementation complexity.

The properties of the planning entities that change during planning must be annotated with the `@PlanningVariable` annotation and also must specify that the values range using one of the following available annotations, which are pretty descriptive:

- `@ValueRangeFromSolutionProperty(propertyName = "propertyNameInSolution")`
- `@ValueRangeFromPlanningEntityProperty(propertyName = "propertyNameInEntity")`
- `@ValueRangeUndefinied`

This is when the Drools Planner concepts come to light. We need to create a class that implements the `org.drools.planner.core.move.Move` interface. Basically, it will represent a change from a solution A to a solution B, but to understand a little more you have to know that local search solves a problem by making a move on the current solution that changes it into a better solution, acting very much like a human:

```java
public class TechnicianMove implements Move {

    private ServiceRequest serviceRequest;
    private Technician technician;

    public TechnicianMove(ServiceRequest serviceRequest,
                          Technician technician) {
        this. serviceRequest = serviceRequest;
        this.technician = technician;
    }

    @Override
    public boolean isMoveDoable(WorkingMemory wm) {
        return ! serviceRequest.getTechnician()
            .equals(technician);
    }

    @Override
    public Move createUndoMove(WorkingMemory wm) {
        return new TechnicianMove(serviceRequest,
            serviceRequest.getTechnician());
    }
```

```
    @Override
    public void doMove(WorkingMemory wm) {
        FactHandle serviceRequestHandle = wm
            .getFactHandle(serviceRequest);
        serviceRequest.setTechnician(technician);
        wm.update(serviceRequestHandle, serviceRequest);
    }

    @Override
    public boolean equals(Object o) {
        if (this == o) {
            return true;
        } else if (o instanceof TechnicianMove) {
            TechnicianMove other = (TechnicianMove) o;
            return new EqualsBuilder()
                .append(serviceRequest, other.serviceRequest)
                .append(technician, other.technician)
                .isEquals();
        } else {
            return false;
        }
    }

    @Override
    public int hashCode() {
        return new HashCodeBuilder()
            .append(serviceRequest)
            .append(technician)
            .toHashCode();
    }

    @Override
    public String toString() {
        return serviceRequest.toString() + " to " +
            technician.toString();
    }
}
```

The Move implementation requires the implementation of three fundamental methods, which we will discuss further.

The `isMoveDoable(WorkingMemory)` method is automatically used by Drools Planner to filter the non-doable moves. A non-doable method is:

▶ A move that changes nothing on the current solution

▶ A move that is impossible to do on the current solution

In this recipe, a non-doable move is when the move wants to assign the same technician to a service request who is already assigned in the current solution. Next, you will see a implementation of the `isMoveDoable(WorkingMemory)` method:

```
@Override
public boolean isMoveDoable(WorkingMemory workingMemory) {
    return !serviceRequest.getTechnician().equals(technician);
}
```

Drools Planner also needs to know how to undo the last move, by simply implementing the `createUndoMove(WorkingMemory)` method, which is shown as follows:

```
@Override
public Move createUndoMove(WorkingMemory workingMemory) {
    return new TechnicianMove(serviceRequest,
                            serviceRequest.getTechnician());
}
```

As you may have already figured out, it should also know how to create a new move by calling the `doMove(WorkingMemory)` method. Inside this method, we assign the current technician to the service request and update the working memory:

```
@Override
public void doMove(WorkingMemory workingMemory) {
    FactHandle serviceRequestHandle = workingMemory
        .getFactHandle(serviceRequest);
    serviceRequest.setTechnician(technician);
    workingMemory.update(serviceRequestHandle, serviceRequest);
}
```

 In a move implementation, the `equals()` and `hashCode()` methods must be implemented. The same change in a solution made by two different moves should be equal, and it must not be broken. Also, you would like to implement the `toString()` method in order to read the logging output.

The next step is about the generation of moves. At this moment, we can only do a single move, but we need to generate a move set. It's up to you and your business case, but you will have to create a move set that can be sequentially combined to reach all the possible solutions.

> The creation of a move set to reach all the possible solutions directly isn't recommended.

The move set is generated with a `MoveFactory` implementation. In this recipe, we used a `CachedMovefactory` and implemented the `createCachedMoveList(Solution)` method to generate the move set. Inside this method, we generated a move for each of the requested services with all the available technicians, generating a full move set with all the possible combinations:

```
public class SelectNextTechnicians extends CachedMoveFactory {

    @Override
    public List<Move> createCachedMoveList(Solution solution) {
        TechniciansSolution techSolution =
            (TechniciansSolution) solution;
        List<Move> moves = new ArrayList<Move>();
        for (ServiceRequest sr : techSolution.getServiceRequests()) {
            for (Technician technician : techSolution.
    getTechnicians()) {
                moves.add(new TechnicianMove(sr, technician));
            }
        }
        return moves;
    }
}
```

Now that we have generated the move set, we have to implement the `Solution` interface using the `SimpleScore` object. The `SimpleScore` object will contain the score of the current solution, which is calculated/recalculated after each step execution, and the best solution founded after the execution will be the one with the highest score.

Next, you will see how the solution was implemented for this example using a `SimpleScore` score implementation:

```
public class TechniciansSolution implements Solution<SimpleScore> {

    private List<Technician> technicians;
    private List<ServiceRequest> serviceRequests;
    private SimpleScore score;

    private TechniciansSolution() { }

    public TechniciansSolution(List<Technician> technicians,
        List<ServiceRequest> serviceRequests) {
        this.technicians = technicians;
```

```
            this.serviceRequests = serviceRequests;
    }

    @Override
    public SimpleScore getScore() {
        return score;
    }

    @Override
    public void setScore(SimpleScore score) {
        this.score = (SimpleScore) score;
    }

    @Override
    public Collection<Technician> getProblemFacts() {
        return technicians;
    }

    @Override
    public Solution<SimpleScore> cloneSolution() {
        TechniciansSolution solution = new TechniciansSolution();
        solution.score = score;
        solution.technicians = technicians;
        List<ServiceRequest> clonedServices = new ArrayList<ServiceReq
uest>(serviceRequests.size());
        for (ServiceRequest sr : serviceRequests) {
            clonedServices.add(new ServiceRequest(sr));
        }
        solution.serviceRequests = clonedServices;
        return solution;
    }

    public List<Technician> getTechnicians() {
        return technicians;
    }

    @PlanningEntityCollectionProperty
    public List<ServiceRequest> getServiceRequests() {
        return serviceRequests;
    }
}
```

 The TechniciansSolution object has to be initialized with an initial solution that will evolve into a best solution.

This custom `Solution` implementation needs to implement four methods, which we will examine further. The first two methods are related to the score property. In this recipe, we used a `SimpleScore` implementation, and its getter and setter methods. Initially, it will be null, but it will be calculated/recalculated after each step execution as was explained earlier:

```
private SimpleScore score;

@Override
public SimpleScore getScore() {
    return score;
}

@Override
public void setScore(SimpleScore score) {
    this.score = (SimpleScore) score;
}
```

The `getProblemFacts()` method has to return all the objects that need to be inserted into the working memory. In this case, all the `Technician` objects have to be inserted but not the planning `ServiceRequest` entity objects, because they will be automatically inserted:

```
@Override
public Collection<Technician> getProblemFacts() {
    return technicians;
}
```

Also, we have to annotate every property in the `Solution` that returns a collection of planning entities with the `@PlanningEntityCollectionProperty` annotation. Instead, if you have a property that returns a single planning entity then just use the `@PlanningEntityProperty` annotation:

```
@PlanningEntityCollectionProperty
public List<ServiceRequest> getServiceRequests() {
    return serviceRequests;
}
```

Finally, the `cloneSolution()` method has to clone the current solution, and this is because most of the solvers need to clone it each time they encounter a new best solution. In this case, we are only cloning the requested services, which are the only facts that can be modified in runtime without the need to clone the technicians:

```
@Override
public Solution<SimpleScore> cloneSolution() {
    TechniciansSolution solution = new TechniciansSolution();
    solution.score = score;
    solution.technicians = technicians;
```

```
        List<ServiceRequest> clonedServices = new ArrayList<ServiceRequest
    >(serviceRequests.size());
        for (ServiceRequest sr : serviceRequests) {
            clonedServices.add(new ServiceRequest(sr));
        }
        solution.serviceRequests = clonedServices;
        return solution;
    }
```

The score calculation is done using score rules, which makes the process of adding more constraints relatively easy and scalable. But before starting to define the rules constraints, we have to declare a global SimpleCalculator shown as follows:

```
global SimpleScoreCalculator scoreCalculator;
```

This scoreCalculator global will be automatically inserted into the working memory and has to be used to calculate the score of the current step. Ideally, this score has to be updated in a single rule using the weights generated by the score rules.

In our example, we can find several constraints, and one such contraint is that ideally the technician must be in the same location as the service request. In the rule consequence, we need to logically insert a new IntConstraintOcurrence fact with a value. In this case the value should be 1, to specify the weight of the broken constraint:

```
rule "sameCity"
    when
        $sd : ServiceRequest(technician.location != $serviceLoc)
    then
        insertLogical(new IntConstraintOccurrence("sameCity", 1,
$sd));
end
```

Another constraint is the technician availability, which must be available to potentially be selected as the best solution. In this rule consequence, we assigned a higher weight than the previous rule constraint because it has more importance:

```
rule "isBusy"
    when
        $sd : ServiceRequest(technician.busy == true)
    then
        insertLogical(new IntConstraintOccurrence("isBusy", 6, $sd));
end
```

Finally, the last constraint is related with the technician skills required by the service requested. As you can see, it has more importance than the location but less than the technician availability:

```
rule "skillMatch"
    when
        $sd : ServiceRequest($neededSkills : neededSkills,
                             $tec : technician)
    then
        Set<Skill> tempSkills = EnumSet.copyOf($neededSkills);
        tempSkills.removeAll($tec.getSkills());
        insertLogical(new IntConstraintOccurrence("skillMatch",
            tempSkills.size() * 3, $sd));
end
```

The last rule is used to calculate the score of the current step, aggregating the weights of the `IntConstraintOccurrence` objects inserted by other rules. This rule was also assigned with a lower `salience` value to be only evaluated after the score rules. Even though the use of `salience` is not the best practice, we need it to control the rule evaluation order to gain performance in the score calculation:

```
rule "hardConstraintsBroken"
salience -1
    when
        $hardTotal : Number() from accumulate(
            IntConstraintOccurrence($weight : weight),
            sum($weight))
    then
        scoreCalculator.setScore(-$hardTotal.intValue());
end
```

Once the score rules are defined, we have to create the solver configuration file. It's a simple XML file that will configure the solving algorithm behavior. There are a lot of possible configurations here, so we will maintain the focus on the choices for this recipe.

The currently available solver in Drools Planner is local search, which can be configured to use Tabu search and simulated annealing acceptors.

The environment mode is used to influence the seed of the `Random` instance used by the solver, which is used by simulated annealing and Tabu search in different ways. Here we assigned the `REPRODUCIBLE` mode, which is the default mode recommended during development:

```
<solver>
  <environmentMode>REPRODUCIBLE</environmentMode>
```

Now, you need to define the solution class in the configuration:

```
<solutionClass>drools.cookbook.chapter08.planner.TechniciansSolution</
solutionClass>
```

Then the available planning entities must be defined in the configuration, of which there is only one in this recipe:

```
<planningEntityClass>drools.cookbook.chapter08.domain.ServiceRequest</
planningEntityClass>
```

Next, the score rules previously created must be configured to be used by the solver:

```
<scoreDrl>/serviceRequestScoreRules.drl</scoreDrl>
```

As you remember, we used a `SimpleScore` in the solution implementation and this must also be configured:

```
<scoreDefinition>
  <scoreDefinitionType>SIMPLE</scoreDefinitionType>
</scoreDefinition>
```

Now, we have to declare which construction heuristic we are going to use to build a good initial solution. In this example, we are going to use the **First Fit** algorithm, as shown in the following code snippet, but there are plenty of possible construction heuristics. The explanation of all of them goes a little beyond of this recipe so I encourage you to read the relevant sections in the Drools Planner official documentation:

```
<constructionHeuristic>
  <constructionHeuristicType>FIRST_FIT</constructionHeuristicType>
</constructionHeuristic>
```

Next, we have to configure how the local search will stop the execution, which is shown in the following code snippet. In real use cases with a lot of data and constraints, the solving process could take forever, so we need to specify how we would like the solver to stop the execution. Here, we are using a simple approach by configuring the solver to stop when a solution has a score equal to zero or the maximum execution steps are reached. It's really particular to the use case, so there isn't any generic configuration:

```
<localSearch>
  <termination>
    <terminationCompositionStyle>OR</terminationCompositionStyle>
    <maximumStepCount>100</maximumStepCount>
    <scoreAttained>0</scoreAttained>
  </termination>
```

The `selector` is the `SelectNextTechnicians` object that was created previously. It's also possible to create multiple `MoveFactory` objects, as it is a good idea to mix fine grained moves and course-grained moves:

```
<selector>
    <moveFactoryClass>drools.cookbook.chapter08.planner.
SelectNextTechnicians</moveFactoryClass>
    </selector>
```

The acceptor is used to activate a Tabu search or simulated annealing and will assign an accept-change value for each generated move. In this recipe, we are using Tabu search and we are going to configure one of the several Tabu types. The solution Tabu is one of the recommended ones because it tends to gives the best results and requires little or no tweaking. The solution Tabu size depends on the available memory, so if you have enough free memory you can try increasing it to obtain a faster execution:

```
<acceptor>
    <completeSolutionTabuSize>1000</completeSolutionTabuSize>
    </acceptor>
```

Finally, we arrive at the `forager` section. A forager has the responsibility to gather all the accepted moves and pick the one that will be the next step and normally will be the accepted move with the highest score. Here, we can configure whether and how the forager will pick the next move early using one of the following values. Using the NEVER value, a move will never be picked early, but there are two more possible values:

- ▶ NEVER: A move will never be picked early. This is the default value.
- ▶ FIRST_BEST_SCORE_IMPROVING: Picks the first accepted move that improves the best score. If there is none, then it behaves exactly the same as NEVER.
- ▶ FIRST_LAST_STEP_SCORE_IMPROVING: Picks the first accepted move that improves the last step score. If there is none, then it behaves exactly the same as NEVER.

  Once we choose a `forager` configuration, we can configure it as follows:

  ```
  <forager>
      <pickEarlyType>NEVER</pickEarlyType>
      </forager>
  ```

In the last step of the solver configuration we have to close the <localSearch> and <solver> tags as shown as follows:

```
    </localSearch>
</solver>
```

 A step is the best accepted move picked by the `Solver` in the current solution, creating a search path to reach to the best solution.

Finally, we can integrate all the previous steps and create a solver execution. In the `main` method of the `BestAvailableTechnician` class, we defined the steps needed to configure a `Solver` and execute it, but it will be explained in detail in the following code:

First we created our technicians and the required services:

```
List<Technician> technicians = new ArrayList<Technician>();
technicians.add(new Technician(Location.WASHINGTON_DC,
    TrainingLevel.JUNIOR, false, Collections.<Skill> emptySet()));
technicians.add(new Technician(Location.MONTANA,
    TrainingLevel.SEMISENIOR, false, EnumSet.of(Skill.HADOOP)));
technicians.add(new Technician(Location.NY, TrainingLevel.SENIOR,
true, EnumSet.of(Skill.JAVA, Skill.DROOLS)));
technicians.add(new Technician(Location.NORTH_CAROLINA,
    TrainingLevel.SENIOR, true, EnumSet.of(Skill.JAVA)));
technicians.add(new Technician(Location.NY, TrainingLevel.SEMISENIOR,
    false, EnumSet.of(Skill.JAVA, Skill.REST)));
technicians.add(new Technician(Location.SAN_DIEGO, TrainingLevel.
SENIOR, false, EnumSet.of(Skill.SCALA)));
```

In this resource assignment problem, we want to choose the best available technician with Java skills and preferably located in San Diego:

```
List<ServiceRequest> requests = new ArrayList<ServiceRequest>();
requests.add(new ServiceRequest(Location.SAN_DIEGO,
    EnumSet.of(Skill.JAVA)));
```

Next, using the solver XML configuration file, we have to build a `Solver` instance:

```
XmlSolverConfigurer configurer = new XmlSolverConfigurer();
configurer.configure("/ServiceRequestSolverConfig.xml");
Solver solver = configurer.buildSolver();
```

Any solver instance needs an initial solution that will be evolved to find the best solution, which obviously doesn't need to be the best:

```
for (ServiceRequest serviceRequest : requests) {
    serviceRequest.setTechnician(technicians.get(0));
}
TechniciansSolution initialSolution = new
    TechniciansSolution(technicians, requests);
```

Once the initial solution is created, assign it to the `Solver` instance and execute the solving:

```
solver.setPlanningProblem(initialSolution);
solver.solve();
```

When the solving execution reaches the end, irrespective of whether it found the best solution or was ended by the termination configuration, we can still obtain the *best* solution that was found:

```
TechniciansSolution finalSolution = (TechniciansSolution) solver.
getBestSolution();
Technician selectedTechnician = finalSolution.getServiceRequests().
get(0).getTechnician();
System.out.println("Selected technician: " + selectedTechnician);
```

As you probably figured out, it's possible that the selected technician isn't the absolute best option, but it should be an effective solution to the problem. Finally, you may want to know that there are many different solutions:

- A **possible solution** is a solution that does or does not break any number of constraints. Planning problems tend to have a large number of possible solutions; however, most of them are worthless.

- A **feasible solution** does not break any hard constraints. Sometimes, there are no feasible solutions, and every feasible solution is a possible solution.

- An **optimal solution** is one with the highest score. There is always at least one optimal solution to a planning problem.

> Don't forget to check the extensive Drools Planner documentation available at `http://www.jboss.org/drools/documentation` where you will find all the available configurations to modify the solver behavior and optimize your planning problem.

See also

- Refer to the *Using a Simulated Annealing acceptor* recipe.
- Refer to the *Terminating the Solver* recipe.

Using a Simulated Annealing acceptor

In some use cases, you can improve the performance by just changing the solver configuration to use the simulated annealing acceptor. In this recipe, we will understand the meaning of these changes.

Getting ready

This recipe will use the *Solving a resource assignment problem* recipe example and will only modify the configuration file in order to improve the performance. Reading it is recommended before continuing with this recipe.

How to do it...

Carry out the following steps to use a simulated annealing acceptor in your Drools Planner project:

1. Open the `ServiceRequestSolverConfig.xml` file created in the *Solving a resource assignment problem* recipe. Locate the acceptor configuration line and modify it with the following configuration:

```
<acceptor>
    <simulatedAnnealingStartingTemperature>5
    </simulatedAnnealingStartingTemperature>
</acceptor>
```

2. Then we have to modify the forager configuration with a lower value:

```
<forager>
  <minimalAcceptedSelection>4</minimalAcceptedSelection>
</forager>
```

▶ That's all. Execute the project and compare the execution performance against the Tabu search.

How it works...

Simulated Annealing is another local search acceptor that behaves in a completely different manner as compared to Tabu search. It doesn't always pick the move with the highest score nor does it evaluate many moves per step. But that applies only at the beginning of the execution, because at the end it gradually turns into a simple local search only accepting improving moves.

This acceptor allows the possibility of picking one of the un-improving moves, depending on its score and the time gradient of the solver termination configuration. With a few changes in the configuration file, we can switch from Tabu search to simulated annealing.

In the first step, we opened the solver configuration file created in the earlier recipe and modified the acceptor with a `simulatedAnnealingStartingTemperature`. The value is the maximum score delta a single move can cause, and this value can be tweaked using the `Benchmarker`:

```
<acceptor>
    <simulatedAnnealingStartingTemperature>5
    </simulatedAnnealingStartingTemperature>
</acceptor>
```

The second step modifies the forager `minimalAcceptedSelection` with a lower value, in this case `4`, which is a value that usually performs better:

```
<forager>
  <minimalAcceptedSelection>4</minimalAcceptedSelection>
</forager>
```

Finally, we can execute the solver in order to check the performance improvement. In this simple use case, we gain a really high-performance execution compared to using Tabu search. But as always, the performance gained will really depend on your use case complexity.

See also

▸ Refer to the *Solving a resource assignment problem* recipe.

Terminating the Solver

One issue with the local search algorithm is that it doesn't know when it finds the optimal solution and it can take a lot of time trying to find it. Drools Planner provides several ways to configure how we want to configure the Solver termination and we will take a look at them in the following recipes.

Getting ready

This recipe will use the *Solving a resource assignment problem* recipe example and will only modify the configuration file in order to configure the solving termination policy. Reading it is highly recommended before continuing with this recipe.

How to do it...

Carry out the following steps to configure the solving termination policy in your Drools Planner project:

1. Open the `ServiceRequestSolverConfig.xml` file created in the *Solving a resource assignment problem* recipe.

2. Locate the termination configuration line and get ready to configure it with any of the discussed options explained in the *How it works...* section.

How it works...

As it was explained in the *Solving a resource assignment problem* recipe, the solving process could take forever when trying to solve a real use case with a lot of data and constraints. So, it will have to be terminated based on criteria such as the maximum execution time, the maximum steps reached, the score reached, when the score doesn't improve in N steps, or terminated manually using another thread. These criteria are explained as follows:

- **Specifying a maximum execution time**: This will terminate the execution when a specified amount of time, in minutes or hours, is reached. If we only want to execute the solving process for 10 minutes, we can use the following configuration:

```
<termination>
    <maximumMinutesSpend>10</maximumMinutesSpend>
</termination>
```

Or, if we want to execute the solving process for 1 hour, then use the following configuration:

```
<termination>
  <maximumHoursSpend>1</maximumHoursSpend>
</termination>
```

- While using this configuration, you will have to keep two things in mind:

  - The time taken by StartingSolutionInitialized is also taken into account. So, if StartingSolutionInitialized takes two minutes then the Solver will have only eight minutes left to execute.

  - The available CPU time in this time period will impact in the number of Solver steps executed, sacrificing reproducibility.

- **Maximum steps reached**: The execution terminates when the maximum number of steps is reached:

```
<termination>
  <maximumStepCount>100</maximumStepCount>
</termination>
```

- **Score reached**: When you know the perfect score of your problem you can use this termination. It will terminate the execution when the configured score is reached:

```
<termination>
  <scoreAttained>0</scoreAttained>
</termination>
```

> ▸ **Unimproved score in the last N steps**: If the score hasn't improved recently then probably it is not going to improve in the next execution step, so we can force Planner to stop the execution:

```
<termination>
  <maximumUnimprovedStepCount>50</maximumUnimprovedStepCount>
</termination>
```

> ▸ **Terminate early using another thread**: A Solver can also be terminated early from another thread executing its `terminateEarly()` method. Of course this cannot be configured as a termination configuration. It can be done just executing the `terminateEarly()` method, shown as follows:

```
solver.terminateEarly()
```

There's more...

The first four Termination configurations can be combined using AND/OR operators to create more complex termination policies. For example, in the Solver configuration file provided in the first recipe, we used a combined termination to stop the Solver once 100 steps were performed or when a step reached the perfect score of our problem:

```
<termination>
 <terminationCompositionStyle>OR</terminationCompositionStyle>
  <maximumStepCount>100</maximumStepCount>
  <scoreAttained>0</scoreAttained>
</termination>
```

See also

> ▸ Refer to the *Solving a resource assignment problem* recipe.

Creating a basic benchmarker

Drools Planner provides a benchmarker that is useful to find the solver type that best fits in your problem domain. It will help you in the process of comparing the performance of solvers creating reports with statistics and information that we can use to tweak the configurations. In this recipe, we will see how to create a simple benchmarker configuration with two different solver types.

Getting ready

This recipe will use the *Solving a resource assignment problem* recipe example and will configure a solver benchmarker in order to compare Tabu search and Simulated Annealing solvers. It's recommended to read the first two recipes before continuing with this recipe.

How to do it...

Carry out the following steps to build a basic benchmarker:

1. Add the following dependency in the `pom.xml` file of the **Apache** Maven project:

```
<dependency>
  <groupId>jfree</groupId>
  <artifactId>jfreechart</artifactId>
  <version>1.0.13</version>
</dependency>
```

2. First, we have to configure the benchmarker with all the solver types that we want to test. Create a `ServiceRequestSolverBenchmarkConfig.xml` file in the `main/resources` folder and add the content available in the *How it works...* section.

3. Create a new `unsolvedTechnicianRequest.xml` file in the `main/resources` folder. This file will contain the entities used in the execution of the benchmarker.

4. Create a `BestAvailableTechnicianBenchmark` Java class file and add the following code to execute the benchmarker:

```java
public class BestAvailableTechnicianBenchmark {

    public static void main(String[] args) {
        XmlSolverBenchmarker benchmarker = new
            XmlSolverBenchmarker();
        benchmarker.configure(
            "/ServiceRequestSolverBenchmarkConfig.xml");
        benchmarker.benchmark();
    }

}
```

How it works...

In the first step, we added the **jFreeChart** library to the project. This is a required dependency needed by the **drools-planner-core** in order to create the summary statistic charts.

After this we have to configure the `ServiceRequestSolverBenchmarkConfig.xml` file with the solver benchmarker suite definition:

```xml
<?xml version="1.0" encoding="UTF-8"?>
<solverBenchmarkSuite>
```

The `benchmarkDirectory` configuration will specify the directory relative to the working directory where the execution results will be stored as graphics and CVS files:

```
<benchmarkDirectory>benchmark-results</benchmarkDirectory>
```

Next, we have to configure the statistics types. In this example, we want to find out how the scores evolve over time (BEST_SOLUTION_CHANGED) and how fast the scores are calculated (CALCULATE_COUNT_PER_SECOND):

```
<solverStatisticType>BEST_SOLUTION_CHANGED</solverStatisticType>
<solverStatisticType>CALCULATE_COUNT_PER_SECOND</solverStatisticType>
```

The `warmUpSecondsSpend` configuration is used to warm-up the hotspot compiler to avoid non-reliable benchmarker results. In this case, it will execute some of the benchmarkers for 30 seconds before running the real benchmarkers:

```
<warmUpSecondsSpend>30</warmUpSecondsSpend>
<inheritedSolverBenchmark>
```

The `unsolvedSolutionFile` configuration defines the name of the file with the definition of the entities used to execute the benchmarks:

```
<unsolvedSolutionFile>
  src/main/resources/unsolvedTechnicianRequest.xml
</unsolvedSolutionFile>
```

Next, we have to define the common solver configuration for all the benchmarkers, as we already saw in the previous recipes:

```
<solver>
  <solutionClass>
    drools.cookbook.chapter08.planner.TechniciansSolution
  </solutionClass>
  <planningEntityClass>
    drools.cookbook.chapter08.domain.ServiceRequest
  </planningEntityClass>
  <scoreDrl>/serviceRequestScoreRules.drl</scoreDrl>
  <scoreDefinition>
    <scoreDefinitionType>SIMPLE</scoreDefinitionType>
  </scoreDefinition>
  <termination>
    <maximumSecondsSpend>20</maximumSecondsSpend>
  </termination>
</solver>
</inheritedSolverBenchmark>
```

Finally, we are ready to define the solver types that we want to benchmark. The solver type configurations added here are the same ones used in the first two recipes, and don't need further modifications:

```
<solverBenchmark>
  <name>TabuSearch</name>
  <solver>
    <localSearch>
      <selector>
        <moveFactoryClass>
          drools.cookbook.chapter08.planner.SelectNextTechnicians
        </moveFactoryClass>
      </selector>
      <acceptor>
        <completeSolutionTabuSize>1000</completeSolutionTabuSize>
      </acceptor>
      <forager>
        <pickEarlyType>NEVER</pickEarlyType>
      </forager>
    </localSearch>
  </solver>
</solverBenchmark>
<solverBenchmark>
  <name>simulatedAnnealing</name>
  <solver>
    <localSearch>
      <selector>
        <moveFactoryClass>
          drools.cookbook.chapter08.planner.SelectNextTechnicians
        </moveFactoryClass>
      </selector>
      <acceptor>
        <simulatedAnnealingStartingTemperature>5
        </simulatedAnnealingStartingTemperature>
      </acceptor>
      <forager>
        <pickEarlyType>NEVER</pickEarlyType>
      </forager>
    </localSearch>
  </solver>
</solverBenchmark>
</solverBenchmarkSuite>
```

The only remaining configuration step is the definition of the entities in the `unsolvedTechnicianRequest.xml` file. This file contains the initial `TechniciansSolution` object in XML format serialized using `XStream`. So, instead of manually writing XML, we can use the following code snippet to create the entities' definitions executing the `toXML(object)` method of the `XStream` object:

```
XStream xstream = new XStream();
String xml = xstream.toXML(initialSolution);
```

This method invocation will generate content that is similar to the following content that we need to save in the `unsolvedTechnicianRequest.xml` file:

```
<drools.cookbook.chapter08.planner.TechniciansSolution>
  <technicians>
    <drools.cookbook.chapter08.domain.Technician>
      <location>WASHINGTON_DC</location>
      <trainingLevel>JUNIOR</trainingLevel>
      <busy>false</busy>
      <skills class="java.util.Collections$EmptySet" />
    </drools.cookbook.chapter08.domain.Technician>
    <!-- more technicians entities definitions -->
    <drools.cookbook.chapter08.domain.Technician>
      <location>MONTANA</location>
      <trainingLevel>SEMISENIOR</trainingLevel>
      <busy>false</busy>
      <skills class="enum-set" enum-type="drools.cookbook.chapter08.
domain.Skill">HADOOP</skills>
    </drools.cookbook.chapter08.domain.Technician>
  </technicians>
  <serviceRequests>
    <drools.cookbook.chapter08.domain.ServiceRequest>
      <location>SAN_DIEGO</location>
      <neededSkills class="enum-set" enum-type="drools.cookbook.
chapter08.domain.Skill">JAVA</neededSkills>
      <technician>
        <location>WASHINGTON_DC</location>
        <trainingLevel>JUNIOR</trainingLevel>
        <busy>false</busy>
        <skills class="java.util.Collections$EmptySet" />
      </technician>
    </drools.cookbook.chapter08.domain.ServiceRequest>
  </serviceRequests>
</drools.cookbook.chapter08.planner.TechniciansSolution>
```

Finally, we are ready to execute the benchmarker using the following code:

```
public class BestAvailableTechnicianBenchmark {
```

```
public static void main(String[] args) {
    XmlSolverBenchmarker benchmarker = new XmlSolverBenchmarker();
    benchmarker.configure("/ServiceRequestSolverBenchmarkConfig.
xml");
    benchmarker.benchmark();
}
}
```

Once the benchmarker execution finishes, it will create the statistics summary files in the
`benchmark-results` folder. Inside this folder, we will find graphics and CSV files displaying
information about how the score evolved over time, the best score summary, and how fast the
scores were calculated for both solver types benchmarked.

For more information about benchmark data don't forget to check the official Drools
Planner documentation.

See also

▶   Refer to the *Solving a resource assignment problem* recipe.
▶   Refer to the *Using a Simulated Annealing acceptor* recipe.

9
jBPM5: Managing Business Processes

In this chapter, we will cover:

- ► Creating a business process manually
- ► Testing your business processes
- ► Creating and executing human tasks
- ► Monitoring a process activity and creating reports
- ► Monitoring a business process with Drools Fusion

Introduction

jBPM5 is the new brand name of the Drools process engine that was previously known as **Drools Flow**. It's a flexible and lightweight Business Process Management (BPM) tool that can be integrated with almost all the other available Drools projects and has primary focus on the BPMN 2.0 specification as the main language to express a business process.

This chapter will primarily focus on the BPMN 2.0 support of jBPM5, modeling different business processes by using the new **jBPM5 BPMN2 Eclipse editor** as the authoring tool. Even when the recipes are not specifically about BPMN 2.0 it are widely used in all the recipes, explaining how to model business processes using the editor.

Creating a business process manually

Commonly, the definition of business process is made by using the jBPM5 Eclipse Plugin or by writing a BPMN2 XML definition, which is complex for most users. But there are certain cases, for example, testing and proof of concepts, which need more flexibility at the time of writing business processes. That is why this recipe will cover the internal jBPM5 API to programmatically define a business process.

How to do it...

In this recipe, we will programmatically create a business process using the jBPM internal API. Carry out the following steps to achieve it:

1. Create a Java project using Apache Maven and add the following jBPM dependencies in the pom.xml file:

```
<dependencies>
  <dependency>
    <groupId>org.jbpm</groupId>
    <artifactId>jbpm-flow</artifactId>
    <version>5.1.0.Final</version>
  </dependency>
  <dependency>
    <groupId>org.jbpm</groupId>
    <artifactId>jbpm-flow-builder</artifactId>
    <version>5.1.0.Final</version>
  </dependency>
</dependencies>
```

2. Once the dependencies are added in your project, you can start to model the business process. As we are only testing this feature, just create a Java class file and add the following code inside a Java main method:

```
String processId = "myCustomProcess";
String eventType = "eventType";

StartNode startNode = new StartNode();
startNode.setName("Start");
startNode.setId(1);

ActionNode actionNode = new ActionNode();
actionNode.setId(2);
DroolsConsequenceAction insertAction = new
```

```
        DroolsConsequenceAction();
insertAction.setDialect("java");
insertAction.setMetaData("Action", new Action() {

    public void execute(ProcessContext context) {
        System.out.println("Script task node executed");
    }

});
actionNode.setAction(insertAction);

Join joinNode = new Join();
joinNode.setId(3);
joinNode.setName("Waiting signal");
joinNode.setType(Join.TYPE_AND);

EventNode eventNode = new EventNode();
eventNode.setName("Event");
eventNode.setId(4);
eventNode.setScope("external");
EventTypeFilter eventFilter = new EventTypeFilter();
eventFilter.setType(eventType);
eventNode.addEventFilter(eventFilter);

EndNode endNode = new EndNode();
endNode.setName("EndNode");
endNode.setId(5);

connect(startNode, actionNode);
connect(actionNode, joinNode);
connect(eventNode, joinNode);
connect(joinNode, endNode);

RuleFlowProcess process = new RuleFlowProcess();
process.setId(processId);
process.addNode(startNode);
process.addNode(actionNode);
process.addNode(joinNode);
process.addNode(eventNode);
process.addNode(endNode);
```

3. Next, we need to define the `connect()` method that is used to create the connections between the nodes. Add the following method in the same file:

```
public static void connect(Node sourceNode, Node targetNode) {
    new ConnectionImpl(sourceNode, Node.CONNECTION_DEFAULT_TYPE,
        targetNode, Node.CONNECTION_DEFAULT_TYPE);
}
```

4. Once the process is defined and its nodes are connected, we are ready to add this process definition into a knowledge base in a way not commonly used, and also to create a knowledge session. The following code should be added in the Java `main` method, after the process definition:

```
KnowledgeBase kbase = KnowledgeBaseFactory.newKnowledgeBase();
((AbstractRuleBase) ((InternalKnowledgeBase) kbase).
getRuleBase()).addProcess(process);

StatefulKnowledgeSession ksession = kbase
    .newStatefulKnowledgeSession();
```

5. Finally, using the `StatefulKnowledgeSession`, we can start the process and send a signal to activate the `EventNode` to complete it:

```
ProcessInstance processInstance = ksession
    .startProcess("myCustomProcess");
long processInstanceId = processInstance.getId();
ksession.signalEvent(eventType, null, processInstanceId);
```

How it works...

In this recipe, we are programmatically defining a business process using the internal API. As you have read before, this process declaration isn't an alternative for a production environment and it should only be used for testing purposes or special use cases.

The modelled process used in this recipe is defined using the following five different nodes:

- Start Event node
- Script Task node
- Catch Event node with a Signal Definition
- Parallel Converging Gateway node
- End Event node

The business process that is going to be created in this recipe is displayed in the following figure:

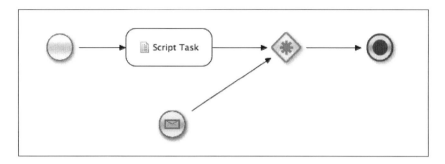

Before starting to declare the process definition, we are going to need the jBPM5 libraries in the project dependencies. These dependencies can be configured adding the following declarations in the pom.xml file:

```
<dependencies>
  <dependency>
    <groupId>org.jbpm</groupId>
    <artifactId>jbpm-flow</artifactId>
    <version>5.1.0.Final</version>
  </dependency>
  <dependency>
    <groupId>org.jbpm</groupId>
    <artifactId>jbpm-flow-builder</artifactId>
    <version>5.1.0.Final</version>
  </dependency>
</dependencies>
```

 There is no need to add the Drools dependencies in your project because they are going to be automatically imported, being jBPM5 transitive dependencies.

Now, we are ready to define the process, instantiating the nodes that are going to be part of it. In this recipe, the process definition and execution are going to be declared inside a Java main method only for demonstration purposes, where we have to choose a process ID and event type ID before starting to define the nodes:

```
String processId = "myCustomProcess";
String eventType = "eventType";
```

All the process definitions begin with the Start Event node's `org.jbpm.workflow.core.node.StartNode` object, which needs a name and a numeric ID:

```
StartNode startNode = new StartNode();
startNode.setName("Start");
startNode.setId(1);
```

Then, we have to declare a **Script Task** node that is implemented using an `org.jbpm.workflow.core.node.ActionNode` object. This node type also needs a numeric ID, and the `Action` that will be executed is shown as follows:

```
ActionNode actionNode = new ActionNode();
actionNode.setId(2);
```

Now, we have to set the action to be executed when the **Action Node** is reached, using an `org.jbpm.workflow.core.impl.DroolsConsequenceAction` object configured to use the Java dialect:

```
DroolsConsequenceAction insertAction = new
    DroolsConsequenceAction();
insertAction.setDialect("java");
```

This `DroolsConsequenceAction` object also needs associated metadata with the action to be executed, which is defined using an `org.jbpm.process.instance.impl.Action` object custom implementation. In this custom `Action` implementation, you will have to complete the `execute(ProcessContext context)` method with your business action:

```
insertAction.setMetaData("Action", new Action() {

    public void execute(ProcessContext context) {
        System.out.println("Script task node executed");
    }

});
actionNode.setAction(insertAction);
```

The Parallel Converging Gateway node is declared using an `org.jbpm.workflow.core.node.Join` object, which needs an ID and name like the other nodes. Also, this kind of node needs the join type, which can be one of the following:

▶ AND: The outgoing connection will be triggered when all the incoming connections have been triggered.

▶ XOR: The outgoing connection will be triggered when one of the incoming connections has been triggered.

For this process, we need an AND gateway and it can be created with the following code:

```
Join joinNode = new Join();
joinNode.setId(3);
joinNode.setName("Waiting signal");
joinNode.setType(Join.TYPE_AND);
```

Now, we have to create the event node using an `org.jbpm.workflow.core.node.EventNode` object with an ID, name, and an external scope:

```
EventNode eventNode = new EventNode();
eventNode.setName("EventNode");
eventNode.setId(4);
eventNode.setScope("external");
```

This event node also needs filters to know to which event signals it must react to be triggered. Just create an `org.jbpm.process.core.event.EventTypeFilter` object, assign the event type previously declared as the event filter type, and add it to the event node filters:

```
EventTypeFilter eventFilter = new EventTypeFilter();
eventFilter.setType(eventType);
eventNode.addEventFilter(eventFilter);
```

The last node we have to create is the **End Event** node using an `org.jbpm.workflow.core.node.EndNode` object and assigning to it an ID and name:

```
EndNode endNode = new EndNode();
endNode.setName("End");
endNode.setId(5);
```

At this point, we have declared all the nodes used in this business process, but they are isolated nodes without any kind of connection between them. So, we have to create the connections using `org.jbpm.workflow.core.impl.ConnectionImpl` objects with the incoming and the outgoing node. In this recipe, we defined a `connect(Node sourceNode, Node targetNode)` static method that creates the connection between a source node and a target node:

```
public static void connect(Node sourceNode, Node targetNode) {
    new ConnectionImpl(sourceNode,
                    Node.CONNECTION_DEFAULT_TYPE, targetNode,
                    Node.CONNECTION_DEFAULT_TYPE);
}
```

Using this helper static method we can start to connect the nodes immediately after their definition. As you can see, we followed the BPMN2 diagram to connect the nodes. There isn't anything too complicated here:

```
connect(startNode, actionNode);
connect(actionNode, joinNode);
connect(eventNode, joinNode);
connect(joinNode, endNode);
```

With all the nodes defined and connections between them, we can finally create our process object using an `org.jbpm.ruleflow.core.RuleFlowProcess` object. This process object only needs a process ID, which was previously declared, and all the nodes that it comprises:

```
RuleFlowProcess process = new RuleFlowProcess();
process.setId(processId);
process.addNode(startNode);
process.addNode(actionNode);
process.addNode(joinNode);
process.addNode(eventNode);
process.addNode(endNode);
```

And that is all! Now, we are ready to add this process definition into our knowledge base, which can be created as you usually do:

```
KnowledgeBase kbase = KnowledgeBaseFactory.newKnowledgeBase();
```

Once we have created a `KnowledgeBase` object, we have to add the process definition using the following code snippet:

```
((AbstractRuleBase) ((InternalKnowledgeBase) kbase).getRuleBase())
    .addProcess(process);
```

Now, with the process definition added into the knowledge base, we can create a new stateful knowledge session to start interacting with our process:

```
StatefulKnowledgeSession ksession = kbase.
newStatefulKnowledgeSession();
ProcessInstance processInstance = ksession
    .startProcess("myCustomProcess");
long processInstanceId = processInstance.getId();
ksession.signalEvent(eventType, null, processInstanceId);
```

And, those are all the necessary steps to create a process definition using the API. This example is included in the book's example source code together with other examples.

For further information about the configuration of other available nodes you can check the jBPM5 source code to discover the implementation the `org.jbpm.workflow.core.Node` object.

Testing your business processes

jBPM5 includes a new helper class to make the task of writing unit testing easy. It comes with several helper methods and assert statements that will facilitate this, which is a tedious tasks sometimes. Take a look at this recipe to know how it could improve your testing process.

Getting ready

In order to use the jBPM5 unit testing integration, you will have to download the `jbpm-bpmn2` module source code from `http://www.jboss.org/jbpm/` or directly browse the source code available on GitHub `http://www.github.com/droolsjbpm/jbpm/tree/master/` to copy the `JbpmJUnitTestCase` Java class in your project.

How to do it...

Carry out the following steps to archive this recipe:

1. Create a Java project using Apache Maven and add the following dependencies to the `pom.xml` file:

```
<dependencies>
  <dependency>
    <groupId>org.jbpm</groupId>
    <artifactId>jbpm-flow</artifactId>
    <version>5.1.0.Final</version>
  </dependency>
  <dependency>
    <groupId>org.jbpm</groupId>
    <artifactId>jbpm-flow-builder</artifactId>
    <version>5.1.0.Final</version>
  </dependency>
  <dependency>
    <groupId>org.jbpm</groupId>
    <artifactId>jbpm-bam</artifactId>
    <version>5.1.0.Final</version>
  </dependency>
  <dependency>
    <groupId>org.jbpm</groupId>
    <artifactId>jbpm-bpmn2</artifactId>
```

```
      <version>5.1.0.Final</version>
   </dependency>
   <dependency>
      <groupId>org.jbpm</groupId>
      <artifactId>jbpm-persistence-jpa</artifactId>
      <version>5.1.0.Final</version>
   </dependency>
   <dependency>
      <groupId>org.codehaus.btm</groupId>
      <artifactId>btm</artifactId>
      <version>1.3.3</version>
      <scope>test</scope>
   </dependency>
   <dependency>
      <groupId>com.h2database</groupId>
      <artifactId>h2</artifactId>
      <version>1.2.128</version>
   </dependency>
   <dependency>
      <groupId>org.slf4j</groupId>
      <artifactId>slf4j-api</artifactId>
      <version>1.6.1</version>
   </dependency>
   <dependency>
      <groupId>org.slf4j</groupId>
      <artifactId>slf4j-log4j12</artifactId>
      <version>1.6.1</version>
   </dependency>
</dependencies>
```

2. Create a Java package in the test folder, for example `drools.cookbook.chapter9`, and copy into it the `JbpmJUnitTestCase` Java file located in the `src/test/java/org/jbpm/` folder of the `jbpm-bpmn2` module source code.

3. Create a new BPMN2 diagram using the BPMN2 editor as shown in the following figure. Add a throw event node with a signal definition in the diagram and save it in the `test/resources` folder. The details about the creation of this diagram will be explained later:

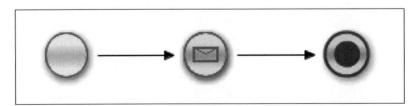

4. Extend the `JbpmJUnitTestCase` with a new Java class named `SimpleProcessTest` and save it in the test package.

5. Add the following code to the previously created `SimpleProcessTest` Java file:

```
package drools.cookbook.chapter9;

import org.drools.KnowledgeBase;
import org.drools.runtime.StatefulKnowledgeSession;
import org.drools.runtime.process.ProcessInstance;
import org.junit.Assert;

public class SimpleProcessTest extends JbpmJUnitTestCase {

    public SimpleProcessTest() {
        super(false);
    }

    public void testProcessWithSignalEvent() throws Exception {
        KnowledgeBase kbase = createKnowledgeBase("processWithSign
alEvent.bpmn");
        StatefulKnowledgeSession ksession =
createKnowledgeSession(kbase);
        ProcessInstance processInstance = ksession.startProcess
            ("processWithSignalEvent");
        Assert.assertNotNull(processInstance);
        assertProcessInstanceActive(processInstance.getId(),
ksession);
        assertNodeActive(processInstance.getId(), ksession, "Catch
Signal Event");
        ksession.signalEvent("mySignal", null, processInstance.
getId());
        assertProcessInstanceCompleted(processInstance.getId(),
ksession);
    }

}
```

6. Now, you only have to execute the unit test using your favorite IDE or from the command line using the **mvn test** command.

How it works...

Unit testing is always an important aspect when you write code, even when business processes are not very descriptive and have a life cycle that behaves according to the use case. jBPM5 includes a helper class to simplify the testing of the process execution that offers several options, which are as follows:

- Methods to create knowledge base and sessions, using a local processes or processes stored in a Guvnor instance
- Easy persistence configuration
- Several assert statements to validate the process execution:
  - `assertProcessInstanceCompleted`
  - `assertProcessInstanceAborted`
  - `assertProcessInstanceActive`
  - `assertNodeActive`
  - `assertNodeTriggered`
- A helper method to restore a persisted knowledge session
- A helper method to obtain the value of variables
- A `WorkItemHandler` to validate the executed work items

In the first step, you added a lot of dependencies needed by the jBPM unit test helper class and most of them are needed to persist the knowledge session. However, if you don't want to add them you can easily modify the `JbpmJUnitTestCase` class and remove the `jbpm-persistence-jpa`, H2, and Bitronix dependencies.

After you have configured the dependencies, you have to copy the `JbpmJUnitTestCase` file located in the `src/test/java/org/jbpm/` folder of the `jbpm-bpmn2` module source code into your project structure, ideally in the `drools.cookbook.chapter9` package.

Now, it's time to create the BPMN2 diagram using the jBPM BPMN2 editor. Create a new diagram named `processWithSignalEvent.bpmn` and save it in the `test/resources` folder.

Throw a Start Event node, a Message Event node, and an End Node in the diagram and connect them using a Sequence Flow connector. The Message Event node has to be associated with a Signal definition (EventType property) and configured with the signal reference in the properties of the node. Also it must be named **Catch Signal Event**. Finally, we only have to modify the name and process ID. In order to achieve this, click on the diagram background and change it to **processWithSignalEvent** on the Eclipse **Properties** view, as shown in the following screenshot:

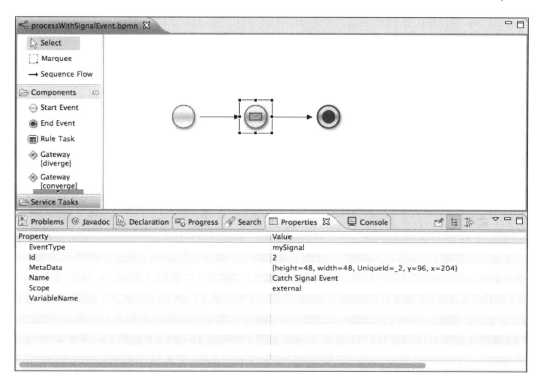

Now, with the BPMN2 diagram ready, you can start writing the unit tests. Create a new Java class named `SimpleProcessTest` and extend the `JbpmJUnitTestCase` class.

Before you start writing a unit test you have to disable the persistence. In this recipe, we are disabling the persistence, but in the examples provided together with the book you will find an example configured to use persistence:

```
public class SimpleProcessTest extends JbpmJUnitTestCase {
    public SimpleProcessTest() {
        super(false);
    }
}
```

Once persistence is disabled, you can define a unit test with the following content:

```
public void testProcessWithSignalEvent() throws Exception {
    KnowledgeBase kbase = createKnowledgeBase("processWithSignalEvent.
bpmn");
    StatefulKnowledgeSession ksession = createKnowledgeSession(kbase);
    ProcessInstance processInstance = ksession.
      startProcess("processWithSignalEvent");
    Assert.assertNotNull(processInstance);
```

```
        assertProcessInstanceActive(processInstance.getId(), ksession);
        assertNodeActive(processInstance.getId(), ksession, "Catch Signal
    Event");
        ksession.signalEvent("mySignal", null, processInstance.getId());
        assertProcessInstanceCompleted(processInstance.getId(), ksession);
    }
```

This unit test uses the helper methods provided by `JbpmJUnitTestCase` to create a knowledge base and a knowledge session. The method to create a knowledge base accepts multiple strings with the BPMN2 filenames and you can also pass a Java Map with processes and rules:

```
KnowledgeBase kbase = createKnowledgeBase("processWithSignalEvent.
bpmn");
StatefulKnowledgeSession ksession = createKnowledgeSession(kbase);
ProcessInstance processInstance = ksession.startProcess("processWithS
ignalEvent");
```

Now, that the process is started you can use the assert statements to validate the correct process execution. The first assert statement used is the `assertProcessInstanceActive` to check the process initialization, passing the process instance ID and the knowledge session as parameters:

```
assertProcessInstanceActive(processInstance.getId(), ksession);
```

In the BPMN2 diagram, we added a Message Event node with a Signal definition after the Start Event node, so at this point of the process execution, the process is waiting for a signal to continue with the execution. This is an ideal situation to use the `assertNodeActive` assert statement to verify that the current active node is the `Catch Signal Event`:

```
assertNodeActive(processInstance.getId(), ksession, "Catch Signal
Event");
```

Now, you have to send a signal to the process to continue the execution. It's commonly done using the following code:

```
ksession.signalEvent("mySignal", null, processInstance.getId());
```

Once the process has been signaled, it finally reaches the End Event node and the process execution finalizes. Again, you can use `assertProcessInstanceCompleted` to verify the correct finalization of the process:

```
assertProcessInstanceCompleted(processInstance.getId(), ksession);
```

As you can see, the `JbpmJUnitTestCase` provides several methods to improve the business processes testing. For more implementations, check out the examples provided along with this book where you will find two more examples, one of them using persistence configuration provided by this helper class.

Creating and executing human tasks

In this recipe, you will see how to integrate tasks that necessarily have to be executed by human actors. jBPM5 provides a special task node based on the **WS-Human specification** to support this special task. Check out this recipe for more details.

How to do it...

Carry out the following steps in order to complete this recipe:

1. Create a Java project using Apache Maven and add the following dependencies to the `pom.xml` file:

```
<dependencies>
  <dependency>
    <groupId>org.jbpm</groupId>
    <artifactId>jbpm-flow</artifactId>
    <version>5.1.0.Final</version>
  </dependency>
  <dependency>
    <groupId>org.jbpm</groupId>
    <artifactId>jbpm-flow-builder</artifactId>
    <version>5.1.0.Final</version>
  </dependency>
  <dependency>
    <groupId>org.jbpm</groupId>
    <artifactId>jbpm-bpmn2</artifactId>
    <version>5.1.0.Final</version>
  </dependency>
  <dependency>
    <groupId>org.jbpm</groupId>
    <artifactId>jbpm-human-task</artifactId>
    <version>5.1.0.Final</version>
  </dependency>
  <dependency>
    <groupId>com.h2database</groupId>
    <artifactId>h2 </artifactId>
    <version>1.2.128</version>
  </dependency>
</dependencies>
```

2. Create a new BPMN2 file using the **jBPM5 Eclipse plugin** and the BPMN2 editor. In this process definition, we added three user-task nodes that were assigned to different actors and were connected using AND gateways, as shown in the following figure:

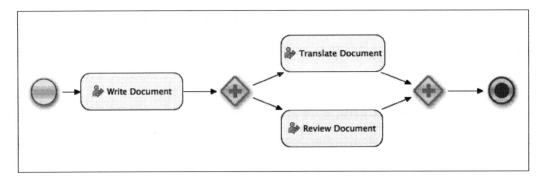

3. Create a `persistence.xml` file in the `resources/META-INF/` folder of your project structure. This file will contain the necessary information to persist and retrieve the human task states using JPA. Inside this file, a `drools.cookbook.jbpm.task` persistence unit will be configured to use an in-memory H2 database as you can see in the following code:

```xml
<?xml version="1.0" encoding="UTF-8" standalone="yes"?>
<persistence version="1.0"
xsi:schemaLocation="http://java.sun.com/xml/ns/persistence
http://java.sun.com/xml/ns/persistence/persistence_1_0.xsd
http://java.sun.com/xml/ns/persistence/orm http://java.sun.com/
xml/ns/persistence/orm_1_0.xsd"
xmlns:orm="http://java.sun.com/xml/ns/persistence/orm"
xmlns:xsi="http://www.w3.org/2001/XMLSchema-instance"
xmlns="http://java.sun.com/xml/ns/persistence">

<persistence-unit name="drools.cookbook.jbpm.task">

<provider>org.hibernate.ejb.HibernatePersistence</provider>

  <class>org.jbpm.task.Attachment</class>
  <class>org.jbpm.task.Content</class>
  <class>org.jbpm.task.BooleanExpression</class>
  <class>org.jbpm.task.Comment</class>
  <class>org.jbpm.task.Deadline</class>
  <class>org.jbpm.task.Comment</class>
  <class>org.jbpm.task.Deadline</class>
  <class>org.jbpm.task.Delegation</class>
  <class>org.jbpm.task.Escalation</class>
```

```
<class>org.jbpm.task.Group</class>
<class>org.jbpm.task.I18NText</class>
<class>org.jbpm.task.Notification</class>
<class>org.jbpm.task.EmailNotification</class>
<class>org.jbpm.task.EmailNotificationHeader</class>
<class>org.jbpm.task.PeopleAssignments</class>
<class>org.jbpm.task.Reassignment</class>
<class>org.jbpm.task.Status</class>
<class>org.jbpm.task.Task</class>
<class>org.jbpm.task.TaskData</class>
<class>org.jbpm.task.SubTasksStrategy</class>
    <class>org.jbpm.task.OnParentAbortAllSubTasksEndStrategy</
class>
    <class>org.jbpm.task.OnAllSubTasksEndParentEndStrategy</class>
<class>org.jbpm.task.User</class>

<properties>
    <property name="hibernate.dialect"
             value="org.hibernate.dialect.H2Dialect"/>
    <property name="hibernate.connection.driver_class"
              value="org.h2.Driver"/>
    <property name="hibernate.connection.url"
             value="jdbc:h2:mem:mydb" />
    <property name="hibernate.connection.username"
             value="sa"/>
    <property name="hibernate.connection.password"
             value="sa"/>
    <property name="hibernate.connection.autocommit"
             value="false" />
    <property name="hibernate.max_fetch_depth" value="3"/>
    <property name="hibernate.hbm2ddl.auto"
             value="create" />
    <property name="hibernate.show_sql" value="false" />
</properties>

</persistence-unit>
</persistence>
```

4. Copy the `orm.xml` file provided in the `jbpm-human-task` library into the
    `resources/META-INF/` folder of the project.

5. Now, we are ready to start interacting with the human tasks, but before starting to instantiate the process, we have to set up the human task service. This process involves several steps, but let's start by creating a Java class and adding it inside a Java `main` method. Add the following lines of code to create the `EntityManager` and the `TaskService`:

```
EntityManagerFactory emf = Persistence
  .createEntityManagerFactory("drools.cookbook.jbpm.task");
SystemEventListener systemEventListener =
  SystemEventListenerFactory.getSystemEventListener();
TaskService taskService = new TaskService(emf,
  systemEventListener);
TaskServiceSession taskSession = taskService.createSession();
```

6. Now, we have to register the users, using `org.jbpm.task.User` objects, into the `org.jbpm.task.service.TaskServiceSession` object created in the previous step:

```
User writer = new User("writer");
User translator = new User("translator");
User reviewer = new User("reviewer");
User administrator = new User("Administrator");


taskSession.addUser(writer);
taskSession.addUser(translator);
taskSession.addUser(reviewer);
taskSession.addUser(administrator);
```

7. At this point, we are ready to start the human task service, in this case using an implementation that uses Apache Mina to communicate with the `TaskClient`. The server is started in a separate thread and delayed by a small amount of time to guarantee the correct initialization:

```
TaskServer server = new MinaTaskServer(taskService);
Thread thread = new Thread(server);
thread.start();
Thread.sleep(2000);
```

8. The interaction with the human task service is done using an `org.jbpm.task.service.TaskClient` object configured with a `TaskClient` Apache Mina Connector. Once the `TaskClient` is configured, it's ready to be connected with the human task service using the `connect()` method and passing the server address and port, which by default is 9123, as parameters:

```
SystemEventListener systemEventListener =
  SystemEventListenerFactory.getSystemEventListener();
MinaTaskClientHandler minaTaskClientHandler = new
  MinaTaskClientHandler(systemEventListener);
```

```
TaskClientConnector connector = new
  MinaTaskClientConnector("client", minaTaskClientHandler);
TaskClient client = new TaskClient(connector);
client.connect("127.0.0.1", 9123);
```

9. Once the client is connected with the server, we can continue creating a `knowledge session` with the process definition created in the second step:

```
KnowledgeBuilder kbuilder = KnowledgeBuilderFactory
  .newKnowledgeBuilder();
kbuilder.add(new ClassPathResource("document.bpmn"),
                            ResourceType.BPMN2);

KnowledgeBase kbase = KnowledgeBaseFactory
  .newKnowledgeBase();
kbase.addKnowledgePackages(kbuilder.getKnowledgePackages());

StatefulKnowledgeSession ksession = kbase
  .newStatefulKnowledgeSession();
```

10. Now, we have to register a custom `WorkItem` into the `StatefulKnowledgeSession` that will have the responsibility to manage the human tasks. The `jbpm-human-task` library provides a ready-to-use `WorkItemHandler` that implements the WS-HumanTask specification:

```
WorkItemHandler handler = new WSHumanTaskHandler();
ksession.getWorkItemManager().registerWorkItemHandler(
  "Human Task", handler);
```

11. With all the required components configured and initialized, we are ready to start the process using the ID specified in the process definition:

```
ProcessInstance processInstance = ksession
  .startProcess("document-publication");
```

12. Once the process is started, we can interact with the human task service using the `TaskClient object` previously created. First, we have to inquire about the tasks available to a user invoking the user's `getTaskAssignedAsPotentialOwned()` method and using a `BlockingTaskSummaryResponseHandler` object to wait for a response for a certain amount of time. Once the human task service responds with the available tasks, we can obtain them by invoking the `getResults()` method from the `BlockingTaskSummaryResponseHandler`:

```
BlockingTaskSummaryResponseHandler taskSummaryResponseHandler =
  new BlockingTaskSummaryResponseHandler();
client.getTasksAssignedAsPotentialOwner("writer", "en-UK",
  taskSummaryResponseHandler);
taskSummaryResponseHandler.waitTillDone(2000);
List<TaskSummary> tasks = taskSummaryResponseHandler
  .getResults();
```

13. As we have only started one process, the response will only contain one assigned task for the user with a *writer* ID. So, the next step is to start the user task, invoking the `start()` method of the `TaskClient` object using the user task ID and the user ID and, again a `BlockingTaskOperationResponseHandler` object to block the execution until you get a response from the server:

```
BlockingTaskOperationResponseHandler startResponse =
   new BlockingTaskOperationResponseHandler();
long taskId = tasks.get(0).getId();
client.start(taskId, "writer", startResponse);
startResponse.waitTillDone(200);
```

14. After you start a human task and complete it, you have to confirm whether the task is completed with the human task service, allowing to the process instance to continue its execution moving on to the next node. To do this, we have to invoke the `complete()` method provided by the `TaskClient` object, which also needs a task ID, user ID, and a `BlockingTaskOperationResponseHandler` object to wait for the human task service response:

```
BlockingTaskOperationResponseHandler completeResponse =
   new BlockingTaskOperationResponseHandler();
client.complete(taskId, "writer", null, completeResponse);
completeResponse.waitTillDone(2000);
```

15. With the completion of the task assigned to the user with the *writer* ID, the process instance moves to the next node, which again is human tasks but in this case assigned to different actor IDs. At this point of the process execution, there are two available human tasks ready to be executed, where each one is assigned to the *translator* and the *reviewer* user ID. These new user tasks can be executed by repeating the previous steps to obtain the available tasks (step 12), start the task (step 13), and complete the task (step 14).

How it works...

Human interaction is an important aspect of the business process because while almost all the work can be executed automatically, there are tasks that really need to be executed by human actors. To solve this, jBPM5 provides a pluggable human task implementation based in the WS-HumanTask specification that allows us to manage the life cycle of these tasks in run-time.

The integration of human actors in the business process needs the following three elements:

- ▶ A business process definition with user task nodes
- ▶ A task management component similar to the one provided by jBPM
- ▶ Human users to interact with the task management component to start the tasks, complete the tasks, claim the tasks, and so on

Before starting to model our business process, we have to create a new Java project using Apache Maven and adding the following dependencies in the `pom.xml` file:

```xml
<dependencies>
  <dependency>
     <groupId>org.jbpm</groupId>
     <artifactId>jbpm-flow</artifactId>
     <version>5.1.0.Final</version>
  </dependency>
  <dependency>
     <groupId>org.jbpm</groupId>
     <artifactId>jbpm-flow-builder</artifactId>
     <version>5.1.0.Final</version>
  </dependency>
  <dependency>
     <groupId>org.jbpm</groupId>
     <artifactId>jbpm-bpmn2</artifactId>
     <version>5.1.0.Final</version>
  </dependency>
  <dependency>
     <groupId>org.jbpm</groupId>
     <artifactId>jbpm-human-task</artifactId>
     <version>5.1.0.Final</version>
  </dependency>
  <dependency>
     <groupId>com.h2database</groupId>
     <artifactId>h2 </artifactId>
     <version>1.2.128</version>
  </dependency>
</dependencies>
```

As you can see, we are adding two new jBPM dependencies that we didn't use before:

- `jbpm-bpmn2`: The BPMN2 specification implementation
- `jbpm-human-task`: The WS-HumanTask specification implementation

Now, we have a project that supports the BPMN2 specification and human tasks management, so we are ready to define our business process. In this recipe, we are using a simple process with three user task nodes that are assigned to three different actors, which is shown in the following screenshot:

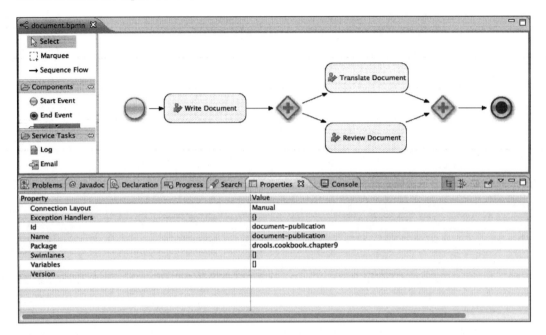

As you can see, we are using the BPMN2 Process Editor from the jBPM5 Eclipse Plugin to author the business process. You can also write the business process using the BPMN2 XML syntax, but it will be really complicated, so I encourage you to install the jBPM5 Eclipse plugin.

Once you have the plugin installed and a new BPMN2 file created, we can start defining the primary properties of the process, such as the package and the process by using the Eclipse **Properties** view and selecting the BPMN2 graphic background.

 It is important to not forget to specify the process ID, otherwise you will get compilation errors.

Now, we can start to model our business process. First, we have to add a user task node by selecting this component from the **Components** palette of the BPMN2 editor and dropping it on our process definition. The minimum information needed by this node is the **ActorId** and the **Name** properties. The last one is only for descriptive purposes. They can be completed in the **Properties** view, as shown in the following screenshot. Once we are done setting the node's properties, we have to connect it with the Start Event node using a Sequence Flow component to create a connection between them.

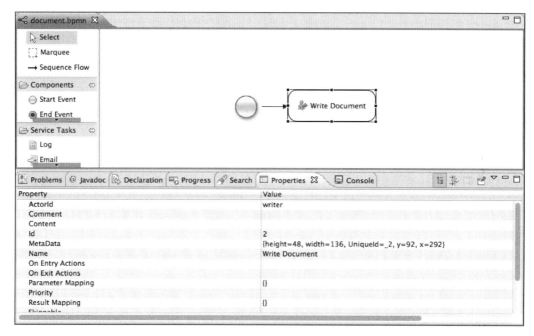

The user task node supports some more properties that can be useful to indicate when the task needs a response from the client to continue with the process execution, assign task priorities, specify if a task can be skipped, and so on. For further information about these properties, you can take a look at the official documentation where all these properties are explained in detail.

Now, we can continue adding the remaining nodes and their connections. As you can see in the following screenshot, we have to add two more user task nodes that are connected using AND gateways. The only important configuration of the user task nodes is the **ActorId** property that should be assigned to *reviewer* and *translator*, respectively. As the last step, connect the second AND gateway with an End Event node to close the business process:

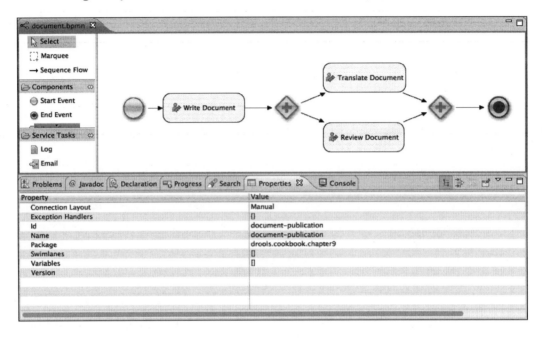

With our business process already defined, we can start configuring the human task management component provided by jBPM5. The jBPM5 engine deals with the human tasks just like other external services that are implemented as domain-specific services. Using this approach, it provides a work item handler to bind these abstract tasks to a specific implementation, which in this case is the WS-HumanTask, but you can implement your custom implementation to use with another human task service.

Human tasks are created when a user-task node is triggered in the execution of a business process, and they contain a specific life cycle. In the following figure, we can see how the WS-HumanTask specification declares the user task's life cycle, where the green blocks (the color version of this diagram is included in the code bundle) define a common execution cycle, and you can also see the variants that can modify the common execution, such as delegating or forwarding task, skipping a task, and so on:

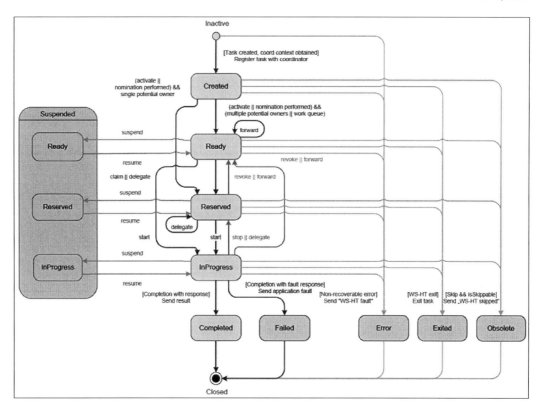

With this minimum idea about a common user-task life cycle behavior we can start configuring the human task service. Here, step 3 and step 4 can be skipped because they are descriptive and do not need much explanation. However, keep in mind that in a production environment, you would like to configure the persistence unit with a non-memory database, such as MySQL, PostgreSQL, MS SQL Server, and so on.

Now we can start writing the code, inside the `main` method of a Java class. First, we have to create a JPA `EntityManagerFactory` using the current persistence unit ID, which will be used to initialize an `org.jbpm.task.service.TaskService` object together with a Drools `SystemEventListener`. The `TaskService` is an independent service that ideally should also be started as a separate service, but for demonstration purpose of the recipe all the services will be started together as shown in the following code:

```
EntityManagerFactory emf = Persistence
  .createEntityManagerFactory("drools.cookbook.jbpm.task");
SystemEventListener systemEventListener =
  SystemEventListenerFactory.getSystemEventListener();
TaskService taskService = new TaskService(emf, systemEventListener);
TaskServiceSession taskSession = taskService.createSession();
```

Now, we have to register the users into the `TaskSession` because the service needs to know all the possible users and groups to avoid errors in the task assignment. The users can be declared programmatically, but you can also use external services that already have the information about the organization structure:

```
User writer = new User("writer");
User translator = new User("translator");
User reviewer = new User("reviewer");
User administrator = new User("Administrator");
taskSession.addUser(writer);
taskSession.addUser(translator);
taskSession.addUser(reviewer);
taskSession.addUser(administrator);
```

As you can see, we declared the three users who were involved in this business process and also an Administrator user who was introduced by the specification, and we must not forget to create and register this user. Keep in mind that this Administrator user can manipulate the task's life cycle but can't be assigned to any task.

Now, we are ready to start the human task service. In this recipe, we are going to use the Apache Mina implementation, but there are more implementations that can be used and are available readily. For example, one of them is using an embedded or external JBoss HornetQ message broker:

```
TaskServer server = new MinaTaskServer(taskService);
Thread thread = new Thread(server);
thread.start();
Thread.sleep(2000);
```

 By default, the `TaskServer` uses port 9123 but it can be easily modified by specifying the port number as the second constructor parameter.

The human task service should also be started as a separate service together with the `TaskService`. As we are only demonstrating how to use it, we can put this wrapper thread to sleep using the `sleep()` method for a little amount of time, so that we are sure that the services are properly initialized.

At this point, we have the human task service initialized, but we also have to configure a `TaskClient` to interact with it. This task client offers a low-level API to communicate with the `TaskService` that isn't the best option for a regular user. Instead, users will prefer to use a more user-friendly GUI such as the Drools Eclipse Task Client Plugin, the jBPM5 Console, or a custom GUI implementation that in the end will be using this low-level API but hiding all these communication details.

As we are developers, we are going to get our hands dirty and interact with the `TaskService` using the low-level API. In order to achieve this, we need to instantiate a `MinaTaskClientConnector` using a `MinaTaskClientHandler` that will be used to connect with the `TaskService` using port 9123:

```
MinaTaskClientHandler minaTaskClientHandler = new
    MinaTaskClientHandler(systemEventListener);
TaskClientConnector connector = new MinaTaskClientConnector("client",
    minaTaskClientHandler);
TaskClient client = new TaskClient(connector);
client.connect("127.0.0.1", 9123);
```

Once the `TaskClient` is connected, we are ready to compile our business process as we usually do:

```
KnowledgeBuilder kbuilder = KnowledgeBuilderFactory
    .newKnowledgeBuilder();
kbuilder.add(new ClassPathResource("document.bpmn"),
                                ResourceType.BPMN2);
KnowledgeBase kbase = KnowledgeBaseFactory.newKnowledgeBase();
kbase.addKnowledgePackages(kbuilder.getKnowledgePackages());
StatefulKnowledgeSession ksession = kbase.
newStatefulKnowledgeSession();
```

The only remaining step in the configuration is the integration of the human task service with the jBPM engine just like any other external service. This integration is possible by registering a specific work-item handler in the `StatefulKnowledgeSession`. This work-item handler, `WSHumanTaskHandler`, is available in the `jbpm-human-task` module and will have the responsibility of communicating with the human task service:

```
WorkItemHandler handler = new WSHumanTaskHandler();
ksession.getWorkItemManager().registerWorkItemHandler("Human Task",
    handler);
```

Finally, we are ready to start a process using the ID of our process definition:

```
ProcessInstance processInstance = ksession
    .startProcess("document-publication");
```

Once the human task service is initialized and the `WSHumanTaskHandler` is registered into the `StatefulKnowledgeSession`, we can start interacting with it by using the `TaskClient`.

The `TaskClient` provides several methods for managing the life cycle of human tasks, which will let us obtain the available tasks for a user or group, start tasks, complete tasks, skip tasks, remove tasks, resume tasks, and so on.

Before interacting with the human tasks, we need to know which tasks are available for the user or group. The `TaskClient` provides a method to let us know all the available tasks for a certain user and language, which also needs a `TaskSummaryResponseHandler` object to retrieve the results and specify the amount of time in milliseconds to wait for a response:

```
BlockingTaskSummaryResponseHandler taskSummaryResponseHandler = new
BlockingTaskSummaryResponseHandler();
client.getTasksAssignedAsPotentialOwner("writer", "en-UK",
  taskSummaryResponseHandler);
taskSummaryResponseHandler.waitTillDone(2000);
```

 The `waitTillDone()` method will hold the execution until a response is completed or for the specified amount of time. This method will return `true` when the response was completed in time, otherwise it will return `false`.

With a successful response, we can obtain the available tasks from the `TaskSummaryResponseHandler` as shown in the following code line:

```
List<TaskSummary> tasks = taskSummaryResponseHandler.getResults();
```

Now that we have knowledge about all the available tasks for the *writer* user, we can start the execution of any of them, but as we have only started one process, we should have only one available task.

This task is already reserved to be executed by the user because the user is the only one with permission to start it. If a task has more than one designed actor then we should claim the task first before trying to start it.

Tasks are started using the `start()` method of the `TaskClient` together with the task ID, user ID, and a `BlockingTaskOperationResponseHandler` object, which behaves in the same way as the handler used to retrieve the available tasks:

```
BlockingTaskOperationResponseHandler startResponse =
  new BlockingTaskOperationResponseHandler();
long taskId = tasks.get(0).getId();
client.start(taskId, "writer", startResponse);
startResponse.waitTillDone(200);
```

Once the user starts a task and completes it, we must notify this to the human task service by invoking the `complete()` method of the `TaskClient` with the same parameters that were used to initiate it:

```
BlockingTaskOperationResponseHandler completeResponse =
  new BlockingTaskOperationResponseHandler();
client.complete(taskId, "writer", null, completeResponse);
completeResponse.waitTillDone(2000);
```

With the task completion, the process instance moves to the next node reaching the Diverging Gateway and creating two new user tasks that are assigned to other actors. These actors are none other than the *reviewer* and the *translator* who are also human and need the document created by the *writer* user to continue the process execution.

From here, we only have to obtain the available tasks for these users and then start and complete them to finish the process execution. For a complete implementation of the process execution take a look at the examples provided for the book.

Monitoring process a activity and creating reports

Business Activity Monitoring (**BAM**) is about real-time monitoring of processes and intervention on the execution, manually or automatically, based on the analysis of the data collected. jBPM provides a BAM module to collect all this available information and store it to create reports.

Getting ready

In order to design and visualize reports, you need to download the **Eclipse IDE** for Java and Report Developers that includes the **Eclipse BIRT** open source reporting tool, from `http://www.eclipse.org/downloads/`. Also you will have to download the MySQL JDBC library driver from `http://dev.mysql.com/downloads/connector/j/` to configure the report's Data Source.

How to do it...

Carry out the following steps in order to complete this recipe:

1. Create a new Java project using Apache Maven and add the following dependencies in the `pom.xml` file:

```
<dependencies>
  <dependency>
    <groupId>org.jbpm</groupId>
    <artifactId>jbpm-flow</artifactId>
    <version>5.1.0.Final</version>
  </dependency>
  <dependency>
    <groupId>org.jbpm</groupId>
    <artifactId>jbpm-flow-builder</artifactId>
    <version>5.1.0.Final</version>
  </dependency>
  <dependency>
    <groupId>org.jbpm</groupId>
```

```
      <artifactId>jbpm-bpmn2</artifactId>
      <version>5.1.0.Final</version>
   </dependency>
   <dependency>
      <groupId>org.jbpm</groupId>
      <artifactId>jbpm-bam</artifactId>
      <version>5.1.0.Final</version>
   </dependency>
   <dependency>
      <groupId>javassist</groupId>
      <artifactId>javassist</artifactId>
      <version>3.4.GA</version>
   </dependency>
   <dependency>
      <groupId>mysql</groupId>
      <artifactId>mysql-connector-java</artifactId>
      <version>5.1.3</version>
   </dependency>
   <dependency>
      <groupId>org.slf4j</groupId>
      <artifactId>slf4j-api</artifactId>
      <version>1.6.1</version>
   </dependency>
   <dependency>
      <groupId>org.slf4j</groupId>
      <artifactId>slf4j-log4j12</artifactId>
      <version>1.6.1</version>
   </dependency>
</dependencies>
```

2. Create two BPMN2 diagrams and save them into the `test/resources` folder of the project. One of the diagrams will be the same as the one used in the previous recipe and the new one will be explained later.

3. The following figure shows the business process with a Signal Event node model:

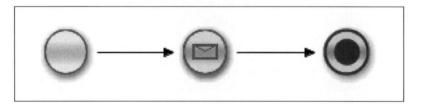

4. The following figure shows a Business process with a Script Task node model:

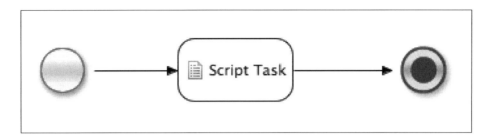

5. Create an `AuditLog.hbm.xml` file in the `main/resources` folder with the following code. This Hibernate mapping file is also available in the `jbpm-bam` module source code:

```xml
<?xml version="1.0"?>
<!DOCTYPE hibernate-mapping PUBLIC
        "-//Hibernate/Hibernate Mapping DTD 3.0//EN"
        "http://hibernate.sourceforge.net/hibernate-mapping-
3.0.dtd">

<hibernate-mapping>

  <class name="org.jbpm.process.audit.ProcessInstanceLog">
    <id name="id">
      <generator class="native" />
    </id>
    <property name="processInstanceId" />
    <property name="processId" />
    <property name="start" type="timestamp" column="START_DATE" />
    <property name="end" type="timestamp" column="END_DATE" />
  </class>

  <class name="org.jbpm.process.audit.NodeInstanceLog">
    <id name="id">
      <generator class="native" />
    </id>
    <property name="type" />
    <property name="nodeInstanceId" />
    <property name="nodeId" />
    <property name="processInstanceId" />
    <property name="processId" />
    <property name="date" type="timestamp" column="LOG_DATE" />
  </class>

</hibernate-mapping>
```

6. Now, you have to configure the Hibernate persistence. Create a `hibernate.cfg.xml` file with the following content and save it in the `main/resources` folder together with the `AuditLog.hbm.xml` file:

```xml
<?xml version='1.0' encoding='utf-8'?>
<!DOCTYPE hibernate-configuration PUBLIC
        "-//Hibernate/Hibernate Configuration DTD 3.0//EN"
        "http://hibernate.sourceforge.net/hibernate-configuration-
3.0.dtd">

<hibernate-configuration>

  <session-factory>

      <!-- MySQL Database connection settings -->
      <property name="connection.driver_class">com.mysql.jdbc.
Driver</property>
      <property name="connection.url">jdbc:mysql://localhost/
jbpmbam</property>
      <property name="connection.username">jbpm_username</property>
      <property name="connection.password">jbpm_password</property>
      <property name="connection.pool_size">1</property>
      <property name="dialect">org.hibernate.dialect.MySQLDialect</
property>
      <property name="current_session_context_class">thread</
property>
      <property name="cache.provider_class">org.hibernate.cache.
NoCacheProvider</property>
      <property name="show_sql">false</property>
      <property name="hbm2ddl.auto">create</property>
      <mapping resource="AuditLog.hbm.xml" />

  </session-factory>

</hibernate-configuration>
```

7. As you can see, Hibernate is configured to persist data against a MySQL database. If you don't know how to install it, how to create schemas, users, and permissions, read the *Using persistence to store knowledge* recipe from *Chapter 2, Expert: Behind the Rules* or configure it to use it against your favorite RDBMS.

8.   Now, create a new Java class file named `BAMReportingTest.java` and add the following code inside it:

```java
public class BAMReporting {

  public static void main(String[] args) throws Exception {
    KnowledgeBuilder kbuilder = KnowledgeBuilderFactory
.newKnowledgeBuilder();

    kbuilder.add(ResourceFactory.newClassPathResource(
      "processWithSignalEvent.bpmn"), ResourceType.BPMN2);
    kbuilder.add(ResourceFactory.newClassPathResource(
      "processWithScriptTask.bpmn"), ResourceType.BPMN2);
    if (kbuilder.hasErrors()) {
      for (KnowledgeBuilderError error : kbuilder.getErrors()) {
        System.err.println(error);
      }
      throw new IllegalArgumentException("Unable to parse
knowledge.");
    }
    KnowledgeBase kbase = kbuilder.newKnowledgeBase();
    StatefulKnowledgeSession ksession = kbase
      .newStatefulKnowledgeSession();
        WorkingMemoryDbLogger historyLogger = new WorkingMemoryDbL
ogger(ksession);

        for (int i = 0; i < 20; i++) {
            ksession.startProcess("processWithScriptTask");
        }
        Random random = new Random();
        for (int i = 0; i < 50; i++) {
            ProcessInstance processInstance = ksession.startProces
s("processWithSignalEvent");
            if (random.nextBoolean()) {
                Thread.sleep(random.nextInt(3000));
                ksession.signalEvent("mySignal", null,
                           processInstance.getId());
            }
        }
        ksession.dispose();
        historyLogger.dispose();
    }
}
```

9. Execute the `BAMReporting` Java `main` method and once the execution ends check the database tables contents, which will look similar to the following screenshot:

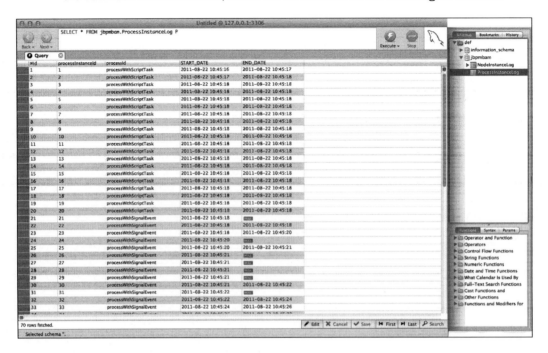

10. Copy the BIRT reports available in the `test` folder `drools-bam` module into your `main/resources` folder and open the `overall_activity.rptdesign` BIRT report file. This report is ready to be used and will generate a report with the number of process instances completed every hour, the currently active process instances, and the average completion time of the process execution, as shown in the following screenshot. Switch to the **Report Design** perspective if it does not automatically open:

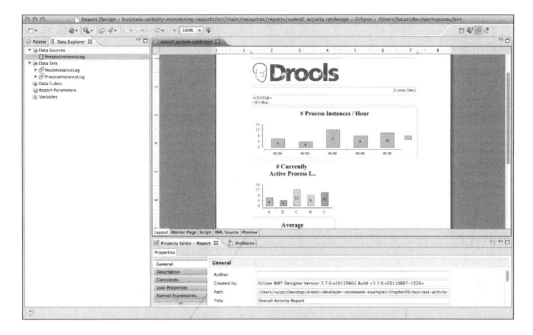

11. Now, you have to configure the **ProcessInstanceLog** report Data Source. Double-click on it, and a new pop-up window will be displayed where you have to add the MySQL JDBC driver using the **Manage Drivers...** option and configure the database URL, and the username and password. Once you are ready, click on the **Test Connection...** button to verify the correct configuration, as shown in the following screenshot:

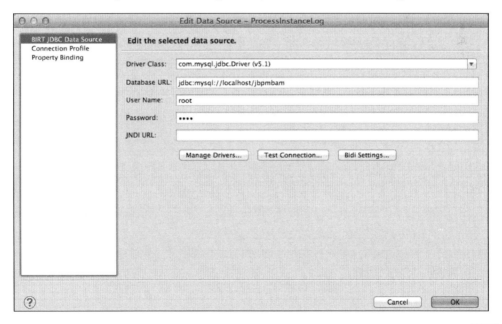

12. The **ProcessInstanceLog** Data Set defines the SQL query used to obtain the information from the database. By default, it tries to retrieve the data from the `public` database. This of course doesn't exist because we configured the Hibernate Connection URL to persist the event information in the `jbpmbam` database. Modify the SQL query displayed in the right side of the dialog to use the `jbpmbam` database, as shown in the following screenshot:

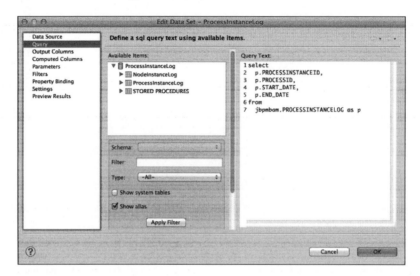

13. Finally, you are ready to generate a report. Click on the **View report** button available in the Eclipse toolbar and a new pop-up will be displayed with the generated report, as shown in the following screenshot:

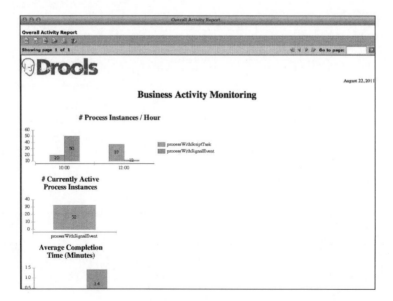

How it works...

The `jbpm-bam` module allows you to add a history logger to the process engine to persist all the related events into the database. Obviously, the history logger needs to be configured with the connection details, but if your application already uses JPA persistence then it can reuse this configuration. With all this information you can configure and analyze the execution of the processes to obtain statistics.

As always, create a new Java project using Apache Maven and add the dependencies as seen in the first step of the *How to do it...* section into the `pom.xml` file.

The newest dependency, and not used in the previous recipes, is the `jbpm-bam` module that will provide the history loggers that are used to persist the event information:

```
<dependency>
  <groupId>org.jbpm</groupId>
  <artifactId>jbpm-bam</artifactId>
  <version>5.1.0.Final</version>
</dependency>
```

This recipe uses two business processes in order to display more data in the final report. One of them is the business process used in the *Testing your business process* recipe, so feel free to follow the same instructions. But the other is a new one, a really simple business process with a Start Event node, a Script Task node, and an End Event node—all of them connected using Sequence Flow connectors. Don't forget to add the classic **Hello world** message in the script property of the Script Task node, as shown in the following screenshot:

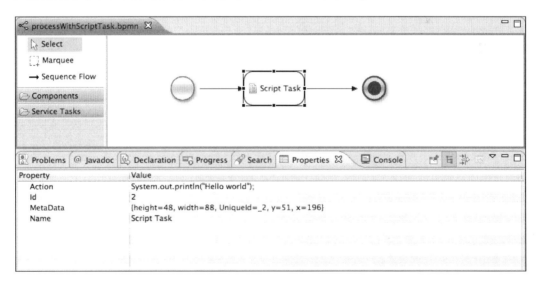

Now, you have to configure all the files related with the event's persistence. Create a new `AuditLog.hbm.xml` file and save it into the `main/resources` folder of the project. The content of this file must be the same as shown in step 3 of the *How to do it...* section, but you can also borrow it from the `jbpm-bam` module. The same happens with the `hibernate.cfg.xml` file, but here you have to modify the connection URL and the username/password with your MySQL database instance configuration.

And now, you are ready to write the code to register the history logger and generate the processes event information. Create a new class named `BAMReporting` and add the following code inside it:

```
public class BAMReporting {

    public static void main(String[] args) throws Exception {
        KnowledgeBuilder kbuilder = KnowledgeBuilderFactory
            .newKnowledgeBuilder();

        kbuilder.add(ResourceFactory.newClassPathResource(
        "processWithSignalEvent.bpmn"), ResourceType.BPMN2);
        kbuilder.add(ResourceFactory.newClassPathResource(
        "processWithScriptTask.bpmn"), ResourceType.BPMN2);
        if (kbuilder.hasErrors()) {
            for (KnowledgeBuilderError error : kbuilder.getErrors()) {
                System.err.println(error);
            }
            throw new IllegalArgumentException("Unable to parse " +
                                                "knowledge.");
        }
        KnowledgeBase kbase = kbuilder.newKnowledgeBase();
        StatefulKnowledgeSession ksession = kbase
            .newStatefulKnowledgeSession();
        WorkingMemoryDbLogger historyLogger = new
            WorkingMemoryDbLogger(ksession);

        for (int i = 0; i < 20; i++) {
            ksession.startProcess("processWithScriptTask");
        }
        Random random = new Random();
        for (int i = 0; i < 50; i++) {
            ProcessInstance processInstance = ksession
                .startProcess("processWithSignalEvent");
            if (random.nextBoolean()) {
                Thread.sleep(random.nextInt(3000));
                ksession.signalEvent("mySignal", null,
                                        processInstance.getId());
```

```
            }
        }
        ksession.dispose();
        historyLogger.dispose();
    }
}
```

The most important thing here is the assignment of the history logger to a knowledge session. In this recipe, we used an `org.jbpm.process.audit.WorkingMemoryDbLogger` object, but if your Drools/jBPM application is already using JPA persistence, you can use another history logger, `org.jbpm.process.audit.JPAWorkingMemoryDbLogger`, which will reuse the JPA persistence configuration:

```
WorkingMemoryDbLogger historyLogger = new WorkingMemoryDbLogger(ksess
ion);
```

Finally, as always, don't forget to dispose of the history logger object:

```
historyLogger.dispose();
```

If you take a look at the database, you will see that two tables were created and populated with the process event data:

The **ProcessInstanceLog** table contains the following information:

▶ **processInstanceId**: The process instance ID of the executed process

▶ **processId**: The process ID of the executed process

▶ **START_DATE**: The start date of the executed process

▶ **END_DATE**: The end date of the executed process

And the **NodeInstanceLog** table will contain the following information:

▶ **type**: The node event type to indicate the enter (value=0) or exit (value=1) of the node in the execution process

▶ **nodeInstanceId**: The node instance ID of the executed node

▶ **nodeId**: The node ID of the executed node

▶ **processInstanceId**: The process instance ID of the executed process

▶ **processId**: The process ID of the executed process

▶ **LOG_DATE**: The event date

The `drools-bam` module contains three different BIRT reports almost ready to be used, as only a few modifications regarding the database connection and the SQL query are needed. You can create your own custom report using the Eclipse BIRT Report Editor, but instead copy the `drools-bam` report files in your `main/resources folder`. The design of a custom BIRT report is, sadly, too complex to cover in this recipe.

Open the `overall_activity.rptdesign` BIRT report file and switch to the **Report Design Eclipse** perspective. As we saw in the screenshot of step 10 of the *How to do it...* section, in the left side of the perspective, you can see the **Data Explorer** view where you can configure the **Data Sources**, **Data Sets**, **Report parameters**, and so on.

By default, all the BIRT report files are pre-configured to use an HSQL database to obtain the data and thus, you have to configure the Data Source to use a MySQL database. Double-click on the **ProcessInstanceLog** data source, and you will a new pop-up window where you have to configure the JDBC driver, database URL, user name, and password. The database URL is a typical JDBC connection URL, where the driver name, the database IP address, and the schema name are specified, as you can see in the following screenshot:

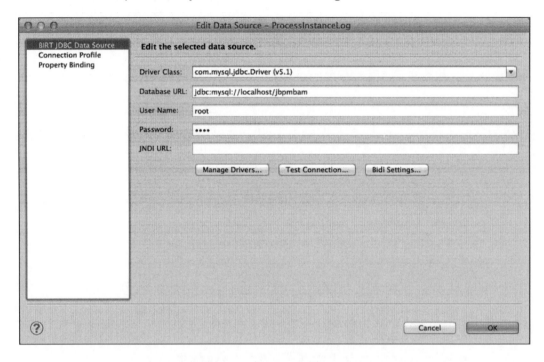

By default the Driver Class combo box will not display the `com.mysql.jdbc.Driver` `(v5.1)` driver. It has to be added using the **Manage Drivers...** option. It's really simple: click on the **Add...** button and locate the directory where you downloaded and extracted the MySQL JDBC library. The following screenshot shows the window dialog were the JDBC driver libraries have to be configured:

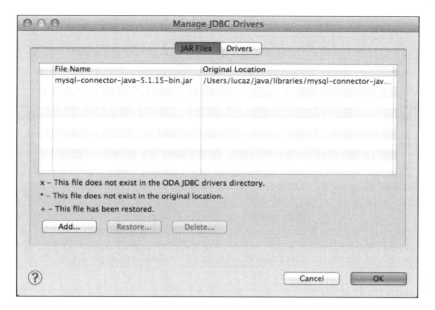

Once the MySQL driver is available, choose it from the **Driver Class** combobox and click on the **Test Connection** button. If you get a connection error check the user privileges and the host permissions.

Then you have to modify the data sets, where the SQL queries are defined to retrieve the information from the `ProcessInstanceLog` data source. In this pop-up window, you only have to modify the current query to obtain the data from the `jbpmbam` database in the **Query Text** section, as shown in the following screenshot. Repeat the same with the `NodeInstanceLog` data set:

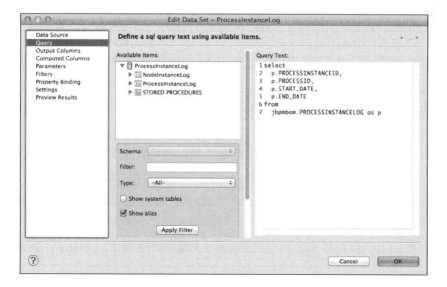

Finally, with the data source and the data sets configured, you can execute the report by clicking on the **View report** toolbar's drop-down button 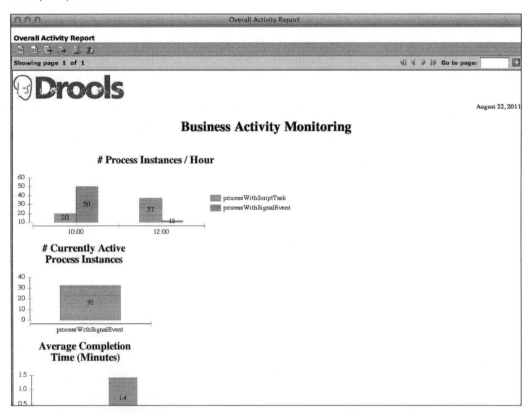. This action will display a window pop-up with the report content in a web viewer, as shown in the following screenshot. This drop-down button also allows you to choose to display it in other formats, such as DOC, PDF, HTML, PPT, and so on:

Lastly, remember that if you want to use the other available reports, you have to do the same modifications.

There's more...

BIRT reports do not necessarily have to be generated by using the Eclipse BIRT plugin. It also offers several integration options supplying several APIs. Check out the BIRT integration official documentation available at `http://eclipse.org/birt/phoenix/deploy/` to understand how to integrate it on a Java standalone/JEE application or directly on an application server.

Monitoring a business process with Drools Fusion

In the previous recipe, you saw how to monitor your business process using the BAM module and generate reports. These reports are useful to take actions, but they can't be automatically executed because it depends on the decisions taken by human actors. In this recipe, you will see how to integrate your business process with Drools Fusion to monitor the business process behavior and make decisions in real time.

How to do it...

Carry out the following steps in order to integrate Drools Fusion and monitor the process execution:

1. Create a new Java project using Apache Maven and add the following dependencies in the pom.xml file:

```
<dependencies>
  <dependency>
    <groupId>org.jbpm</groupId>
    <artifactId>jbpm-flow</artifactId>
    <version>5.1.0.Final</version>
  </dependency>
  <dependency>
    <groupId>org.jbpm</groupId>
    <artifactId>jbpm-flow-builder</artifactId>
    <version>5.1.0.Final</version>
  </dependency>
  <dependency>
    <groupId>org.jbpm</groupId>
    <artifactId>jbpm-bpmn2</artifactId>
    <version>5.1.0.Final</version>
  </dependency>
</dependencies>
```

2. Create a new `withdrawalProcess.bpmn` BPMN2 diagram file in the `main/resources` folder of your project using the BPMN2 Process Editor, as shown in the following screenshot:

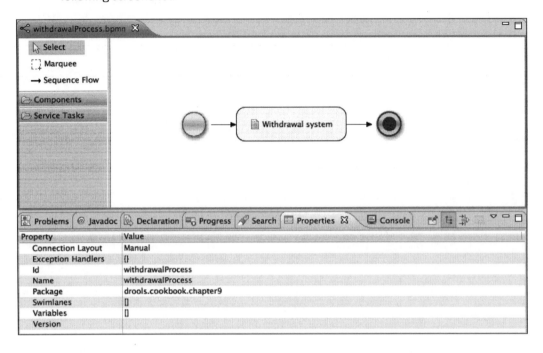

3. Now, you have to create the rules to react to the events generated by the process execution. Create a new `withdrawalRules.drl` DRL file in the `main/resources` folder of the project with the following code:

```
package drools.cookbook.chapter09;

import org.drools.event.process.ProcessStartedEvent;

declare ProcessStartedEvent
    @role(event)
    @expires(1h)
end

rule "More than 10 withdrawals in less than one hour "
dialect "java"
when
  Number(processesCount : intValue > 10)
    from accumulate(e : ProcessStartedEvent(
    processInstance.processId == "withdrawalProcess")
    over window:size(1h), count(e))
then
  System.err.println("Warning: more than 10 withdrawals" +
  "in the last hour. Processes count: " + processesCount);
end
```

4. Create a new Java package, for example `drools.cookbook.chapter09`, and create a new `CustomProcessEventListener` Java class file implementing the `org.drools.event.process.ProcessEventListener` interface shown as follows:

```java
package drools.cookbook.chapter09;

public class CustomProcessEventListener implements
ProcessEventListener {

    private StatefulKnowledgeSession eventKsession;

    public CustomProcessEventListener(
                    StatefulKnowledgeSession ksession) {
        eventKsession = ksession;
    }

    public void beforeProcessStarted(
                            ProcessStartedEvent event) {
        eventKsession.insert(event);
        eventKsession.fireAllRules();
    }

    public void afterNodeLeft(ProcessNodeLeftEvent arg0) {
    }

    public void afterNodeTriggered(
                    ProcessNodeTriggeredEvent arg0) {
    }

    public void afterProcessCompleted(
                            ProcessCompletedEvent event) {
    }

    public void afterProcessStarted(
                            ProcessStartedEvent arg0) {
    }

    public void beforeNodeLeft(ProcessNodeLeftEvent arg0) {
    }

    public void beforeNodeTriggered(
                    ProcessNodeTriggeredEvent arg0) {
    }

    public void beforeProcessCompleted(
```

```
                                ProcessCompletedEvent arg0) {
    }

    public void afterVariableChanged(
                    ProcessVariableChangedEvent arg0) {
    }

    public void beforeVariableChanged(
                    ProcessVariableChangedEvent arg0) {
    }

}
```

5. Finally, create a new `BusinessMonitoring` Java class in the same Java package with the following code. Keep in mind that the `KnowledgeBase` is configured in STREAM mode and the `StatefulKnowledgeSession` is configured to internally use a pseudo-clock to simulate the time elapse between the events' insertion into the knowledge session. The code used in this step is as follows:

```
package drools.cookbook.chapter09;

public class BusinessMonitoring {

    public static void main(String[] args) throws Exception {

        KnowledgeBuilder kbuilder = KnowledgeBuilderFactory
          .newKnowledgeBuilder();
        kbuilder.add(ResourceFactory.newClassPathResource(
          "withdrawalProcess.bpmn"), ResourceType.BPMN2);
        kbuilder.add(ResourceFactory.newClassPathResource(
          "withdrawalRules.drl"), ResourceType.DRL);
        if (kbuilder.hasErrors()) {
          for (KnowledgeBuilderError error :
                            kbuilder.getErrors()) {
                System.err.println(error);
          }
          throw new IllegalArgumentException("Unable to parse "
                                    + " knowledge.");
        }
        KnowledgeBaseConfiguration config =
          KnowledgeBaseFactory.newKnowledgeBaseConfiguration();
        config.setOption(EventProcessingOption.STREAM);

        KnowledgeBase kbase = KnowledgeBaseFactory
          .newKnowledgeBase(config);
```

```
kbase
.addKnowledgePackages(kbuilder.getKnowledgePackages());
KnowledgeSessionConfiguration conf =
   KnowledgeBaseFactory
      .newKnowledgeSessionConfiguration();
conf.setOption(ClockTypeOption.get("pseudo"));

StatefulKnowledgeSession ksession = kbase
   .newStatefulKnowledgeSession(conf, null);
SessionPseudoClock clock = ksession.getSessionClock();

CustomProcessEventListener listener =
   new CustomProcessEventListener(ksession)
ksession.addEventListener(listener);

for (int i = 0; i < 20; i++) {
   clock.advanceTime(20, TimeUnit.SECONDS);
   ksession.startProcess("withdrawalProcess");
}
for (int i = 0; i < 20; i++) {
   clock.advanceTime(30, TimeUnit.MINUTES);
   ksession.startProcess("withdrawalProcess");
}

ksession.dispose();

   }

}
```

6.   As the last step, just execute the Java `main` method to see what happens.

How it works...

The first step is the creation of a new Java project using Apache Maven with the jBPM5 dependencies. As you can see, these dependencies are most commonly used in any jBPM5 project. Remember that the jBPM dependencies will transitively add the Drools dependencies in your project, and this means the Drools Fusion support.

Once the Java project is configured with the required libraries, you have to create a new BPMN2 diagram using the BPMN2 Process Editor. Save it as `withdrawalProcess.bpmn2` in the `main/resources` folder of the project and add a Start Event node and a Script Task node with an End Event node connecting them using Sequence Flow connectors. Don't forget to specify the process ID, which must be `withdrawalProcess`. This BPMN2 diagram is really simple and does not depict a real scenario, where the validations would be more sophisticated. The process definition could have a Timer Event that could resume the process execution if it didn't receive a cancelation from the monitoring business rules.

Now, it's time for one of the most relevant steps of this recipe. The following rule will be used to react to the `ProcessStartedEvent` facts inserted into the knowledge session by the `CustomProcessEventListener` listener object, which was defined in the fourth step of the *How to do it...* section but it will be explained later:

```
package drools.cookbook.chapter09;

import org.drools.event.process.ProcessStartedEvent;

declare ProcessStartedEvent
    @role(event)
    @expires(1h)
end

rule "More than 10 withdrawals in less than one hour "
dialect "java"
when
    Number(processesCount : intValue > 10)
        from accumulate(e : ProcessStartedEvent(
        processInstance.processId == "withdrawalProcess")
        over window:size(1h), count(e))
then
    System.err.println("Warning: more than 10 withdrawals" +
    "in the last hour. Processes count: " + processesCount);
end
```

The `org.drools.event.process.ProcessStartedEvent` fact was declared as an event and with an expiration offset of one hour. With this fact metadata declaration, it's now possible to correlate events using temporal constraints. Also, they will be automatically managed in the knowledge session to retract them when the event expires.

The conditional part of the rule will count all the inserted `ProcessStartedEvent` facts from the process with ID `withdrawalProcess` over a time-based sliding window of one hour and will execute the consequence when more than 10 `ProcessStartedEvent` facts are inserted. Basically, this means that if in one hour more than 10 `withdrawalProcess` processes are started, then the rule consequence will be executed, just printing an error message. Of course, in a real implementation this rule should be more sophisticated and match processes started by the same user. Consequently, the rule could send an e-mail notification, an alert to the fraud monitoring department, or directly cancel the withdrawal process.

Once the business process and rules are defined, you have to integrate them. In order to achieve this, you have to insert the event generated when a process is started into a knowledge session. This is easily done using a custom `org.drools.event.process.ProcessEventListener` implementation that will insert the generated event when the `beforeProcessStarted` method is invoked by the same knowledge session. This `ProcessEventListener` implementation internally holds a `StatefulKnowledgeSession` that contains the business rule created in the previous step, and also the business process. Ideally, the business processes and the rules must be in separate knowledge sessions to decouple the execution and create a kind of process supervisor engine, but for the purpose of demonstration both business resources will be in the same knowledge session:

```
public class CustomProcessEventListener implements
ProcessEventListener {

    private StatefulKnowledgeSession eventKsession;

    public CustomProcessEventListener(StatefulKnowledgeSession
ksession) {
        eventKsession = ksession;
    }

    public void beforeProcessStarted(ProcessStartedEvent event) {
        eventKsession.insert(event);
        eventKsession.fireAllRules();
    }
    // remember to implement the other methods
}
```

Finally, you are ready to write the `BusinessMonitoring` class to integrate all the previous steps. Inside the Java `main` method a `StatefulKnowledgeSession` is created using a `KnowledgeBase` configured in STREAM mode, with the business process and the rules files. This knowledge session is also configured with a `KnowledgeSessionConfiguration` object to use a pseudo-clock to simulate the time elapse between the events' insertion:

```
package drools.cookbook.chapter09;

public class BusinessMonitoring {

    public static void main(String[] args) throws Exception {
        KnowledgeBuilder kbuilder = KnowledgeBuilderFactory
            .newKnowledgeBuilder();
        kbuilder.add(ResourceFactory.newClassPathResource(
            "withdrawalProcess.bpmn"), ResourceType.BPMN2);
        kbuilder.add(ResourceFactory.newClassPathResource(
            "withdrawalRules.drl"), ResourceType.DRL);
        if (kbuilder.hasErrors()) {
```

```
                    for (KnowledgeBuilderError error : kbuilder.getErrors()) {
                        System.err.println(error);
                    }
                    throw new IllegalArgumentException("Unable to parse " +
                                                    "knowledge.");
            }
            KnowledgeBaseConfiguration config = KnowledgeBaseFactory
                .newKnowledgeBaseConfiguration();
            config.setOption(EventProcessingOption.STREAM);

            KnowledgeBase kbase = KnowledgeBaseFactory
                .newKnowledgeBase(config);
            kbase.addKnowledgePackages(kbuilder.getKnowledgePackages());
            KnowledgeSessionConfiguration conf = KnowledgeBaseFactory
                .newKnowledgeSessionConfiguration();
            conf.setOption(ClockTypeOption.get("pseudo"));

            StatefulKnowledgeSession ksession = kbase
                .newStatefulKnowledgeSession(conf, null);
            SessionPseudoClock clock = ksession.getSessionClock();
            CustomProcessEventListener listener = new
                CustomProcessEventListener(ksession);
            ksession.addEventListener(listener);

            for (int i = 0; i < 20; i++) {
                clock.advanceTime(20, TimeUnit.SECONDS);
                ksession.startProcess("withdrawalProcess");
            }
            for (int i = 0; i < 20; i++) {
                clock.advanceTime(30, TimeUnit.MINUTES);
                ksession.startProcess("withdrawalProcess");
            }
            ksession.dispose();
        }
    }
```

Also, one of the most important code lines in this code snippet is the registration of the CustomProcessEventListener into the knowledge session.

The execution of this Java main method will simulate several process initializations using the SessionPseudoClock to simulate different time elapses between the process executions. When these processes are executed they will trigger the rule's consequence when the rule condition generates a rule activation, displaying several messages in the console indicating that there's a potential violation of the process execution.

Index

Symbols

A

B

CXF Endpoint 147

D

data enumerations
creating 72-74
working 74, 75
datasource
configuring 46
creating 46
debianServer object 12
declarative model
creating 69
declare keyword 11, 123
DEFAULT 130
doMove(WorkingMemory) method 218
DriverManagerDataSource bean 180
DRL file 14
Drools
setting up, Spring used 169-174
Drools 5.2 141
Drools 5.2.0.Final release 7
Drools API
custom classloader, using in knowledge agent
51-54
duplicated facts, discarding 49, 50
JPA persistence, using for storing knowledge
42-47
knowledge, monitoring with JMX 61-64
knowledge sessions, marshalling 37-39
knowledge sessions, unmarshalling 40
quality of rules, verifying with Drools Verifier
54-60
Drools application
Apache Camel, integrating 183-189
event stream processing mode, setting up
132
facts, declaring as events 120, 121
testing, pseudo clock used 124-127
Drools beans 171
Drools business rules engine
configuring 169
drools-camel library 186
Drools Classloader 16
Drools commands
executing, from JMS queue 197-205
DroolsConsequenceAction object 242

Drools developers 141
Drools Eclipse Plugin 21
Drools Expert 7
Drools Flow 237
Drools Fusion
about 122
reference link 139
special clock implementation 124
used, for monitoring business process 279-
286
drools-grid 187, 193
drools:grid-node 144
Drools Guvnor5.2.0
downloading 98
DroolsGuvnor instance 143
Drools JBoss Rules 5.0 Developers Guide 7
Drools JPA persistence
configuring, Spring module integration used
175-183
drools:kbase 144
drools:ksession 144
Drools marshallers 163
drools-persistence-jpa dependency 42
drools-persistence-jpa module 42
Drools Planner
about 207
benchmarker, creating 231-236
jFreeChart library, adding 232
simulated annealing acceptor, using 227-229
solver, terminating 229-231
working 215
drools-planner-core 232
Drools Planner official documentation 224
Drools QuartzHelper 29
Drools Rule Language (DRL) 8
Drools Server
about 141
configuring 141-143
deploying, in JBoss AS 5.x 149-151
knowledge services, configuring 142
multiple endpoints configuration 142
working 143, 144
drools-server.war file 165
drools-spring module 170, 193
Drools SystemEventListener 261
Drools Verifier 54

E

Eclipse BIRT
  downloading 265
Eclipse IDE
  downloading 265
emergency-channel entry-point 127
EmergencyInCourse fact 127
EmergencySignal 127
emergency system rule 127
End Event node 240, 243
Enterprise Integration Patterns (EIP) 186, 188
EntityManager
  about 182
  creating 254
EntityManagerFactory
  creating 47
EntityManagerFactory object 47
EntityManager provider 45
entry-points
  about 127
  creating 127-129
  working 130
EnvironmentName.ENTITY_MANAGER_FACTORY 47
EnvironmentName.TRANSACTION_MANAGER 47
equals() method 209
equals(Object obj) method 49
equals objects
  discarding, when inserting 49, 50
ERROR severity types 58
event
  correlating, temporal operators used 137-139
EventListener 17
EventNode 240
event stream processing mode
  setting up 132-136
example code
  downloading 8
execute(ProcessContext context) method 242
ExecutionResults object 160

F

FactHandle object 51, 196

facts
  declaring 8-12
  declaring, as events 120-123
  declaring, XML used 12-16
FactType object 12
Field value pop-up 88
FileOutputStream object 39, 61
FileSystem class 106
FireAllRulesCommand 152, 195
FireAllRulesCommand object 153
fireAllRules() method 21, 22, 24
fireAnalysis() method 58
fireUntilHalt() method 24, 26
First Fit algorithm
  using 224
flight-arrival entry-point 126
flight average speed rule 136
flight-control entry-point 131
FlightStatus event 121, 126
FlightStatus facts 131
Frameworks Integration System 197
From Collect Patterns
  about 76
  using, in Guided BRL Editor 76-80
  working 81
from entry-point operator 131

G

getAttribute() method 66
getBean(beanId) method 175
getBinaryPackage(String packageName) method 116
getBySeverity() method 58
getCalendars() KnowledgeSession method 29
getFactType method 12
getFields() method 12
GetGlobalCommand 153
getInputStream() method 117
GetObjectCommand 152
GetObjectsCommand 153
getProblemFacts() method 221
getResults() method 255
getTaskAssignedAsPotentialOwned() method 255
GitHub
  URL 245

Thank you for buying
Drools Developer's Cookbook

About Packt Publishing

Packt, pronounced 'packed', published its first book "*Mastering phpMyAdmin for Effective MySQL Management*" in April 2004 and subsequently continued to specialize in publishing highly focused books on specific technologies and solutions.

Our books and publications share the experiences of your fellow IT professionals in adapting and customizing today's systems, applications, and frameworks. Our solution based books give you the knowledge and power to customize the software and technologies you're using to get the job done. Packt books are more specific and less general than the IT books you have seen in the past. Our unique business model allows us to bring you more focused information, giving you more of what you need to know, and less of what you don't.

Packt is a modern, yet unique publishing company, which focuses on producing quality, cutting-edge books for communities of developers, administrators, and newbies alike. For more information, please visit our website: www.packtpub.com.

About Packt Open Source

In 2010, Packt launched two new brands, Packt Open Source and Packt Enterprise, in order to continue its focus on specialization. This book is part of the Packt Open Source brand, home to books published on software built around Open Source licences, and offering information to anybody from advanced developers to budding web designers. The Open Source brand also runs Packt's Open Source Royalty Scheme, by which Packt gives a royalty to each Open Source project about whose software a book is sold.

Writing for Packt

We welcome all inquiries from people who are interested in authoring. Book proposals should be sent to author@packtpub.com. If your book idea is still at an early stage and you would like to discuss it first before writing a formal book proposal, contact us; one of our commissioning editors will get in touch with you.

We're not just looking for published authors; if you have strong technical skills but no writing experience, our experienced editors can help you develop a writing career, or simply get some additional reward for your expertise.

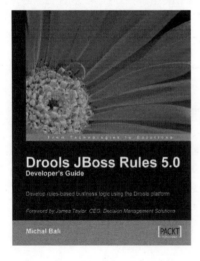

JBoss Drools Business Rules

ISBN: 978-1-847196-06-4   Paperback: 304 pages

Capture, automate, and reuse your business processes in a clear English language that your computer can understand

1. An easy-to-understand JBoss Drools business rules tutorial for non-programmers

2. Automate your business processes such as order processing, supply management, staff activity, and more

3. Prototype, test, and implement workflows by themselves using business rules that are simple statements written in an English-like language

Business Process Management with JBoss jBPM

ISBN: 978-1-847192-36-3   Paperback: 220 pages

A Practical Guide for Business Analysts

1. Map your business processes in an efficient, standards-friendly way

2. Use the jBPM toolset to work with business process maps, create a customizable user interface for users to interact with the process, collect process execution data, and integrate with existing systems.

3. Use the SeeWhy business intelligence toolset as a Business Activity Monitoring solution, to analyze process execution data, provide real-time alerts regarding the operation of the process, and for ongoing process improvement

Please check **www.PacktPub.com** for information on our titles

Printed in Great Britain
by Amazon.co.uk, Ltd.,
Marston Gate.